A Good Man with a Dog

A Game Warden's 25 Years in the Maine Woods

ROGER GUAY

with KATE CLARK FLORA

Skyhorse Publishing

Skyhorse Publishing books may be purchased in bulk at special discounts for sales promotion, corporate gifts, fund-raising, or educational purposes. Special editions can also be created to specifications. For details, contact the Special Sales Department, Skyhorse Publishing, 307 West 36th Street, 11th Floor, New York, NY 10018 or info@skyhorsepublishing.com.

Skyhorse® and Skyhorse Publishing® are registered trademarks of Skyhorse Publishing, Inc.®, a Delaware corporation.

Visit our website at www.skyhorsepublishing.com.

10 9 8 7 6 5 4 3 2 1

Library of Congress Cataloging-in-Publication Data is available on file.

Cover design by Tom Lau
Cover photo credit: Jolyne Guay

Print ISBN: 978-1-5107-0480-0
Ebook ISBN: 978-1-5107-0481-7

Printed in the United States of America

This book relies on the author's memory of true events. As such, it is a purely personal recounting, reflecting his opinions and recollections. Some names and identifying details of individuals were changed to protect their privacy.

We just do what all public safety personnel do—enforce the laws, assist the injured, and deal with death. We just do it in the middle of the woods, in the middle of the night, in the middle of the winter. And everyone we meet is carrying a gun.

I can't paint. I can't build things. I have no gifts when it comes to doing anything creative. But I can find people.

—Roger Guay

This book is for all the great, brave men and women who have taken the oath to preserve natural resources and have made it their life's mission, both present and past. We are a unique group of folks because we hear a different drum beating in our hearts. Embedded in us is this undeniable call to be the keepers of the fields, forests, and waters of the land we love. This thing that burns inside us drives us to keep going in the toughest conditions, risking our lives so that the torch we were handed makes it to the next generation and to the next.

I dedicate this book to two men who persevered in the Maine Warden Service with me as the Class of '86.

Daryl Gordon, my classmate, my friend, my working partner. A man who shared his faith and taught me how to have a personal relationship with God, the Creator. Daryl lost his life while flying his warden plane on patrol in northern Maine. He gave the ultimate sacrifice. I never hear a plane flying off in the distance and don't think it is him keeping an eye on me. My big brother.

Rick Stone, my classmate, my friend, a great man, a warden recovery diver, a faithful man of God who gave his all every day until God called him home. Rick died due to cancer a few years ago.

These men were men of honor. Shining examples of dedication, honor, and humility. They are both legends with whom I was privileged to serve.

—Roger Guay

To all the great men and women in law enforcement who have so patiently and generously shared their stories and their time. And, as always, to my patient husband, Ken Cohen, who puts up with my riding around in trucks, asking strangers to share their stories.

—Kate Clark Flora

CREED

Recognizing the responsibilities entrusted to me as a member of the Warden Service of the Department of Inland Fisheries and Wildlife of the State of Maine, an organization dedicated to the preservation of the fish and wildlife laws of Maine, I pledge myself to perform my duties honestly and faithfully to the best of my ability and without fear, favor, or prejudice. I will wage unceasing war against violation of the fish and game law in every form and will consider no sacrifice too great in the performance of my duty. I will obey the laws of the United States of America, and of the State of Maine, and will support and defend their Constitutions against all enemies whomsoever, foreign or domestic. I will always be loyal to and uphold the honor of my organization, my state, and my country.

CONTENTS

CO-AUTHOR'S NOTE

A few years ago, a retired Maine game warden named Roger Guay sent me an email. He said that he'd always been told he had good stories to tell from his twenty-five years as a warden. People kept urging him to write them down, but he had no idea how to go about it. He was contacting me because he'd read a book I'd written—*Finding Amy: A True Story of Murder in Maine*. Roger and his brilliant chocolate lab, Reba, had participated in the search for murder victim Amy St. Laurent's body. He said he liked the way I wrote about the investigation and the wardens' work. He wanted to know if we could talk.

That was beginning of a beautiful friendship. I was in the midst of writing about another missing murder victim ultimately found by the warden service and their trained K-9s. Roger had been part of that search as well. I needed his expertise and he needed mine. Our subsequent conversations showed me that he truly did have great stories to tell.

In the beginning, it looked like it was going to be a lighthearted book. Those stories were anecdotes about fish and wildlife enforcement, about what it's like to be a rookie and the adrenaline high that comes from beating the bad guy. But as we drove the back roads around Greenville, Maine, in his green pickup, and every corner we turned had a story, I got ever deeper insights into the challenges and demands involved in being one of Maine's off-road public safety officers.

Roger's story wasn't just about fish and wildlife enforcement or the rigors of wilderness rescue. It was the story of a life shaped by dedication to protecting cherished resources for future generations. It was the story of the patience, endurance, and ability to "read the woods" required to find those who have become lost—and bring them safely home. It was the story of the powerful relationship between a handler and his dog, and how the team became an invaluable resource for finding those lost or dead in the woods, and, ultimately, finding crime victims whose bodies had been hidden or buried in Maine's vast tracts of wilderness.

Those of us who live in a world where going into the woods might mean a few hours of hiking or a trip to a civilized campground have little concept of what the warden's life involves. The job is never nine-to-five. It can be day or night, or day *and* night, or even many days on end. Like many public safety jobs, it can go from peaceful to full-bore intensity in the time it takes the radio to crackle. An enforcement day may go from driving back roads in a truck to an intense emergency rescue of plane crash victims who have to be put on a stretcher, carried half a mile through the woods, and walked through an icy pond to a waiting floatplane.

Hunters, boaters, and the drivers of off-road vehicles carry guns. Poachers are active after dark and do not want to be caught. Snowmobilers may get lost somewhere on hundreds of miles of trails and may not be reported missing until night has fallen. They may be driving a powerful machine drunk at 2:00 a.m., when charging through a checkpoint seems easier than getting caught. ATVs allow quick access to wilderness areas that could take days to walk to, and corresponding access to protected ponds, making both enforcement and rescue bigger challenges.

The big woods can be beautiful but deadly, as hikers or skiers may find on remote parts of the Appalachian Trail or in Maine's own Grand Canyon, Gulf Hagas. Searches for the lost have a reality-driven intensity—those not found within three days will very likely die. A small child who has wandered off has far less time than that.

In blizzards and ice storms, day or night, in summer's heat and winter's chill, enforcement and rescue must go on, and a lifetime of facing danger, dealing with the injured, and finding the dead takes its toll. From his rookie days in Washington County, where people drove curiously past his house to get a look at the new warden, to the chaos of New Orleans after Katrina, this is a story of dedication, service, damage, resilience, friendship, and recovery.

It has been my privilege to help tell it.

—Kate Clark Flora

PROLOGUE

New Orleans, Louisiana
Six weeks after Hurricane Katrina

We were a cadaver dog team, Wayde Carter and I, along with his German shepherd, Buddy, and my Lab, Rader. In New Orleans on loan from the Maine Warden Service to FEMA to help them locate the bodies of people still missing, we mostly worked in the Ninth Ward. On this particular day, though, we were working in a neighborhood where the houses were still upright and had attached roofs.

Six weeks after the devastation of Katrina, it was nasty in New Orleans. We worked in a world of mold, mildew, spilled chemicals, decomposing animals and body parts, sewage, and thick black slime. Our job, and the dogs' job, involved crawling through rubble heaps and through buildings that had been swept off their foundations, tipped on their sides, ceilings downed, walls buckled, and the interiors looking like they'd been agitated in a washing machine.

Around us, the whole city was out of control. No traffic lights. Few street signs. No social order. There was random violence and gunshots during the day, roving gangs and gunshots all night long. I'd spent my career dealing with people who carried guns. Some of them angry. Some of them drunk. Some of them both. And I was about to have one of the scariest moments of my life.

Because the city was so dangerous, the first rule in the Big Easy after Katrina was never leave any rescue vehicle unprotected. It was my turn to stand and guard the truck while Wayde and our support team went down the street with our list of missing persons, looking for the address of a name on the list. Our dogs, Rader and Buddy, were in their crates in the back.

I was standing beside the truck with the driver's door open so I could hear radio calls, staring out at desolation, a city in ruins. Everything around me was still waterlogged, the heavy smell of rotting garbage and sewage not letting me forget the death and destruction that was everywhere.

Then I saw this car coming down the road, an old beat-up junker in need of a muffler. There was no reason for anyone other than us to be here. No one could live here or work here. But the car stopped in the road, facing me, and the driver sat there, staring at me in a very unusual manner. Usually people passing just glanced up and looked away, but this guy—his eyes locked right on me.

A chill went up my spine. Maine game wardens have all the powers of police and I'd policed an armed population for more than two decades, more often than not alone with no backup for twenty to fifty miles. I'd seen that stare before and I knew what it meant. Those eyes were looking for death.

Seconds passed, then the driver abruptly pulled over about twenty yards away, still facing me. All I could see were his eyes. No face, just those eyes with that look, the look of no return.

My heart jumped.

Time stopped.

Keeping his eyes fixed on me, he popped the driver's door wide open and stood behind it. He thought I couldn't see him, but I could see his hands moving and I knew exactly what he was doing. I could only see half the picture from my vantage point, but over the years I had observed this motion replayed hundreds of times, watching hunters in the field and during warden stops. There's no other hand motion like that. He was loading a gun. From my experience, I could even tell that he was loading a revolver because of the way he held his arms—the left arm locked steady, holding the gun, the right elbow moving up and down, putting the rounds in the cylinder.

Each time he dropped in a bullet, he looked up at me.

Within a millisecond, twenty years of my own training, training younger wardens, and dealing with people with guns, activated the "Go Mode" sequence, telling me: *Make no mistake, you are about to be in a fight for your life.* All the signs were there: the death look in his eyes, the stance a person takes when exiting a vehicle with a gun, the way the body acts as it anticipates taking the shot and bracing for the gun recoil.

All these things were going through my mind, I thought, *I'm not here in a law enforcement capacity, but thank God I've got my gun.* I could see that this was not a good situation. This guy was going to shoot me just because I was there. Because he could tell from my uniform and the Maine Warden Service crest on the truck that I was some kind of law enforcement. He was just going to park his car, get out, and kill himself a cop.

This was so messed up. I'd driven here from Maine to help, not to get in a gunfight with someone I'd never exchanged a single word with. But my training and experience taking down people with guns were telling me that things were about to go to hell and none of it was within my control. All I could do was react.

As I went into tunnel vision, time slowed to a crawl. The only things in motion were his hands and mine. The man had no face, just eyes. Everything in my mind was moving in slow motion and at super speed at the same time. My focus was fixed on him, on eyes and hands and how he moved, while my brain was saying *Don't lose the visual!* and running through a list of questions. *What if this goes down? Where am I going? Where do I move? Where is safety?*

Safety was getting as much metal as possible between us. I slid into the truck and across to the passenger side to put the engine between us. On TV, they use doors, but in reality, car doors aren't very good at blocking bullets.

I drew my weapon—a .357 SIG that held fourteen rounds—from its holster slowly so he couldn't see me do it; I didn't want him to know how ready I was.

Seeing that I had some cover, he left the comfort of his car door and started to quarter me, to cut the angle to expose me to his shot and give me no place to hide. A long black trench coat covered his left hand. At the waistline, his right hand was positioned for the draw and fire.

Look for the gun, my brain said, cycling the orders of engagement, moving up the force continuum, looking for the key elements to establish deadly force. I needed to see the gun. I picked the point that my bullets were going strike his chest.

As he moved around, angling so he could fire through the open truck door, I finished sliding across the front seat and slid out the door on the other side. As he was cutting the angle, I was working toward the back of the truck, still trying to put as much steel as possible between us.

I've been through a lot of pretty hairy situations, and I knew we were within seconds of it going down as he came around the edge of his door, in that trench coat with his hand tucked into it and wearing that stare. I didn't think about hollering for someone to help me, calling back Wayde or the fire fighters who were with him, or doing anything other than locking in on what that guy was doing and what was about to happen. I was 100 percent locked in to tunnel vision. That man was the only thing in the entire universe.

Suddenly, my trance was broken by ferocious growls and barking from the back of our warden truck as Wayde's shepherd, Buddy, lit up. It wasn't some kind of *bark, bark, bark*. He started roaring, a totally aggressive explosion. The whole truck started rocking. Rader, my chocolate Lab, joined in. They could sense what was happening and the whole truck rocked as they tried to protect me. The roar of their voices echoed through the empty streets.

That guy stopped dead in his tracks. Then he pulled his stare away, turned his back on me, and just walked away down the street, leaving his car behind.

When the other guys came back five or six minutes later, I was still shaking. I tried to recount what had just happened and realized that I could not describe my attacker beyond white and male. All I could remember were his eyes, his hands, and a dark trench coat. It was in the seventies that day; that coat was just there to conceal the weapon.

They looked at each other, and at me, and said, "What do we do?"

In a normal situation, if that had happened to one of us in law enforcement, there would be an investigation to find out who that person was. Given this type of behavior, it was likely that he was going to go and hunt down someone else. He might do this until he'd satisfied that urge to kill a cop. But this was post–Katrina New Orleans. There was no law enforcement.

So we all just shrugged and said, "Nothing. It's just another day in New Orleans," and went back to the task at hand.

PART I

ROOKIE YEARS

CHAPTER ONE

A Loss and the Call to Serve

I didn't set out to become a game warden. When I was a boy growing up in the small Maine town of Jackman, on the Canadian border, hunting and fishing were my primary activities and the woods, streams, and lakes were my playgrounds. Back then, I didn't consider poaching a crime. Nobody I knew did. The game warden was the enemy, and the crime was getting caught.

I still relish all those wild years of running around, doing what I wanted, breaking rules while looking over my shoulder for the game warden. But during my teenage years, two significant things happened that changed my thinking and started me down the road to becoming a warden. Not only did my views of wardens change, my whole way of looking at fish and game changed.

The first thing that was a major influence on my decision to become a warden, something that has stayed with me through all these years, happened while I was in the hospital for a bad ear infection.

There was a gentleman sharing the room with me. He was just a huge man, strong, outdoorsy, muscle from head to toe. I was in there for a couple of days and so we got to talking quite a bit about hunting and fishing and sharing our stories about places we'd been, and things we'd done. What struck me, from his side of the conversation, was how valuable being able to enjoy fish and wildlife was to him. He was a really impressive guy, and he got me thinking about things I'd always taken for granted.

Then, at one point, they came in and closed the curtain. Of course you hear everything through it; it was just a piece of cloth. And what I heard them telling him was that he had cancer and he didn't have much time to live. I remember our conversations, after that, because we had long talks, lying in our beds side-by-side. He wasn't lying there talking to me about how important his work was or how much money he made. He'd just been told he was dying, and what he wanted to reflect on was the value of fish and wildlife in his life, and how important it was that that be available for people in the future. He talked about that moment when his son got his first deer, and about getting his own first deer, about the trips they went on together. For him, that was the value of life more than money or possessions, more than anything.

He was a young man, probably in his early forties. I was a teenager used to taking all that for granted. He really changed my philosophy. For me it was like: Boom! Suddenly I had this new awareness of what was important to that man. Even though hunting and fishing was also an important part of my life, I'd never paid attention to its value before. For the first time, the idea came into me that the special opportunities fishing and hunting can provide had real value and were something worth devoting your life to protect.

The second event that turned my thinking around was losing my dad in a boating accident. It was just before my eighteenth birthday. He and my Uncle Lawrence, who had come up from Massachusetts, had gone fishing out on Turner Pond. Normally, I would have gone with them, but I'd just bought a new .22 pistol and wanted to try it out. I was out target shooting with it when they drove by and beeped.

When they didn't come home that night, we figured that they'd gotten done late and gone to stay with my Uncle Ernest out in Holeb. We didn't think anything of it until the next morning, when I called my uncle on the radio phone and he said they hadn't come to his house. That's when we knew something was wrong.

I drove out to the pond and found their vehicle parked there with the ropes still hanging off, just the way they'd left it to go fishing. There was no sign of them. It was a beautiful, crystal clear September day. I remember yelling for my dad on the shore and only hearing my echo in return. As I walked the shoreline calling for him, an owl answered me and landed on a limb in front of me. It was a very surreal moment. The leaves were changing and it was beautiful and terrifying at the same time.

It seemed like it took hours for my uncle to get there. When he arrived, he went to the Turner Pond Camps, found a canoe, and picked me up at the landing. We found their overturned Old Town canoe washed up on the opposite shore. When we flipped it over, we found a dead trout and my dad's hat. My uncle, who was a deputy sheriff for Somerset County at the time, went back to Holeb, where there was a radiophone at the mill, and called the sheriff's department and Glen Feeney, the local warden.

At that time, it hadn't been clarified under Maine law that recovery work was under the game warden's jurisdiction, as it is now. It was kind of a "whoever got there first" thing. So the sheriff's department came up with their divers and started dragging the pond, which completely silted up the water. It wasn't until that afternoon that the warden service came and brought their divers and a whole lot more expertise. When the silt settled, they found the anchor, and stuff from the canoe. They recovered my uncle but they couldn't find my dad.

Now, this whole recovery process wasn't a matter of hours. It was a matter of days. As I remember it, they found my uncle on the second day. While this was going on, all we could do was wait. In the absence of facts, we substituted false hope, doing what I now think of as the "maybe this or that happened" drift away from what the facts were telling us.

At the wardens' suggestion, my two brothers-in-law and my cousins, Rene and Joe, and I kept busy searching the woods, searching the woods line and the edges of the pond, thinking that maybe he'd made it to shore and had hypothermia and couldn't move or something. That kept us occupied while they were doing the dive work.

When all this was happening, during those awful and endless days of waiting and watching, I saw a side of the wardens I'd never seen before. I learned that the wardens weren't the enemy after all; they truly cared and were incredibly professional. They gave their all to those days of searching with no complaints or excuses. Our whole family had never seen that side of them before.

In particular, I remember a warden diver named Charlie Davis, who was especially compassionate at that time. Although my uncles were there, and my sisters' husbands, it was Charlie Davis who played the role of father figure for me, which I badly needed at that time. He took the time to let me sit in his truck and explained the whole process, how their search was going to work, what they were doing, and what was coming next.

I can remember my hopeless feeling, especially after those first few days of searching when nothing was coming up and I had more questions than could be answered, and how, during that lengthy search, my sense of time literally stopped. In the midst of that, through his patient explanations and his presence, Charlie Davis became somebody who steadied me. He took the swirl of anxiety I was feeling and brought me back into the present. I didn't necessarily need to sit down and talk to him every five minutes. It was his demeanor—so calm and competent—as much as his words that indicated to me things were under control. After a while, I only needed to see him there—knowing that he cared and had the time for me was enough. We'd built a rapport and I trusted him.

What I learned from Charlie during those days became something I would carry with me into similar events throughout my career. I learned that people in a search situation with a bad likely outcome needed someone affirming and calming to help them focus where they needed to be. The sort of conversation Charlie had with me, which I learned to provide for other people, went like this: *Listen, this is what we need to worry about right now. We are going to get divers here. We are going to start the search. We are going to put teams running the shoreline and we are going to concentrate on finding him. That's what we are going to do today.*

During that initial phase of the search when they're coming to grips with the idea something really bad has happened and it's not looking like it's going to end well, people will get overwhelmed. Their minds go in many different directions. What about funeral arrangements, or calling people? They're thinking about finances. They're thinking about how they're going to get back home, especially if they're on vacation. They're thinking about how they're going to tell people. Considering what they might have done differently to change the result. All of this stuff just comes rushing in and when they're in the middle of a situation, they can't figure out how to process all of it. They fill their minds so full that they can't focus on the immediate circumstances.

Because I've been there, I understand what people go through during a search, especially during those early hours. From how Charlie dealt with me, I learned that in situations like this we've got to grab them and say *STOP*. Bring them into the here and now and tell them: *You've only got to worry about where you are right now and what needs to be done today.* We try to help them ward off all the other stuff that is coming at them and put them in a place where they can sit safely for a minute, and then we let them know we're going to help them work through it step by step. I say: *We're not going to deal with that right now. We're going to be here right now, and you need to be here right now. Telling your family—we can help you with that. But you don't need to be grabbing more than you can handle right now.*

Once we build that connection with them, just like Charlie did with me, they can see that we're going to help them. We'll get them where they need to be, help them make the calls that need to be made, and walk them through things step by step. We help them see that they don't have to deal with it all at once. And it makes all the difference in the world to them.

The other critical thing the wardens taught me then that made a huge difference in my understanding of them was that they had the expertise to ask the important questions. When the sheriff's department got there, they just went to work dragging the pond. But when the wardens came, they gathered information to help conduct an effective, focused search. One of the things Charlie asked me was where, in that three-hundred-acre pond, my father and my uncle liked to fish. Where were their favorite fishing spots? That helped them focus the search on the area where my dad and uncle were finally found.

It was three days before they finally found my father. Only then did it become real.

One of the hardest things I've ever done in my life was to separate from my uncle after they found my father's body, drive home by myself, and have to tell my mother what had happened. That job was left to me, only seventeen at the time, even though I had several adult relatives involved in the search. My mother was a tough, unemotional person. She had no reaction. She just went silent, leaving me to follow suit and put my own emotions on the shelf. I was at that stage where my dad and I were butting heads over issues like what I wanted to do with my life versus what he wanted me to do. Now everything was just left hanging where there could never be any resolution between us.

I remember my feelings then—half shock and half kinda lost. It was such a surreal thing. One minute he was driving by, honking and waving, and the next, he was gone. Just that quickly and the whole world turned a hundred and eighty degrees. When it happened, my brain's ability to function clearly went away and all these things just came pounding in on top of me and completely overwhelmed me. In those days, my dad worked the night shift at the railroad station and would walk home. My bedroom was near the front door and I would always hear him come in after midnight. After his death, I would still wake up around midnight and listen for him to come through the door.

Now I've been on the other side of that scenario so many times. I bring a lot of my own experience to these situations that lets me understand what people are going through. It took three days to recover him, so I know, firsthand, what it feels like during those days when someone is missing. I've carried that with me on every search I've gone to, and I think it's motivated me, maybe harder than most people, because when I've gone out the door on something, it's been personal to me.

My conversations with the man in the hospital left me with an understanding of how valuable fish and wildlife were in people's lives and the recognition that you can't put a dollar sign on the experience of hunting and fishing. That's what started me in the opposite direction. From my love of the outdoors and from the way I'd grown up, I was kinda going in that direction anyway. Then this man's passion pushed me over. I started taking the whole fish and wildlife protection thing much more seriously, because I was beginning to understand its value. Then those days with the wardens when my father was lost and they were searching for him showed game wardens in a totally new light—both in the way they brought their outdoor knowledge to the search process, and in their compassion and understanding under devastating circumstances. That pushed me even further toward the warden service.

Still, my high school yearbook quote was: *Can you imagine Roger Guay being another Glen Feeney?* Glen was our local warden. So that transition didn't happen right away.

CHAPTER TWO

Deputy Warden and the Academy

Before I was accepted at the academy, I started as a deputy warden, acting as a backup when they needed extra hands. It gave me a taste of things to come and a chance to see whether I really wanted the job.

My first test, as deputy warden, was to issue a summons for dogs roaming at large. The area warden in Lincoln, Norman Moulton, sent me to this lady's house to give her the summons, knowing exactly what would happen because he'd dealt with her many times before. This lady went crazy on me. She started yelling things I'd never heard before in my life. She hadn't showered for two months, she had long, greasy hair, missing teeth, she was smoking, and the reek of the house poured out through the open door. It was horrible. She was a very nasty woman, with nasty dogs, but I issued that summons.

When I got back, Moulton grinned and asked, "How did it go?" I told him all my body parts were intact. And passed the first test.

Another time, during my deputy days, I was involved in a night hunting case that ended up with a high-speed chase going backward down a road. Night hunting is the use of artificial lights for the purpose of hunting wild game, and it's a big deal, from a wildlife protection stand-point, because using those lights paralyzes the game, blinds them so they don't move. You cannot illuminate wildlife from September 1 through December 15. Using the lights, having a loaded firearm in the vehicle, discharging a gun at night, putting out bait to lure deer in to a hunter—they're all crimes. Catching a night hunter, to a warden, is like catching a drunk driver to a cop. Everyone celebrates when they catch their first night hunter.

It was Thanksgiving night, and we'd heard this guy was going to be night hunting, so we set up by the field to wait. Sure enough, it wasn't long before these guys come driving by with a big spotlight out the window. We pulled in behind them and were following them without lights. We had cut-off switches to cut off our brake lights and our running lights. So we came up alongside 'em and Norm Moulton put on the blue lights.

My job was to shine the flashlight into the cab and get into their truck before they could do anything with the gun. To charge someone with the crime, you need lights, a weapon, and ammunition. Often, hunters would run so they'd have time to pitch the bullets out the window, removing one element of intent, and thus moving fast was critical. We came up right beside them, hollered "Wardens!" and told them to stop. Instead of stopping, the guy threw his truck into reverse, so we threw ours into reverse too. Now we were both backing up, side-by-side, and we had to be going thirty-five miles an hour in reverse. Those trucks were just whining. It was slippery. Pretty soon, our bumpers locked, and we all went sliding into the ditch.

I bailed out and rushed up to the passenger side. The passenger was just muckling onto his rifle, trying to get it up so he could unload it. He was doing that because it was illegal to have a loaded gun in your vehicle, and they were running because night hunting carries a minimum mandatory thousand-dollar fine, three days in jail, and loss of the weapon.

When I came around the vehicle, I could see the gun and I could see what he was doing. I can tell the hand motion when someone's loading or unloading a gun. Everything was unfolding lightning fast. I was racing the clock not only so he couldn't get that gun unloaded but so he couldn't use it against me. I popped the door and I grabbed the rifle and snapped it away from him. We got him out and up against the vehicle, and it was a total adrenaline rush like you cannot believe. That was my introduction to the warden's world, and it will be with me forever.

After we got done, the game warden looked at me and he said, "How did you like that?"

I couldn't even hold a cup of coffee, I was still shakin' so bad, and I said, "Oh, it was good."

It turned out it was okay, though, showing that I was shaking like a leaf. A few weeks earlier, he and I were working our way back into this field, expecting a poacher might show up. Then a guy came in on foot. We were sitting in the truck, it was pitch black, and all of a sudden, poof! Everything lights right up in front of us from someone using a hand-held spotlight, what we used to call a Q-beam. We bailed out of the truck, and the light goes off and we were like: What happened? Then we ran along the edge of the field, trying to find the guy. Our jackets were made of nylon at the time, and he's making this rustling sound, *rustle, rustle, rustle*, and he turned around, looked at me, and said, "Twenty-five years and I still shake every time."

That total adrenaline thing: pretty much anytime you step into that realm of confrontation, it comes up. And working in the world we did, everyone carried guns, and it was always close and personal.

It took me several years to get accepted at the academy. The warden service wasn't adding many officers. Some years there were no classes at all and all of the classes were small. Even after I passed the test, it was eighteen months before I actually started training. Finally, I got the word that I'd been accepted to the academy. It was really exciting, but first I had to go and take a polygraph.

I had to go up to Caribou, Maine, about a three-hour drive. I got up at four in the morning, threw the kids in the car, and Jolyne and I drove up there. Now, when you're going to take a polygraph, every bad thing you've ever done in your life runs through your mind and I had the whole three-hour drive to dwell on that. When I got there, they wired me up and give me the list of questions they were going to ask so I had even more time to think about what I'd done. The process was first they'd ask me the questions with the machine off, then turn the machine on and go through the questions again. By then, I'd had all this time to think about it, and built up all this stress.

I told them everything I ever did. I just dumped it all right out—all the rabbits I'd snared and fish and birds I'd shot even when it wasn't hunting season—just spilled out every bad thing I'd ever done. They didn't really care. What they really cared about was if I was trying to evade or lie about something. (Later on, when I did background checks on two people for the warden service, I told them: *Don't lie because the last thing you want to do is to lie on the polygraph.* No one is perfect, especially when they're teenagers. They didn't listen, and they blew those polys.)

So I passed my polygraph, and had to go to the academy in Waterville for nearly twenty weeks of training. That was a very scary move. By that time, I had a family and a job and I was really putting everything on the line to become a warden. I'd waited years for this and knew it was what I wanted. But it meant a pay cut, and I had a family to support. I would lie in bed at night thinking, "What have I done? I quit my job for this. Now what if I don't make it?"

It was wintertime, and every morning we'd run the streets of Waterville. Outside in the streets. Six or seven miles. Snow, rain, ice, misery. We were building up to our final run, a ten-miler that we had to do, while at the same time, the state police cadets were doing their running inside in the Colby College gym. I'd known that wardens were tough, but this really drove it home.

I was so mean and lean back then, and my metabolism was so high, that every morning, about five miles into the run, my stomach would flip because I had no fuel. Every single morning, partway through, I'd end up on my knees, being sick. And every morning, my friend Richard Stevens, who was training to be a Passamaquoddy tribal warden (later, he became the tribal governor), would pick me up by my T-shirt and he'd troll me for a while until I got my wind back. As this progressed, there was this tree that was at the five-mile mark, and it became a signal, a trigger. I'd just start thinking about it and it would happen.

One of the things we did was intensive swimming, which was not fun. It was a poorly heated pool and I had no body fat at all. We'd just swim and swim and swim. One day they threw a big brick in the bottom of the pool, twelve feet down, and we had to retrieve it. When I went down and got it, I dislocated my shoulder. Man, that hurt! I came up out of the water like a porpoise, and they grabbed me and popped it back into place. I couldn't use my arm for a couple days. It was miserable. At least I got few days off from running.

People tend to see game wardens and think, oh, the little green men riding around in trucks who are going to screw up my day. But that rigorous training isn't just to make us fit. We run outdoors in bad weather because we work in bad weather. Enforcement operations or rescue and recovery operations may take many strenuous hours, even days. We swim in chilly pools because chances are we're going to find ourselves working in freezing water. You have to go out on the ice, and sooner or later you're going to fall through and you've got to be prepared to deal with it.

We learn high-speed pursuit driving. Firearms. Self-defense. First aid. Search and rescue. Map and compass. We learn to read the woods—tracking and looking for disturbances in the vegetation—because that's our beat.

We train in the dark as well as in the daytime because poachers work in the dark. Because lost people don't conveniently get lost and found during daylight hours. Because as human beings, we're not very comfortable with doing stuff at night, and that's something we need to get over. Get over it ourselves and understand the effect of darkness on human behavior. For us, it's not just about *being* in the dark; it's about functioning in the dark. In reality, it's just the absence of light that you have to adjust to, but it affects how people move and what they do and how they think. Senses are heightened, focus is more intense, there are fewer distractions.

The culmination of that training was a week of hands-on training on Swan's Island, a small mid-coast Maine island, about one mile by three miles. There was an old farm complex there with two houses. No water or electricity. That week on Swan's Island was about the wildest thing I'd ever experienced in my life. All the senior wardens were playing the bad guys and we were sent there to catch them. Things were running 24/7, just like they would be when we were on the job. We did everything: lost hunter scenarios, night hunting, and ATVs. One of the things they told us was that sometime during the week we were going to get into a knock-down, drag-out fight with someone. We never knew when it was coming, so we were always on the lookout. I'm 5' 9" and my battle took place with 6' 2" warden Mike Morrison during a night hunting stop. Mike and I retired on the same day and worked a lot together, as he was in my section.

There were six of us trainees that week, two Passamaquoddy wardens and four of us. Daryl Gordon and I were bunkmates at the academy and we were assigned to be working partners on the island; he later became a warden service pilot and died in a crash while I was working on this book.

Daryl had kind of become my big brother at the academy and would end up playing a huge role in shaping me as a warden. He was older, about thirty-five at the time, and had grown up in Hartland. A Vietnam vet, he'd seen a lot of combat, so he was very used to hunting things in the dark that were dangerous. The possibility of anything popping up at any time was his norm. Because he was cool with that, our days on Swan's Island turned out beautifully for me because his demeanor and approach to things helped keep me calm and focused.

During that week, they were simulating the real world. We would get all kinds of calls, anything from a sick raccoon call to an injured ATV rider to missing people. And those calls could come in any time, day or night. At one point, we got a call on the radio that said people in the farmhouse had just heard someone fire at a deer.

Just like they'd said we could expect we were going to be in a fight, at the beginning of the week one of the lieutenants in charge of the program had told us, smugly, "Sometime this week, I'm gonna take a deer right out from under your noses and I'm going to drive away with it. No one has ever caught me. I've been doing this for twelve years and no one has ever caught me. You're gonna watch me drive away with a deer."

Keeping that from happening became a real challenge to us. Daryl and I got down there where the shots had been fired and ditched our truck in the woods. We went in on foot and hid in the high grass in the ditch and waited. Then a car came down the road, slowed, and popped the trunk. People came out and milled around. They did that two more times.

Daryl and I were lying on the ground, watching. Then the car came back a fourth time, and we saw a guy heading toward the car, dragging a deer. We'd already gotten to the point where we didn't really need to talk much. We'd developed an unspoken understanding about how we'd operate, so when we saw that, we just took off running. The way we were positioned, he was going to get the guy heading for the trunk of the car, I was going to get the driver. Daryl grabbed the guy just as he reached the trunk, spun him around and threw him to the ground, while I went right through the driver's window, grabbed that guy, and spun him to the floor of the car on the passenger's side.

It was awesome. We arrested them—Dave Peppard, the district warden for that area, and Lieutenant Langdon Chandler—and put them in handcuffs. The lieutenant, he started getting really feisty. Well, we had two kinds of cuffs that we were using: regular cuffs and flex cuffs. Flex cuffs have a solid piece of metal in the center. If someone starts giving you a really hard time, you just grab those flex cuffs in the middle and twist. It puts all the pressure on the wrists and it really hurts. Daryl knew how to do that. We'd already arrested Lieutenant Chandler earlier in the week and he'd kicked out the radio in our truck, so this time we put him in the truck bed. He started kicking, and I just reached down and twisted. By that point, he'd been cuffed so many times throughout the week that his wrists were pretty sore, so I just had to apply a little bit of pressure and got immediate compliance. We were walking on air after we pulled that one off. It was the high point of the week.

During that Swan's Island week, they gave us another scenario around night hunting. There was a complaint that a farmer had heard shots at the back end of his field after dark. When the call came in, we had an hour, hour and a half of daylight left. This was in June. Most of the students took a break after supper, but Daryl and I decided to go look at this place and figure out where the shot was. We looked and saw there was no way they could walk down the field and take that shot without the farmer seeing them. The only way was if they came by boat. So we looked, and sure enough, we found a mark where a boat had been pulled up onto a beach. This was where they were going to be.

So later they called us out, and Daryl and I went and sat by that little scrape mark on the beach. Sure enough, right after dark, the boat came up the river, they went up in the field and they fired, and when they came back to the boat we grabbed them and handcuffed them.

It's a funny mix, the work we do. Our training goes in two directions: one part is all about protecting fish and wildlife and the other part is all about saving people. That's a pretty complex set of challenges. And we have to train to do both of those things well. We have to have that basic foundation of woods knowledge to carry us, and we build on that.

CHAPTER THREE

First Patrol

I'll never forget my first days as a game warden. I grew up in Jackman, in western Maine on the Canadian border. It was a real small town and a place where everybody got along. Then I landed in Princeton, way over on the eastern side of the state, with a patrol sector that included a tribal reservation. I quickly discovered there was a lot of animosity between the tribe and law enforcement, particularly with game wardens. This was all new to me. People in Jackman feared and respected wardens but didn't hate them like I was seeing here. It was such a different environment. I'd never seen people hate game wardens. Hate *me*.

I had so much to learn. My days as a deputy warden had given me a taste of the job; now I had to adjust to the highs and lows of doing it every day. The job demanded patience for the many hours of sitting necessary to catch a poacher. It required stamina for lost person searches that sometimes took days. I needed to get used to handling those incredible adrenaline highs that came from confrontation, and the necessity to go on working hours after the post-adrenaline surge would leave me drained and weary. Among the biggest challenges was becoming the guy I'd spent my youth trying to avoid, now that I was seeing it from the other side.

My first day, I was driving through the reservation, going toward Topsfield. It was about seven in the morning and there was a little boy playing in the ditch. He was probably four or five years old, didn't have a stitch of clothes on, and he looked at me and flipped me the bird. Right then I said to myself, *hang on to your hat, buddy, 'cause this is going to be a ride.* I mean, that child, at that age, already hated game wardens.

That was a real rude awakening to me. I thought: *I am in a different part of the world and a different culture here.*

When you're a warden in woods country, you're an important figure, whether you realize it or not. A lot of people talk about you at the dinner table. They want to know as much about you as they can. It's kind of a law enforcement thing. But also, they want to be able to recognize you before you recognize them. When we moved to Princeton for my first patrol, the first night we were at the house there were all these people driving by to see what we were like, checking to see what our personal vehicle was like, literally driving into the yard and turning around. It was kind of like a parade.

Jolyne would go into the market and walk toward the deli, and all conversation stopped. She got a kick out of it. She also got a few notorious poachers to wave to her by just adjusting her visor when they passed each other on the road.

I was very fortunate, though, that in our warden academy class we had someone from the Passamaquoddy tribe go through with us. He helped me so much in understanding his culture, so I could get an idea of how things really worked. One thing I figured out right away was that while we had no authority to deal with fish and game violations that occurred on tribal lands, they were always sneaking across the line because that's where the game was. So what I started doing, which had the biggest benefit, other than catching them, was working with the kids. I did some speaking engagements at the school—classes, really, in some of the useful things wardens did that would appeal to outdoorsy youth—things like using maps and compasses and outdoor survival techniques. I really worked hard to break that cycle of hatred toward game wardens. I kinda had to put the hardcore enforcement aside a little bit to get through the door to work with that generation of kids. But with Richard's help, I made some pretty good friends, and I like to think it made a difference.

From the challenges of that first patrol, I learned one of my most important life long lessons: if you're open and willing to learn, the people you meet can teach you a lot. They can give you different windows into the world. I remember Timmy Bacon, this older guy who lived at Grand Lake. He had been a deputy warden in his younger days, and he sat there one day and told me he was mad at the state biologists.

I said, "Timmy, what's wrong with the biologists?"

And he said, "Those guys think they know all about this river and what's best for the fish." He went on and on about Grand Lake Stream. Finally he looked at me, and he said, "I've lived on this river for eighty-two years, and I'll tell you exactly what I know."

"What's that, Timmy?"

"I don't know a damned thing about this river. It changes every day."

That's what I've enjoyed most about twenty-five years of doing this—the people I've met on the road. But back then, I was so green I didn't know anything.

One thing we—we, meaning the wardens, but in those early days, specifically me and Daryl—got involved in, out there in Washington County, was being the "back woods" backup for local law enforcement. Sometimes, especially around the time the tribal checks came out, things would get pretty crazy. I remember one night, the cruiser that was chasing a car had lost them through a series of intersections on woods roads. Well, I knew the person they were chasing and I kinda knew where he would go. So we were headed that way and we came around a corner and there was the drive shaft of a car lying right in the middle of the road. The car had missed the turn and gone off a bridge, and the drive shaft caught on the abutment of the bridge and it blew back into the middle of the road.

The car was down below in the bushes. The occupants were getting out of the car, so we ran down to stop them before they got away. I put my hand on one guy's shoulder, and he turned around, ready to swing at me, and he stopped, and he said, "Oh, I'm sorry. You're a game warden. I thought you were one of the town cops." And he apologized and was just as nice as he could be.

Some of the stuff that we had happen was beyond my wildest imaginings. We had a high-speed nighttime chase that ended up on the ice on Pocomoonshine Lake. The Princeton officer had stopped where the guy he was chasing had driven out onto the lake. He didn't want to take the police cruiser out onto the ice, so we came down with a snowmobile. I knew the kid that we were chasing; he was a pretty wild boy, so when we hopped on the snowmobile, I got on behind the driver because you can't drive a snowmobile and use your firearm because your gun hand is also your throttle hand. So I was on the back, riding shotgun. We were on the ice, chasing their lights, and they were trying to hide behind little islands. When they saw us, they headed for the far side of the lake.

We had officers hiding out over there, waiting for them. So they got them stopped and we pulled up on the snowmobile. This kid, he was probably in his twenties, he said, "How come there's two of you on the snowmobile? How come you guys did that?"

I said, "Think about it a minute . . . if, for example, you're driving a snowmobile and you're going to try and shoot a coyote," because I knew he'd done that, "what's the problem?"

There was a moment of recognition as he said, "You can't keep the sled moving and shoot 'cause it's the wrong side."

And I said, "There you go."

It's always a mix. Policing fishermen, catching night hunters, moose hunters, bear hunters. And then there were the searches for lost people.

Back in the pre-GPS world, and before I had my dogs, lost people still had to be found, like the search for Nellie Tibbets.

We were working a big case involving the illegal trapping of bear, been working it for a while. We'd just found all the illegal traps that we were looking for, and we were going home to get our gear—food, drink, sleeping bag, flashlight, radio, and of course a can of Vienna sausages—so that we could sit on those traps and wait for the poachers to show up. We figured they'd come and check 'em at daylight. We went on the FM radio, and they were talking about this missing lady out of Lincoln who'd left in her car and never returned. They were broadcasting the description and stuff. My partner at the time was Daryl, and we looked at each other, and we said, "We'll be looking for her before we get home."

Sure enough, we were almost home and we got the call that they'd found her car near Danforth, that she was not in it, and off we went.

We'd been trained in these major searches using the overhead management team and the whole command structure at the academy, but this was the first time I'd actually participated in one. It was my first hands-on introduction to how the overhead team worked and what actually went into the science of searching and all the tools it took to get the job done.

Those tools would include the planning, the mapping, figuring out the sections of the map that had the highest probability of finding the missing person based on the information that we had, planning the logistics of feeding all the searchers and housing them and getting them water and lunches and things like that. There would be a person who was going to deal with the press and communicate to them the essential details of the search, such as who they're searching for, that person's description and habits, the point last seen, and getting the word out in case the person had been seen.

The highest probability areas would be identified through what is known as a Mattson Consensus.[1] We would use it pretty much on any of the larger scale searches. What we would do is take all of the information we had, then pool all of our experience and knowledge and our gut feelings. We would test that gut as kind of a community gut—what does our collective experience tell us?—then put what we'd agreed

---

1   The Mattson method was the first consensus method used in land search and rescue. First published in the spring 1976 issue of *Search and Rescue Magazine* by creator R. J. Mattson, this is how the concept of determining the Probability of Area using a consensus of experts was first conceived.

were the most likely scenarios on a piece of paper and score the highest probability areas to help plan our search.

The search for Nellie involved typical Washington County terrain. Big swamps, cedar ridges, big woods country all crisscrossed with logging trails, ATV trails, snowmobile trails. There was lots and lots of water—ponds, lakes, and streams—so it was difficult to break the search up into neat blocks of land.

Back in those days, the first three days of a search, we went all out. Statistically, one thing that drives the intensity of these searches in the early days that they're missing is that if someone's lost in the woods, after three days there's a 90 percent probability of them being deceased, so the push was really on. You'd clear a block, you go back and get a new assignment and you just keep doing that. You might get an hour's break to eat and have coffee, but otherwise it was non-stop, on your feet searching, dawn to dark. In the pre-GPS era, we used physical features and a lot of string to identify the blocks we'd searched and ensure that our searches were thorough. What we were doing in this case was grid searching, slow, painstaking step-by-step lines to carefully cover all the ground. Times like this really brought home why they'd been so tough at the academy.

Over those three days, what complicated our search was that she was evading us. That's a fairly common occurrence; I've seen it happen a lot over the years, especially on searches for elderly people or those with Alzheimer's. They get lost and then when the searchers come out they hide because all that noise, the helicopters overhead and stuff, scares them. In her mind, Nellie was at a physical place. I think she believed she was at her dad's camp.

Here's how we ended up finding her. One of the wardens working in the command post went for a walk to clear his head a little bit. He walked down a skidder trail and he saw footprints made by bare feet. We took a big team and swept them through the area where he'd seen that footprint. And we found where she was hiding. She was close to where the vehicle was, probably within a half mile.

I remember trying to drive home from that after getting virtually no sleep for those three days. I was completely wiped out. My feet were all blistered. It was just like I was drunk. In fact, at one point during the search I fell asleep just sitting there. I woke up when a log truck roared by. Thus, once we were finally done, I went home, went to bed, and I don't know if I moved for two days.

People tend to think of Maine as one generic block, but the terrain across the state in Washington County is very different from where I grew up. What you have for terrain out there is mixed. As you get closer to Machias, you roll into the blueberry barrens, and you've got that coastal environment, and as you get inland heading north from Calais, you're getting into spruce fir and lot of hemlock stands, and rolling hills and pretty substantial swamp areas. A lot of water, and then you start getting into what we call "the big water," the Grand Lakes, and Big Lake, and Princeton, and the West Grand, East Grand, with logging roads going everywhere. Because it's not mountainous, it's very easy territory to get lost in because you don't have visuals to sight on.

We did have a lot of lost hunters, the first couple years, and then we'd have to go and dig them out. I was good with a compass, because I'd done a lot of timber cruising—evaluating timber stands for harvesting and figuring out the value of timber in blocks—so I was adept at digging lost hunters out of the woods. This was in the pre-GPS era, so we pretty much used the old style system of firing a shot. You'd listen for the answering shot, hold your compass out, line your dial where you heard the shot, get your bearing, and take off, staying on that line.

With GPS today, it's no problem because it can keep recalculating your route, but back then, when you offset from your line, you had to count your steps, pacing it out and pacing it back to get back on your line. Another thing that would happen that made finding these people difficult was that when the hunter could hear you, he'd start moving so you'd find him somewhere off the line.

The bigger trick was coming back, because if you were off, you'd miss your vehicle. What you'd do is, if you had his buddy with you,

you'd leave him at your truck. You had your radio, and you'd put your radio on the one channel that was just a local channel, and you'd tell the buddy: "At some point, I'm going to contact you, and I want you to flip the siren," because you'd get into swamps and water and you couldn't keep that straight line. If you had the guy at the truck with the siren, you could hear it and know, okay, that's the way to come out.

Of course, just to make it more complicated, we'd nearly always learn about lost hunters at the end of the day because that's when their buddies, or their family, would realize that they were lost. Then the call would come in to us. Always after dark, when we couldn't fly a plane over. Or even later at night just when we'd turned the TV off to go to bed.

It's very interesting, finding people who are lost, because often, two things would happen. They're always very glad to see you. Always, pretty much the first thing that came out is "Thank God." But, because their egos were bruised by getting lost, a lot of the guys, right after that, would say, "Well, I was just gonna sleep here and come out in the morning anyway. You didn't have to come looking for me."

I'd say, "All right, you can stay here and I'll go back."

And they'd go, "Oh, no, that's okay. Now that you're here I'll come out with you."

I never had one stay 'til daylight. They all followed us out.

CHAPTER FOUR

Blowing Things Up and Calming Things Down

Another of the adventures of my rookie years was learning to use dynamite. They don't do this anymore, but we used to drive around with a box of dynamite in our trucks, half a case in the back and blasting caps in the dashboard. We never thought twice about it. We needed to know how to use it. I remember the first time they were training us how to use dynamite. The instructor took us to this old beaver flowage. He placed the charge and set it off, and all of a sudden rocks the size of softballs were raining all over the place. Everyone was scrambling and trying to find a place to hide. What we learned from that was you had to be really be careful when you set it off because you never knew what was under there. Sometimes it would be all mud, which could absorb the blow, sometimes it would go straight up and then start raining rocks. Sometimes it got so bad you'd crawl right under the truck.

We had detcord, which looks just like rope but burns really fast. When we wanted to set off multiple charges at the same time, we'd connect it with this cord. We could cut trees with it. Wrap it around a tree with a blasting cap, drop a tree right there. Wrap it around a moose or something, floating in the water, to sink it. That was one of the big things we did with dynamite, trying to sink dead moose. It's what we were told to do. It never worked, though. All it ever did was spread it all over the place. But it was great in theory.

Back then, we used to blow up beaver dams. I had this one particular beaver problem—the beaver had built a dam right under a bridge, and attached the dam to the main support beams of the bridge so the dam was right up against it. Very problematic to remove because of the proximity of the dam to the bridge. I couldn't get underneath it to work with a lever to break it loose because of deep water and its location beneath the bridge. In an effort to weaken the dam so that water pressure would break it free, I used quarter sticks of dynamite, and I would slide one down and pop it.

Well, I did that three or four times and had no luck, so I went from quarter to half. Still no luck. Finally, I had one stick left and the dam hadn't budged. I didn't want to go back and have to report that I'd failed, so I said what the hell? I taped this dynamite onto the stick, and shoved it down in there as far as I could, and I attached my wires. I got back with my little roll of wire, took my battery pack, attached the wires, and *Wham!* That bridge went in a million pieces. I blew that bridge completely to China.

See, when you're using dynamite, like we learned with those flying rocks, what matters is how hard the bottom is, because that's what puts the energy upward. I had managed to put that stick all the way to the hard-packed bottom. On the other tries, I hadn't managed to get down that far, but I'd punched a few holes in the dam, which had opened it up, so that time I managed to get that stick all the way down. It was all ledge underneath that, so all that power had come blasting up. I don't think there was a piece of that bridge more than three feet long left. In three seconds the entire bridge was gone. It was impressive. It really was.

I couldn't go back to the state and say, "Hey, I blew up the bridge." I picked up all the evidence that dynamite was there, like the little pieces of paper that the caps come in, and I went back. There was a senior warden who had a camp on the other side of that bridge, and he was the one who really wanted us to take care of that beaver dam. I came back to the office. I went upstairs and said, "Hey, the bridge went out. You're going to have to go around the long way." That's all I said, and I walked out.

Another time, we were in Washington County on Route 9, the road they call "The Airline" that goes from Bangor over to Calais. They'd just tarred it and put in these big new culverts. There was a brand new culvert, about an eight-footer, and beaver had built a dam in there. Again, it was a big dam, so we figured a whole stick would be needed to clear it. We stuck a charge in it. We stood on the highway, cars were going by, we had a stick of dynamite at the end of the culvert, and we were waiting for a lull in the traffic so we could blow this thing up. Finally, the lull comes and we blew it up.

The whole road rippled. You know the pilgrim guns? The blunderbusses? That's exactly what that culvert looked like. All the rivets were popped out of the end of the culvert, it was splayed right out. We were looking at each other and then this gush of water came through.

Blowing things up was fun, but what I was really learning, during those early years, was that the call of duty was a fact of life, a lot of those calls could be scary, and when you're a game warden, your own plans can always be pushed aside. The general public has absolutely no idea what it's like to live a life where our schedule never belongs to us. Day, night, light, dark, winter, summer, whatever the weather—everything can always be tipped on end while you're trying to live a normal family life. When the call comes, you have to go, and so much of what you end up dealing with is life and death. Even when you go out into the woods with poachers and fisherman, they carry guns. Everyone carries guns into the woods. Every day, you always deal with that element. Much of the time, you are all alone. It might take backup hours to get there.

As a game warden, I always had to have that in mind—how I was going to approach any situation. I had to think that through, and I always had to go into the game with a plan, because if something went bad, I was on my own. So I had to really look hard at the situation before I acted. Sometimes, even when the law was violated, and I really wanted to make that arrest or issue that summons, I couldn't. I had to step back and say, all right, today's not the day enforcement's going to happen. I'm gonna pull back, get some more people, and come back in.

When you're a young officer, you tend to be more aggressive and push that envelope a little harder. It's experience that teaches you what you need to know. I learned that from scary situations like this one. What happened was that as I was driving along, a guy with a gun stepped out into the road. I stopped to check him because I knew from past experience that anytime I saw him in the woods, there was likely to be a fish and game violation. It was almost like breaking the law was part of his recreation. What I didn't know was that on this particular day he was with a bunch of other people who were still back in the woods and they had a deer drive going.

A deer drive is when some hunters line up and force the deer to move to shooters who are standing in place waiting. Deer drives are very dangerous. Back in the 1930s and '40s there were lots of fatalities from driving deer, which is why Maine outlawed it. So I was checking him out, we were having a conversation, and all of a sudden, these guys who were just at the edge of the tree line, six, seven, eight guys, stepped out and they surrounded me. The accepted gun protocol is muzzle pointed away from everybody, but every one of them had their guns pointed at me. Casually, not at the shoulder, but every one had his finger on the trigger and his gun pointed at me, and I was in the middle.

These weren't your usual poachers. These were bad boys—a couple of them were big-time drug dealers—and I'd caught them in a deer drive. This was their entertainment, to just go out there with big guns and kill some things. Bad, bad boys and I was all alone. I realized I was in way over my head and if I just chirped the wrong way, things could go badly. I had to go real easy, let things de-escalate, bring it down to a level where we could all walk away. If I'd gone for my gun, I would have been dead, and this for just a class E minor infraction, so I had to gracefully step back and they finally backed off.

It was extremely frustrating, because I'd put such a lot of time into trying to catch these guys, but I had not seen enough to initiate enforcement action—they saw me before I could catch them. However badly I wanted that arrest, I had to accept that I wasn't ten feet tall and bulletproof. By letting the situation go from very dangerous to casual, both sides knew we would fight this battle another day.

CHAPTER FIVE

Learning Patience and the Long View

Looking back, I can see that in those early days some pretty wild things happened. Here's another case that left me with an "Oh my God!" adrenaline rush. Long before we had our Operation Game Thief hotline, we would get calls about this or that person night hunting. Pretty often, these callers were not motivated by righteous indignation or a desire to protect wildlife. It was more likely that they'd had a disagreement with the person they were reporting, or were simply jealous that he was a more successful poacher. Mostly we'd just answer the phone and an anonymous voice would deliver the information and hang up.

We got a call that there was some night hunting taking place on Musquash Stream. This stream flows into Big Lake, and on the western shore of Big Lake there's a section that's tribal lands and then the stream kind of meanders away and goes up to paper company lands and into a pretty remote area.

We had information that someone was night hunting, but that's about all we knew. This was in early fall, Septemberish, and all of our deer decoys were fall decoys, which meant that their hides were brown. Those wouldn't work, because an experienced hunter would know that a September deer's hide is red. Luckily, we had a small deer that had been hit by a car. Knowing that we needed it, we skinned it and salted the hide and then tacked it onto a piece of plywood to make it look like a summer deer. Up close, it would never fool anyone, but at a distance of twenty or thirty yards, if you were in a hurry, you might think it was a deer.

We put that together and then we went up Musquash Stream. There was one access road going into that country where we could carry boats down to the stream. We had to be very careful, because we didn't want to go up the stream and get "bumped" by someone who might see us. Bumped is the term we use for when the wrong person you want to see sees you in the last place you want them to see you, so they know you're working 'em. That was one of the challenges, anytime you worked water. You can't hide when you're going up a stream.

We'd gone in on a side road, carried our boat down to the water, and covered it with camouflage parachutes we used as tarps. We had the motor all set to go. There were four of us, and the game plan was that if a boat did come by night hunting, we'd pick up our boat, throw it in, start it up, and see if we could catch 'em.

We put the decoy across the stream on the other side, about twenty yards into the marsh, so if they shot, they'd be shooting away from us. The way the stream doglegged, we could get in trouble pretty quick if we weren't careful. It was open, flat, marsh country around there. We got there just before dark, set up the boats and the decoy, and sat.

Sitting quietly and waiting was a huge part of the job, and patience wasn't something I had a lot of when I first came on. It was something I learned from working night hunters. From September to December, we wardens would put in literally hundreds of hours waiting to catch them. It's because night hunting was such a big deal, and so dangerous, that wardens always talked not about how many years they'd worked but how many falls they'd survived. The gun that was used on the deer could easily be used on you. Night hunters were notorious for not identifying targets before shooting. Or they might shoot you as a reflex, or deliberately, or because they're drunk.

Now, in our mind's eye, we were expecting the boat to be coming upstream, from Big Lake going up. We didn't anticipate what was about to happen.

About an hour into darkness, we could see a spotlight coming from the upstream side. It took forever for it to get to us, because that stream meandered like a worm, but we could watch it coming toward us, that spotlight sweeping the marsh, and sweeping the marsh. It was a total adrenaline surge, as we were waiting. Waiting. Poised and ready to go.

Finally, after what seemed like three hours, and was probably about ten minutes, the boat came by. The light went across the marsh and caught the reflector eyes we'd put in the deer. The light just clipped it and then instantly shut off. The engine of the boat shut off and there was this absolute silence. We heard the click of a rifle being loaded, the bolt being closed. Then, for a split second, the light came back on, and the rifle fired. You could see the muzzle flash, and a big roar rolled across the open marsh, echoing everywhere.

As soon as they fired, the light went off. At that point, we were about twenty or thirty yards away. We grabbed our boat and threw it in. We didn't have any lights on, but there was all this thrashing and banging. I'm sure they were trying to figure out what was going on. We got the boat launched, and of course, it didn't start on the first pull, like we'd primed it to. But it started on the second pull. I was in the bow, and Daryl was in the stern and soon as the motor started, I put my flashlight on and started hollering for them to put their hands up, saying, "Game warden. Game warden. Put your hands up."

They were drifting down the stream. We were probably about twenty yards apart. I had my flashlight on the bowman of that boat, when, all of a sudden, about the third time I said it, it clicked who we were, and I saw he was reaching down for the gun. Our motor was accelerating, we were moving at a pretty good clip, but I didn't notice that because I was only focusing on the guy with the gun. Within a second, we collided, nose to nose, with their boat. The impact pushed me out of my boat and into the other boat just as the guy was coming up with the rifle.

When I went into their boat, my whole focus was on where his hands were and where my hands were. He and I flipped to the back of the boat, and the scramble was on for that loaded rifle. I had the advantage, because I was on top, so I pinned the rifle down with my right hand and kind of pushed my arm into his neck hard enough so he had to let go of the rifle and use his hands to push me away. Not something planned on my part, but it worked perfectly, because first and foremost I needed to get that gun secured. I believe it was a .308 rifle, safety off, fully loaded, and ready to go.

Once I was able to get that gun, I pulled back, and he stayed there.

There was a lot of screaming. I don't know if Daryl had his gun out or not; I'd gone into tunnel vision at that point. I didn't get back to normal until I'd pulled the clip out and ejected the round out of the chamber. Once I separated the guy from the gun, things calmed down and he was not a problem to deal with. It was just critical to get that thing away from him. Our guys on the shore had a spotlight trained right on him, so the two guys in that boat must have felt like they were surrounded. So at that point, everything de-escalated.

We towed them right to shore. We wanted to get them where there were two more wardens right away. I believe I stayed in their boat and we put the rifle in our boat. We really never want to handcuff some-body in a boat, unless we put a lifejacket on them. That's bad form. But once they were on shore, we patted them down and handcuffed them. I think I came off the high about twenty minutes after we landed.

So now we had two prisoners, two boats, four wardens, and it was the middle of the night. We had to take them to Machias to the county jail, which was about an hour away, and take their seized boat to Princeton. We had one truck with a trailer, so we took their boat and loaded it. It was brand, spanking new. We had a couple extra trucks in the area, so we used one truck to send them to jail, another to shuttle their boat to Princeton, which was about a twenty-minute drive, and then we came back for our boat. It was a long, long night. But we got 'em.

It was what every young game warden dreams of. But it was also probably the most vulnerable moment I had ever experienced. We're trained, tactically, to always have something to get behind, and to always have an escape route. In a boat, we've got nothing.

Then there are the rules about when we can use force to defend ourselves. Being the responder is worse because you always want to have the upper hand—action beats reaction every time—and yet, in law enforcement generally, you can't do anything until you have a reasonable fear for your life. The magic words are imminent danger or imminent bodily injury.

In this case, the guy in the boat, it's interesting what I can remember clearly. Sometimes when people see a game warden and they just did something bad with a gun, their first instinct is to unload the gun and hide it. That is a very clear thing. You see it over and over in your career, their attention goes from you to the gun, and it's rarely the *I'm coming up with my gun, 'cause I'm going to shoot you* look that I got from him. You can tell the difference, your brain articulates that difference at a very quick pace. This guy in the boat was all about going for his gun. He was not going back to jail.

What I didn't know, when we were struggling over that gun, was who I was dealing with. This guy had recently gotten out of prison for beating someone almost to death with a baseball bat. I didn't find out until we had him in jail that the suspect going for his gun had already almost taken another life. In that time and era, we didn't have the computers we have now where I could have found out his whole criminal history. Then I realized that yeah, had it been just Daryl and me in the boat, and if they weren't being lit up from the shore, it would have been a bigger fight. The guys on the shore were important because the two men in the boat couldn't tell how many of us there were. And subconsciously, sitting on the water and with nowhere to hide, even though this was happening at the speed of light, I think they realized that they were going to lose.

That was one of those moments where, after it was all done and I really got to process it, I thought *Wow, that could have been very bad*.

The next day, a gentleman called me who owned the boat—a brand-new, expensive boat—and I could hear his wife screaming obscenities in the background. I told him, "Well, I have a boat. I don't know if it's yours 'cause I haven't run the registration yet. If we don't enter it into evidence, you stand a better chance of getting it back, but right now, we've seized it." So the two offenders went and pled guilty the next Monday, turned themselves in to get the guy his boat back.

Rookie years. I was 100 percent fearless. Not smart enough to be scared. That was really, really a dangerous event.

The importance of taking the long view, and of educating people about preserving resources instead of just catching them and writing summonses was really brought home to me the first fall that I was in Princeton. I was right out of the academy and gung ho to start catching bad guys. My first hunting season as a warden, we were working night hunters and I was between these guys and what they thought was a deer. What they thought was a deer was me, in the woods, moving a set of eyes to make them think they were seeing a deer. It was a very dangerous situation, and as I was moving along to make it look like that "deer" was moving, I fell in a hole and dislocated my shoulder. I ended up out of commission for six weeks.

One day I went to the post office, and there was a retired game warden, Dale Speed, who worked there. He could tell I was really bumming. My first fall on the job and I was sidelined. He looked at me and he said, "Young man, if writing summonses was going to stop people from breaking fish and game laws, it should have worked a hundred years ago." He said, "You've got to think about it. I know you're fretting because you're not out catching bad guys, but there's a lot more to it than that."

I realized that he was talking about another part of our role. He was talking about what I was trying to do with those school kids. Community policing. He was talking about the part of the job that involved educating people about why we were doing what we were doing. That really brought it home to me.

I said, "You're right. That's the fun part—catching bad guys. But I've got to look at the bigger picture."

Here's the philosophy behind enforcement: We know we're not going to catch all the bad guys; we're there as a deterrent, to keep people honest. What you find with respect to fish and wildlife in

Maine—and I assume it's that way in other states as well—is that nice people commit fish and wildlife crimes. It's kind of a cultural thing. It's been the practice in their family for years. My own family was that way. People in Maine don't necessarily think of poaching fish or wildlife as a crime. The crime is getting caught by the game wardens. A lot of these poachers that I've dealt with absolutely love fish and wildlife. That's their entire life, and they don't realize that they're destroying what they love the most by not respecting it.

Our job is to educate them. To make them understand, for example, that if someone goes to a pond to fish and gets greedy and cleans it out, takes more than their limit, takes the undersized fish, takes everything they can catch, then the next year, when they go there, they've got nothing. We're the conscience of these people. We get them to look at the reality: that if they don't take care of this, they'll lose it. That was a big part of my job. When I dealt with people in poaching situations I'd tell them: My job is not to leave fish and wildlife for you, it's to leave it for your grandkids. My job is done if your grandkids get to enjoy the same outdoor resources that you have. You put it in that context, they usually catch on and begin to think *maybe I'm not in the right here.*

The job is also about dealing with people who are selfish and want it all for themselves, right here and right now, who don't care about other people or the future. Then we have some people who are completely indifferent, who aren't there to enjoy fishing or hunting but are killing just for the sake of killing, and that's a whole different thing.

So, we're the conscience. We're the people who are there to make it happen. Our philosophy of deterrence is that you must give people the impression that you are everywhere and you are likely to step out at any time.

PART II

PROTECTING FISH AND WILDLIFE

CHAPTER SIX

Night Hunting

I worked a lot of my early cases in Washington County with Daryl Gordon. Both of us were on our first assignments—Daryl had Woodland and I had Princeton, and when we could, we had each other's backs. Daryl was a bigger guy—the guy who'd carried the .50-caliber rifle on patrol in Vietnam. His military training gave him a confidence and judgment that was invaluable—to him and to me in the situations we sometimes found ourselves in. Times where, as was so often the case in warden work, things could spin on a dime, its danger or its complications, and we had to spin right along with it. Daryl also taught me a lot about reading signs that people had been in the area. About reading what was in front of us in the field—tracks, broken branches, etc.

He was a blunt man. Not easy to get along with. He had this intimidating look he could do, a look that could say volumes without saying a word. If he didn't like you, you knew it. Where our skills were complimentary was that I could be more diplomatic. I was good with people. So he'd play bad cop; I'd play good. I was Catholic, from a town where everyone was Catholic; Daryl was a Baptist who openly witnessed for his religion. But we were close. From the start we had an almost uncanny ability to read each other's minds and a level of trust that let us handle things without stopping to discuss them. A great thing when we had to respond to dangerous, rapidly changing situations.

Like me, he loved being a warden. We lived and breathed it every day.

We had had a report about night hunters out Calais way who were using shotguns from some tree stands. They were not using lights, but they were luring deer in with apples, and they'd put dry sticks around the base of the tree stand so they could hear the deer when they came in to the bait. Baiting, of course, using apples or something to draw in deer, was illegal during hunting season.

This technique would only be used by good, extremely experienced night hunters. According to our information, the guy who'd organized it had bragged that he'd never be caught. But these guys had made one fatal mistake: They had made their brags in the mill community—Calais was a mill town because of the Georgia Pacific plant. The story kind of circled around and came back to us. There are always people who really want to see the guy who's bragging all the time taken down. There was a tremendous amount of poaching going on in Washington County, so at that time we'd pretty much go out every day with our lists, prioritized according to who were the worst offenders. When this news came to us, right away the braggart went from somebody down in the middle of our list right to the top.

We knew what was going on, but we didn't know where, so we started looking really hard. Out behind the town of Woodland, there was an old railroad bed that went all the way to Princeton. About halfway out, there was an island with spruce trees in the middle of a big marsh. We poked around, found a foot trail out to that island, and when we got out to the island, we found bait, and sticks, and the tree stand.

It was a very difficult place to conduct surveillance because it was so open, so we had to resort to a little warden ingenuity. What we did was take a moose telemetry collar, which works with a magnet. If you put a magnet on it, it will deactivate the collar. Take the magnet off and it gets turned on so you can track the moose. So we buried it at the base of a tree, and put the string to the magnet almost chest high on the trail, knowing that deer could come back and forth on that trail without disturbing it, but a man coming down the trail would push the branches out of his way and activate the device.

Then we took my car, my little Subaru, Daryl, me, my wife, and all the kids, and we drove down the road. We had the telemetry monitor, a little antenna that when you point it picks up the signal and kind of gives you a direction. These monitors are used for tracking moose for research. When the little monitor in the car went off, we'd know that we'd got someone out on the island. So we're driving by, holding the monitor out the window, and it starts beeping.

This was early afternoon. Our plan had been to get in there before dark, before the hunters came in. Now it got complicated because they were already on the island, in the blind, with guns. And we had nowhere to hide.

We couldn't go up over the road, 'cause we'd be seen, so we drove until we got to a point where there was a big culvert, and Daryl and I rolled out of the car on the opposite side of the bank, rolled down the bank, and crawled through the culvert. Then we lay there on the bank and waited for dark.

My wife, Jolyne, and the kids went home, the kids a little freaked because we'd just rolled out and we were gone. Jolyne said they asked, "We're just going to drive away and leave Daddy and Daryl here?"

When it got dark, about eight o'clock, we started moving toward the island. We saw a quick flashlight flash from one of the tree stands, and then they started coming out. Daryl and I were waiting on either side of the trail. How we're trained to do this kind of a stop is this: Daryl will be the lead man, he's going to step out and confront them. I'm behind them, at an angle, for two reasons. One, so that if there's a shooting confrontation, I'm not in his line of fire. Two, if they turn to run or try to escape, it's 99 percent likely they're coming to me.

As they were coming toward us, it was deathly quiet, there wasn't even a breeze, and I could hear the branches pinging on the gun barrels. They were carrying shotguns, which are a lighter metal, and it's a very distinctive sound.

Because we work in a world where people carry guns, and we're often confronting them when they've done something wrong, it's warden practice to work in the dark and not turn on our lights until the last minute. We do this for several reasons: to preserve the element of surprise, and to be sure we're close enough to quickly get them under control. So when they were close, Daryl stepped out, put the light on, and said, "Game warden, hold it. Drop your guns."

At that point, all we could see were two figures. One of them immediately dropped his gun, but the other one was turning with his shotgun and going right toward Daryl. I was at that angle that I could see what he was doing and I just ran for him. I hit him at full speed, right above the knee, took him right out, and he went down into a big bog with me on top of him. His gun went flying. He's screaming because he's in pain. It turned out the guy had just had knee surgery and he was on worker's comp. But he could still climb tree stands and shoot deer.

Once we got control of them, we handcuffed him. But now we were kind of perplexed, because there was no vehicle. So I grabbed hold of the kid, who was not handcuffed, the guy's nephew who was about eighteen. As I walked him toward the road, I said, "How'd you get here?"

He said, "We got dropped off."

I said, "Your ride coming soon?" And he just nodded.

I realized then that I was wearing exactly the same camo coat as the guy with the bad knee, so I grabbed the kid and we stood there, and sure enough, pretty soon this car came chugging up the rail bed, and goes right by us. I said to the kid, "How are we going to make it stop?"

He said, "It'll come back." And sure enough, it came back and beeped the horn. So I grabbed him by the arm, keeping him between me and the car. He was so shell-shocked, I could move him any way I wanted to. We popped out of the bushes and went over to the car, and as soon as I got to the car, I grabbed the door, leaned in, and said, "Game warden, hold it."

It was the injured guy's wife, and she had their kids in the car. As I popped the door open, she hit the gas. I grabbed her arm and she was coming out of the car, and there were kids screaming in the back seat. It was bad. Luckily, it wasn't a place where she could go very fast. Finally, she stopped. We got her out and got her up in front of the vehicle, got her under control and checked for weapons. Once we realized there were no weapons, we took the keys and let her get back in the car and talk to the kids.

Then the guy with the bad knee came running over to her, and he goes, "Honey, we have been lost."

She says, "What?"

And he says, "Honey, WE have been LOST."

She says, "What do you mean?"

And he repeats, "We have been lost."

Finally, she says, "I have been looking for you everywhere."

They started with this whole story of how they got lost the day before, scouting for deer, and they weren't the hunters we were looking for. What we needed to do was confirm that those lights we saw across the bog were from the two people we'd arrested. So we had another warden, Debbie Palman, come in with her K-9. At this point, the warden service had very few working dogs, just Debbie's and one other. Her dog, Anna, tracked them back to tree stand A and tree stand B and showed their story was false. It helped us put together an awesome case. It also was the point where I began to see how useful dogs could be in warden work.

Another night hunting case involved a guy who worked in the Georgia Pacific mill, in upper management. Poaching was one of his pastimes. We had gotten a lot of intelligence that he was night hunting, so one night we put the decoy deer out on this back road. We knew he had a scanner. We had information that he was listening to our every move, so once we got into position, and got our decoy deer set up, we signed off to home, each one of us separately, a few minutes apart, which would have been the norm.

It wasn't half an hour later, here comes this truck, creepy-crawling up the road. There was an apple tree in the field, and we'd kind of set the deer in front of it. So the truck stopped, jigged toward the field to light up the target, and fired.

Now, we had put a camouflage parachute over our truck. Quick as anything, we pulled the parachute off—Daryl was driving and I was the wingman—and headed up the road, driving without lights of course, and the parachute got caught in the drive axle of the truck. Luckily, we caught up to it quickly, before that parachute could cause too much trouble, put the blue lights on, and it stopped. We bailed out, got him out of the vehicle and arrested him, and the scanner was sitting right there.

We got him flat. Stopped, shot the decoy, what's your defense? So he ended up pleading guilty. Our intelligence sources in that mill kept us apprised. He had to go to jail—three days in jail, thousand-dollar fine, and he lost his weapon and his right to have a hunting license for two years. When he came back from jail, they'd put black crepe paper over his office windows and they were playing "Jailhouse Rock" on the intercom.

That was a good catch because this poacher wasn't one of those guys who needed to poach to survive; this was something he did for entertainment. Poaching because he could. It was the rush.

Because a person of his stature was poaching to brag, when we caught him, it made a lot of people in the mill very happy. People who saw this started calling us with other information, as in, you got him, now you need to get so-and-so. It really opened doors to some great intelligence for us.

It can be pretty scary, and dangerous, going after night hunters. I remember one time we were following up on a report about night hunting at a camp up in Dover. This other warden, Mike Eaton, the fastest walking human on the planet, and I were walking in the warden way, no lights, just making our way through the dark. We were a couple hundred yards from the camp and suddenly, *Kapow!* We started running down the road and when we got in closer, we can see the camp and that there are lights in the apple orchard right behind the camp. So we slithered right in, right in along the edge of the camp, and once we got a line on them, we made a plan—you take this one, I'll take that one. Well, the guy I grabbed, he was holding his arm out, stiff, so I knew he was holding something in his hand. I couldn't see it but I knew he had a gun. The rule of survival is always get your hand on the gun so they can't point it at you, and get them to the ground as quickly as you can. So I screamed at him to get down and drove him to the ground hard.

I was laying on top of him, and I was looking, and I didn't see the gun. I knew he had a gun, and he had one hand underneath him. I yelled, "Where's the gun? Where's the gun? I want that gun."

He was panting and gasping, and he said, "I dropped it. I dropped it."

I said: "Don't move."

I grabbed him by the elbow and then I grabbed his hand, and I said, "You move your hand out ever so slowly." I got his hand out where I could see it, and I said, "All right." I moved a little bit off him and I said, "Roll up."

The gun was right there underneath him. A loaded handgun with the safety off.

What we didn't know until this had gone down was that while we were outside with these two guys, the guy with the rifle who'd fired the shot we heard was inside the camp. When we learned there was another guy, Mike rushed the camp, and there was the third guy inside with the gun and he didn't know what to do with himself. He'd just shot a big doe right between the eyes. They all went to jail.

Sometimes, like in that case, the danger you're in doesn't hit you when things are happening, it hits you after everything is under control, leaving you with an adrenaline rush that lingers for an hour or more after.

In some cases, if we don't catch them quickly before they drive away, getting the evidence can be the big challenge. This is where being able to "read the woods" comes into play. Out in the woods, we're often looking for very small things, for the small disturbance, the faintest track, the slightest difference in the landscape. That was the case with another night hunting scenario. We had the decoy out, and this truck came by with a special light rig. They lit up the rig and fired at the decoy, but when we tried to stop them, they took off and it turned into a high-speed chase.

We were trying to find their vehicle, which had gone off onto a gravel road. Finally we found them and stopped them, but when we checked the vehicle there were no guns. There was just a light skim of snow on the gravel, just the slightest skim of white. The other wardens were interrogating them, and the guys didn't have anything to say, so I just started walking. I don't know why, just that over time, I'd developed these instincts about things.

It was maybe eight or nine at night. I started backtracking and I came to a little intersection just down around the corner. Not being in a vehicle, but standing there with a flashlight held low to the ground, I could see just a faint turn where a vehicle had gone down that road. I started down that road and I could see where the vehicle had stopped. This was something I could never see from up in my truck, I had to be on foot, but they were going down that road so fast there was a lot of heat in the tires, and if I held the light right, I could see a melt spot where that vehicle had stopped.

I looked closer. There was a little hummock, and I could see where someone had stepped there and then hopped into a little fir thicket. I got to pawing around in the fir thicket, looking for the guns, and there was a rubber boot. Inside the boot was a grouse. This was on Sunday, when there's no hunting, and the grouse was still warm, so it had to have been shot that day.

Then, since we still needed to find those guns, I poked around a little bit more. There was a big old pine log. And I was thinking, *Where would I hide something and not leave tracks?* I looked carefully at the log and I could see heel marks, so I looked down at the end of the log. There was a duffle bag with three gun barrels and the spotlight sticking out of it. The guy's name was right on the bag, so I called in on the radio and I said, "Hey, I just found the guns. Is your suspect named Lucas? Because the bag I just found has the name Lucas on it."

The guy was sitting in the front seat with his arms folded, and when he heard that, he just folded over, banged his head on the steering wheel, and said, "Wardens around my area wouldn't have found that." That was a sweet, sweet find.

It's not all bad guys slaughtering animals, thank goodness. Sometimes there are chances for compassion, and teaching moments, like this one. I laugh every time I remember it.

We were working night hunters, up toward Kokadjo, which is a town north of Greenville with a sign that reads "Welcome to Kokadjo, population not many," and Allen Stehle, my deputy, and I had a decoy set up. It moved, its tail flipped, it looked just like a real deer at night. It was a real foggy, rainy night. We were along the side of the road, and we kept seeing this beam of light. You know how, with a flashlight, you run a light up in the fog and you can see that beam from a long way away? Kind of like those searchlights at the beginning of a Hollywood movie? It was like that. I kept seeing this light sweeping the sky from behind us, and I'm looking at it and wondering, *What is that?*

Finally, we knocked the decoy down, so it wouldn't be shot while we were away, and we started walking down the road. We saw the light sweep again, coming from down a little side road. It was black and raining and we had no flashlight on, just kind of slithering along like game wardens do, and we came into a clearing and there was a camper there. It was deer season, and a lot of people had come up hunting.

We were standing outside in the dark. We could hear people inside the camper talking, it sounded like a couple of dads and kids. Pretty soon a guy came out and went to the bathroom, right next to the camper. Then a young boy stepped out with a spotlight, waving it all around, which you can't do during deer season, because illuminating wildlife is not allowed.

Then the father came out and went to the boy, and he said, "You'd better not do that, the game warden's gonna get you."

At that point, I was literally the length of a truck away from the boy, and I figured this was perfect, I had to do it. So I put my light on, and I go, "Game warden," and everybody just froze. Just froze. They didn't move. They didn't breathe. And I went up to the boy, and I took the spotlight, your basic thousand candlepower spotlight, and I said, "Now let me guess, guys. You're here hunting, right?" And the father nods. "And you have guns in that camper, right?" He just nods his head. "So," I said, "what we're doing here with the spotlight is called night hunting, and that's a thousand dollars and three days in jail. So from now on, gentlemen, we use the little flashlight."

The boy was also holding a small flashlight, and I took it from his hand and held it up, "We use the little flashlight to go to the bathroom, and we leave the big light inside the camper and we don't shine it around. Now, are we clear with that?"

He never spoke, he just nodded his head. I handed him back the lights. We turned off our lights and disappeared into the black night, and as we walked away a little voice came from behind us: "Have a n-n-nice night."

CHAPTER SEVEN

Have Moose, Will Travel

Because game wardens spend their lives in the woods dealing with wildlife, we're acutely attuned to changes in our environment. One of the changes I saw over the years was the effect of so much logging on the deer population. The invention of modern logging equipment and poor deeryard management in the early years of intense logging left few quality areas where deer could survive during the winter, thus resulting in smaller and smaller deer herds. As the deeryards were gradually destroyed, the deer population that had attracted so many hunters to Maine every year dwindled or moved away, and a moose population, which feeds on the small growth that grows up in logged areas, moved in.

People sometimes call moose "swamp donkeys." They look like they're made out of all the spare parts. They are very ugly.

This happened up on the Number Four Mountain Road near Kokadjo. Some people happened to be driving down the road and saw a guy dragging a chain into the woods. Being neighborly, they stopped, and parked, and asked him if he needed help. He said no, he'd just shot a moose. Then they asked if he needed help getting it out, and he said no, so they just drove off down the road. But something about it seemed funny, so they turned around and came back and found that the guy had jumped in his truck and taken off, leaving the chain behind.

When they looked around, they found two dead moose lying there, a cow and a calf, so they called us and gave us a plate number. I took my chocolate lab, Reba (a dog you will hear more about later), in to where the two dead moose were, on an evidence search. She found one spent casing for a 7mm Magnum in a slash pile, so we knew we were looking for a 7mm Mag. It's a big shell.

Now, shooting two moose is bad. Driving off and leaving two moose to rot in the woods makes it much worse. So we were out looking for this guy—the plate number gave us a name and vehicle information—and I happened to see him driving down the road. I pulled him over, and he and his wife were sitting there, and everything was cool. I said, "You guys moose hunting?" And he said, "Yeah." And I said to him, "Sir, what do you have for guns aboard?"

He said, "Oh, my wife has a .30-06 right there."

"Any other firearms? What else do you have for guns?"

And he repeats, "My wife has a .30-06."

I could see a case with the butt of a gun sticking out of it, and I asked, "What about this?"

I directed him right to it and he said, "Oh, that's a 7mm Magnum."

I said, "Sir, I need you to come with me for a minute."

He came and sat in my truck and I said, "I really need to talk to you about this moose that's up the road that's been shot."

All of a sudden, he took his sunglasses off, set them on the dash, and he started banging his head against the window, wigging right out, screaming at the top of his lungs, "I shot the moose! I shot the moose!"

Meanwhile, my sergeant came by and he stopped and looked at me, like, *Roger, what are you doing to this guy?* I said, "It's okay, we're all set, boss."

So then the guy told me the story. He said, "My wife wanted to shoot the moose because she had the permit. So we saw the moose, and she got out, and went down, and she shot. And the moose went down, and we're jumping and hugging and so happy, and I looked down, and the moose was standing up again and starting to leave. And my wife said no, she wanted to shoot it, and I didn't listen to her, I shot it, and then, when we went down there, we had two dead moose. Then the car came along while I was trying to drag one out and I just completely panicked."

Meanwhile, his wife was being interviewed by my sergeant, and she was saying, "Now I'm going to have to slit my wrists. Commit suicide."

Finally I told him, "Listen, this is not the end of the world. You made a mistake, but this is not a life-ending event." So we worked it through and we worked out a plea agreement that everybody could live with, and it wasn't the end of the world. But his reaction was so sudden. He was laughing and chuckling and then he took his glasses off and he was screaming and banging his head against that window.

They did lose their licenses as part of the deal—I think they lost them for two years—and they paid a fine for the moose because they left them. That was a part of it. You don't leave two moose to rot in the woods that could feed families.

It happens like that, though. Lots of people are hunting for a deer or moose to help with food through the winter, but others? We see people up here just killing and killing. We had a couple young fellows that were in the Marines, up from over Waldoboro way, down near the coast, who went on kind of a moose killing spree. This was all happening around two or three in the morning. They shot a cow and a calf, took the hindquarters and the straps, threw it in their truck. Then they drove a couple miles down the road and killed another moose, and they were in the process of cutting that one up when a border patrol officer happened to come by. He saw the truck and stopped and found these hindquarters piled up in the back of the truck.

When they saw him, they took off on a dead run into the woods, and the manhunt was on. We had all available officers on the hunt, about seven or eight of us. We knew they were Marines trained in evasion tactics, so we knew it was game on. That search started around two in the morning and went on all day. Wardens and dogs. They'd made their way to the road and kept hiding when they heard a vehicle coming. The next afternoon, they caught 'em way down by 201. They'd gone about twenty miles.

Of course, we had all their identification, their military IDs, in the truck that they'd left behind. It turned out that they were AWOL. They were like a week overdue. They weren't concerned about fish and wildlife penalties, they were only concerned about what the Marine Corps was going to do to them. So we called and got hold of their commanding officer, and after they served their three days in the county jail, the Marine Corps picked 'em up.

When we interviewed them, we learned that they apparently were trying to act like Robin Hood, riding around, spreading moose meat to everybody who needed it.

The laws about moose hunting keep changing. In my early days, you could shoot any moose; now your permit is area-specific. North of the Golden Road, they're allowed to shoot calves. In the Greenville area, it's bulls only. The permits are assigned to zones, and you have to tag your moose in your zone at the first tagging station you come to. I've got a real interesting story about that. About tagging. And, I suppose, about wildlife CSI.

The title of this chapter comes from a case I worked years ago involving a moose that was shot up near Greenville and tagged way across the state in Washington County where the shooter had a permit. That day, I happened to have a filmmaker with me, so the investigation got recorded and ended up on television. It demonstrates how often a warden also has to be a detective, and sometimes a pretty persistent one.

I was up north of Greenville, and I saw some men who had just shot a bull moose loading it onto a truck. My suspicions started when I asked, "Where were you when you shot?" and all of a sudden, everybody pointed in different directions. That automatically told me something was wrong here.

The case ended up involving detectives from the Maine State Police, including my friend Kenny MacMaster and Detective Jay Pelletier. Once I asked the guys about shooting the moose and got those conflicting answers, I let those hunters go and started looking around a little more. We weren't able to get tire track prints for the four-wheeler they were using because it had rained overnight. But we had the drag marks that told the story, and we had found witnesses to the killing of two moose—a bull and a cow—at the same time right in that area.

The witnesses told us that they had seen the men using a four-wheeler to drag the cow moose away. It was illegal to kill a cow moose in that area; the permits were only for bull moose. We had a description of the truck—a white Ford Ranger pickup—that they'd used to haul that cow moose away, and the witnesses, who were up there bird hunting, told us that when the truck hauled that moose away, the moose didn't have any antlers.

This case became a splendid example of the value of dogs in evidence searches, and of something few people even know we do, which I would call "warden service CSI." It was a nasty, rainy day the next day when I took my dog, Rader, in and let him go to work. Dogs will naturally go to the death site because of the blood. He quickly led me to the places where the two moose had been killed. Once you've seen it a few times, it's pretty easy to tell where a moose that's been shot has fallen. Where the wound is, you get a ring, or circle with a lot of blood. It's one of the things a warden looks for when trying to see where a moose ended its journey. Only one paunch, where they'd dressed the bull, but not far beyond that, there was another site with blood and hair on the ground, and it looked like someone had used a four-wheeler to haul a second moose away. And only one of those moose had been tagged.

Once you've got the spot where the animal fell, you look for the trajectory of the shot. Often, that's a two-step process. From the spot where the moose fell, you next find the spot where that moose was shot, which will be marked by cut fragments of hair and a spray of hair from the exit wound. From those two spots, which the dog is very adept at locating, we can run a line and determine where the shooter was standing. For locating and searching the spot where the shooter was standing, I'll give the search command "gun," which tells the dog to look for anything with human scent, gunpowder, or brass. From the information at those two death sites, Rader and I located the two shooting sites.

Then I brought in the state police, and we treated it just like any other crime scene. We collected spent shells the dog located from the two different shooting spots, and we collected blood and hair samples from the kill spots and from the places where the moose had been hit.

Of course, from the shells the dog located, we knew the type of rifle that had been used, and we had the name and address of the person who had tagged that bull moose. So, since we knew he had been hunting with whoever tagged the cow moose, we started with him. The wardens and the state police went and questioned him. Through him, we found the guy who owned that Ford truck, and he insisted that he had shot that cow moose in Aurora, out in Washington County, where he had a permit that allowed him to shoot a cow moose. Our records showed that he had tagged that moose in Washington County. The rifle recorded as the one used to kill that cow moose matched the shells we'd found in the Greenville area.

We had a warrant to search for moose meat, firearms, equipment, the truck, ATV, photos, or ammunition. We took blood and hair samples from the back of his truck, and confiscated some of the moose meat for tissue samples, and put together a real good case. Debbie Palman, the warden service wildlife forensics specialist, was able to analyze hair and tissue samples. Ultimately, we were able to prove that both moose were shot by the same gun, both in the Greenville area, and both by the same shooter. They'd come all the way up to Greenville, shot that cow moose illegally, used that four-wheeler to haul it up a mountain a mile and half away, and then loaded it and trucked it all the way across the state to tag it where it was legal. I guess they never thought we'd go all CSI on 'em, but with the help of a clever brown lab, we had everything we needed to show that moose was shot illegally.

I drive through the Greenville area, and every roadside has a story. Sometimes the story is about bad guys willfully breaking the law, like those Marines, or the hunters who hauled that moose away to be tagged in Washington County. Sometimes the story is just about people making a mistake.

Now, outside of Greenville, along Route 6/15 West, is a state game preserve where you can't hunt. I came by there during moose season, and I saw a car parked down on the road leading in with the doors open. You see a car with the doors open, it might mean someone's in trouble, so I parked and went down to see what was up. Well, I was walking down the road—walking in my quiet warden way so they couldn't hear me coming—and a little way ahead I could hear a man talking to his son. This man was explaining how God has blessed him by letting him shoot this moose today, how God is so wonderful, and I was walking toward him, hearing him say this to his son—the boy was about ten—and there was this moose, dead as a doornail in a game preserve.

I was thinking, *Oh, this is not good*. I came up to him, and I said, "Sir, could you come with me for just a minute?" We walked out to the end of the road. I pointed to the sign that says "STATE GAME PRESERVE," and the guy started bawling. He was bawling his eyes out. I can see how it happened. He saw the moose, his eyes were on the moose the whole time, and he never noticed the tiny black sign.

I knew I had him. So I called the office and found he had already called because he had an antlered moose permit and he thought the antlers were too small. He'd already reported himself. I just happened to stumble onto him.

What I knew, because of the location of the preserve and the highway, was that this was a moose that we were going to end up dragging off this highway after a truck or a car hit it, because we always got that happening in that area. So I called my lieutenant, Pat Dorian, and laid it all out. I told him I could see what happened, there was no intent to break the law whatsoever, and this was a moose we were gonna end up dragging off the highway anyway, what did he think? And he said okay.

So I went back to the guy and his son, and I said, "Now, this is a really good example of where you told the truth and how important the truth is." Because I had to make it a teachable moment. His father was so upset, I was going to bring this back around. I said, "You tell the truth, and we can come and see what happened, and we can understand how this whole thing was an accident and you had no intent to break the law. Sir, your job now is to load that moose and go tag it. Do you hear me?"

He said, "Yes, sir, yes, sir." And he was out of there.

And you know, I could tell. They didn't have much. Their car was an old beater. He did not need to go to jail for that. It just wasn't the right thing to do. You had to have compassion. I see all these people slaughtering animals just for fun, not even taking them for food, and then this man was so grateful.

I could tell moose stories all day, and every one would be different. Sometimes, the best part of the story happens when the case goes to court. There was an old-time woodsman, a hermit who lived alone, a classic Maine poacher. When he needed something to eat, he would go out and shoot it. Dan Carroll, a warden in Sebec, and I were working together. It was in the spring, maybe March, and we were just out bebopping around like wardens do at that season, checking out some logging roads, and we saw some tracks going into the woods. It had snowed a little bit and it looked like there was some blood melting into the snow, so we got out and looked and we saw that a cow moose had been shot and quartered up. And the unusual thing was that the tongue had been cut out, which I'd never seen before.

So we started working in the area. We talked to the logging crews, and they mentioned an old beater car that had come in the day before, two guys in it, and gave us a description of one that resembled our woodsman. They said he had a big heavy beard and he wore heavy wool pants, the kind that we call "woolies," the standard winter dress of a lot of people in the wintertime in Maine. Woolies are quiet (not nylony), so people like to hunt in them, and they don't hold moisture. He became our suspect right away.

We went back to the scene, and sure enough, we saw raspberry bushes and clinging to them were tufts of green wool, so we photographed that. We found where the moose had been shot, and we were pretty sure that it had been shot with a .30-30 rifle. We did a little more digging and were able to find a person who could confirm that our guy had been out in that car that day and was wearing those wool pants.

We wrote a search warrant and executed it the next day. We went into his camp, and there's a fry pan with a hunk of meat in it, cooking, and there's a cat on the floor, eating a piece of moose meat, and in the refrigerator, which is like an old, small gas refrigerator, there's blood oozing out of the bottom even with the door closed. There's moose hair stuck to the piece of meat in the fry pan, stuck all over it.

We opened the refrigerator, and everything was there, including the moose tongue. The moose had been deboned in the field and the meat had been transported in burlap bags. All of the fibers and stuff from the bags were stuck to the meat. It was just horrendous.

We wrote him a summons, seized all the evidence, caught up with the other guy, arrested him, and when we got to court a few months later, the woodsman stood up and said, "I'm not guilty."

The judge said, "Okay, we're going to have a trial."

We got to the point where we entered the moose tongue as evidence. I'll never forget this. The accused was sitting there, and he raised his hand, like he was in school. And the judge kept looking at him, and finally the judge said, "You have something to say, sir?"

He said, "I don't want to waste anyone's time. I'm guilty. I did it. I like moose tongue."

This was before the time of Judge Benoit in Skowhegan, who had a pretty stiff gavel when it came to fish and wildlife stuff, so the judge asked us, "How big was that animal?" He was trying to figure the per pound value of the moose because he was going to order restitution to the state for the value of the moose, along with the fine.

We said, "Oh, it was about an eight-hundred-pound cow moose."

The defendant put his hand up again, and said, "That moose wasn't over four hundred pounds. I've killed a lot of 'em. I know what they weigh."

CHAPTER EIGHT

Famous Fishermen

Wild Maine salmon and wild trout are among Maine's most precious resources. There's nothing like the experience of catching that rare five-pound brookie, even if it is only in a catch and release pond. We've got a lot of protections in place for these special fish, trying to save them for future generations, and it has been a constant battle throughout my career to protect this resource from fishermen who don't think the rules apply to them.

I remember back when I was brand new, right out of the box, issuing my first summons for fishing. Grand Lake Stream has a big dam where the stream starts. It leaves West Grand Lake and it flows into Big Lake. Probably five or six miles of river there. It's a stream, it's not a river. This stretch of water—Grand Lake Stream—is one of those "elite" fishing spots where the more professional people like to fish, the sport fishermen. They're generally more catch and release type people.

There's a fishway along that dam. Any place that has a fishway dam, you can't fish within one hundred fifty feet of that dam, because the fish all ball up there, waiting to go upstream, and you could jig 'em.

With jigging, the fish doesn't really bite, you just drape the line across their backs and hook 'em. Often fishermen will use treble hooks or multiple hooks, and as soon as they feel something move, they'll give a jerk and they'll hook them in the belly or the side. To prevent that from happening in a place like that, there are two posts across from each other on the downstream side of the riverbank (where the salmon gather to go up the fishway) that signal where the one-hundred-fifty-foot mark is.

So, in a typical game warden move, I was in the alders watching this guy casting. Where the current comes off the dam, it breaks and does a backflow, a circular motion. I was watching this guy and he was casting his line right on that one-hundred-fifty-foot mark, and letting it catch the current and drift right into the fishway.

I'd just spent something like twenty weeks in the academy, and here was my first apprehension of a violator. I was just shaking with anticipation. I watched him do it quite a few times. While I was watching, he didn't catch a fish. But I didn't wait all that long. In my later years, I might have waited a little bit longer, but I was ready to go right away.

I waited until he had the line completely into the fishway, and I walked down over the bank. One of the guys who was casting, fishing legally, looked over to his buddy, and he made a circle with his hand, telling his buddy he saw a badge. I walked up to this guy and I stood right behind him, and I said, "Good evening, sir. I need to check your fishing license."

He jumped, and he was so startled he threw his fly rod into the water. Probably a four- or five-hundred-dollar rod and he just flipped it right into the air and threw it into the water.

I told him to get his rod. He had waders on, so he waded in and got his rod, and then I reeled it in, checked that it had a fly on it, hooked it up, and wrote him a ticket. The other guys were quite happy to see that happen, because they were upset to see what he was doing. The guy started to tell me that it was unfair for me to give him a ticket, he wasn't going to keep a fish if he caught one. Then he told me he wrote books about wildlife. He gave me his whole life history. And I looked at him, and I didn't say it, but I was thinking, *You don't understand,*

*mister. I've just been twenty weeks sitting at the academy, waiting for
this moment. You're not a catch and release client, buddy. Not today.*

He was thinking about his ruined day. All that mattered to me was,
Press hard, so it will go through five copies.

Just like with wildlife poaching, a lot of our tips about fishing come
from other fishermen or people whose livelihood comes from fishing in some way. These are people who understand the importance
of preserving the resources. We had a tip line called Operation Game
Thief, and one day we got a tip that some dentists, a group of annual
out-of-state fishermen who were staying at a local sporting camp,
were stockpiling a lot of fish. Our information was that the dentists
were way over their legal limit and would be leaving Princeton with a
van full of salmon. The limit was two salmon per day, and you couldn't
have more than one day's limit in your possession. Otherwise you had
to eat it, or catch and release. You couldn't stockpile.

Our tip said they were planning to leave very early in the morning,
like four thirty or five in the morning, to avoid any road checks that we
might have set up. We had a description of the vehicle, the boat, everything. So we set up on the road real early that day and sure enough,
right around five in the morning, here comes that van.

We pulled in behind it, Daryl and I, flipped our blues on, and they
wouldn't stop. For about five hundred yards, the van kept going, fish-
tailing all over the road. Finally it stopped. We told 'em right up front
that we'd gotten a game thief tip that they were in possession of a lot
of fish and we needed to check it out. They said, okay, sure, go ahead
and look. The cooler's right in the back. So we opened the cooler and
sure enough, there's their legal limit of fish, nothing more.

So we think, well, we're going to look a little closer.

I reached my hand down among this bunch of clothing and dun-
nage, and I could feel something ice cold and slimy. I pulled it up
and sure enough, there was a bunch of salmon. So we started moving stuff around, and then we were finding fish everywhere. When
they weren't stopping, it was because they were hiding their fish.

Everyone had gotten out of the van except this one older gentleman who was sitting in the seat behind the passenger side, and he was not moving. The seats had those little curtains on the bottom, so you couldn't see the base.

I said to him, "Sir, I need to check under that seat," kind of gently implying, "Sir, I need you to step out so I can search," And he didn't move, he didn't do anything. He just sat there. Finally, I said, "Sir, I need to check under that seat." He just rolled his eyes and gave me that look. When he moved aside, I lifted that little curtain up, and the space under that seat was just packed with salmon.

I want to say they had at least thirty salmon over the limit. Big salmon. A huge amount. And this wasn't their first trip. They'd been doing this as a yearly event.

At that time, standard procedure was to bail them right in the field. Non-residents from out of state, we would actually take the money for the fine on the spot, and they would sign a bond promising to appear or relinquishing the money from the bond for their fine. We left there with a pretty big chunk of change, and we never saw the dentists come back again.

Nobody does that bonding in the field anymore. But that came in really handy near the Canadian border. You had to be fifty miles from a courthouse before you could do it. So, if you caught a Canadian, his buddy might go home, get the money, and come back. But it isn't done much anymore, because nobody carries money.

Fishing can be a real bonding experience for fathers and their children. But sometimes, the adults forget to include the children in the fun, occasionally to their detriment. Like the little boy who ratted out his dad. It was on East Grand Lake, early January, and I was walking the shoreline, checking fishermen. I came across a group of fishermen with several kids, and watching them I saw that every time a flag would go up on the ice fishing trap, indicating a fish had hit the bait, the adults would run, and the kids weren't getting any chances to catch fish. (On an ice fishing trap, there is a spring-loaded flag that is triggered by a fish grabbing the line. When the line is tugged, the spring is released and the flag pops up. Everyone runs for a "tip up.") So, at one point, after checking their licenses and chitchatting with them, a flag went up, all the men took off running, and this little boy was left standing there next to me.

Without even thinking, I said to him, "Well, where are all your fish?" and he said, "We're hiding all the little ones at camp; as soon as we catch the little ones, they run 'em right to camp." And I realized that they weren't showing us all the fish they had. I said, "Oh, that's good. That's good."

So the next morning, we had a road check set up where we'd check all the fishermen coming out of that area, kind of like you'd set up for OUI (operating under the influence). Their vehicle came through, and we got a tremendous over limit and a lot of very short fish. Like thirty undersized salmon. Salmon had to be a minimum of fourteen inches and lake trout had to be eighteen inches, and half of their fish were undersized. They had kept everything they caught.

That little boy was sitting in the truck. I waved to him and he waved back, and we just had this great moment together. His dad never figured it out, that we had this connection. And it probably cost the dad a lot of money.

After many years in this business, it's easy to think there will be no more surprises. But sometimes there are. Like who the poachers are and how determinedly they go about it. This incident took place in Greenland Brook, which is on the southern end of East Grand Lake, and it involved smelts. The traditional way to catch smelts is with a dip net. They're small, about five and a half or six inches long, and they come up the stream to spawn at night in the shallows of the brook. Greenland Brook is a closed brook, which means you can't dip smelts there. It's closed because smelts are the major forage for salmon and lake trout; they're what feed the game fish so the game fish can grow big, and as such they're a very important part of the fisheries chain in Maine, especially on these bigger lakes.

We knew the smelts were running, and this was a prime place for poachers to go, so I sat on this brook from probably nine at night until two in the morning, curled up in a sleeping bag. I had to be somewhere in the morning, so I couldn't stay all night. I'd had a couple of people come down to look. They knew the stream was closed, but they were still coming down to look to see if they were spawning.

Well, toward the end of the evening, this lady came by, and stopped and looked, and drove away. Then she turned around, came back, and stopped again. She never dipped or anything, and then she drove away. At that point, I had to leave. I hated to, because I figured she was going to come back and dip, but I had to because I had a commitment the next day.

My truck was hidden a long ways away—it was one of the things wardens did so poachers wouldn't spot the truck and know we were around. I hiked through the woods to it and drove out, and the woman I'd seen was pulled over at the side of the road, not far from where I'd been sitting. I stopped and got out to make sure she was all right. I asked her if she had any smelts. She said yes. She had a cooler full of smelts. A lot of people keep live smelts, because they take them to fish with or they catch them to sell for bait. But they can only have a quart unless they have a special license, which she didn't have. She had her limit alive in the cooler, which she showed to me. I went and checked the back of the truck.

As I walked back to my truck, I noticed that she had a bucket on the other side, the passenger side, and that her air cleaner cover, from her engine, was sitting on top of the bucket. It had slid over a bit, and I could see the little silvery tails of a bunch of smelt. So I said, "What's that?"

She just got this look of horror on her face. She had a whole bucketful, which is about four or five quarts. It was an unusual thing; she was a lady probably in her sixties, not somebody you'd expect to be out all night long chasing smelts and taking over limits. Had that air cleaner cover not slipped I never would have seen them. So I captured her. That was my big catch of the night. And she got a ticket.

CHAPTER NINE

Whirly Bobbers and Finger Dippers

The area around Greenville has many special regulation ponds. These are fly fishing or artificial lure-only waters, designated that way by the Maine Legislature to preserve the wild brook trout populations in these ponds. Special regulations protect designated ponds and rivers so that they always have quality fish in them to reproduce. These ponds are never stocked. The trout are all wild. These bodies of water are harder to fish but provide for better quality of wild fish.

I've said this before, but the point can't be made too strongly—these ponds are a fragile resource and a few fishermen's carelessness or selfishness can have a major impact on trout populations and on the future of fishing for present and future generations.

I remember my first case, when I came back to Greenville, on a beautiful little fly fishing pond. It was a lovely, sunny day. Of course, hot, bright sun is not conducive to good trout fishing. Fly fishing works best on dark, cloudy days.

I had worked my way into my little hidey-hole there, and I looked out through my scope and saw an elderly couple out there fishing in the bright sun. I didn't think too much of it. I just kept eating my lunch, watching them with my scope, and pretty quick they start looking all around. It's a real telltale thing. You see their heads turning. Then the binoculars came out and they scanned the shore. Then the binoculars were lowered, and he reached down, and I could see he had a hand line. I saw him putting a worm on the hook, and then spinning it around and dropping it over the side. Pretty quickly, he caught a trout. Caught another one. Pulled it up, and then he handed the line to his wife and she started fishing with it. He had another rod, and he put a big gob of worm on that and dropped it over the side.

I watched, and I watched, and soon they had five or six trout over their limit, caught 'em all on worms. Every few minutes, he took out the binoculars and scanned the shoreline. Then they started to pack up. I noted which pack he put the fish in, and then I booked it around the pond so I was on the landing when they came in, and I said, "How was the fishing today?"

"Oh, good. Good," he said. "My wife really beat me today. She had the magic fly."

"I'm sure she did," I said. "I'll check your licenses." So they handed me their licenses and I said, "I think we've gotta have a little discussion here."

They said, "Oh?"

And I said, "We've got to talk about hand lines, and that little baggie of extra trout that you have in that blue bag right there."

She got all huffy and said, "Why aren't you out here catching REAL poachers?"

I said, "Well, you know, I can only catch so many at a time, and today . . . you're it."

So I got their pack, and I got the fish out, and oh, my was she sputtering, she was almost foaming at the mouth. And I said, "Ma'am, this isn't a really good time to have this conversation. You don't have to say much. You can save all this conversation for when you get to court. That's the time to really do it, because I saw what I saw and you're not going to change my mind. That's not going to happen."

That kind of toned her down a little bit.

What we called them was whirly bobbers and finger dippers. You'd be watching one person in a canoe and everything was good, and you'd watch the next guy, and all of a sudden he'd start whirling the line. Not casting it, like he would with a fly, because he had a big gob of worm on the end of that fly, and if he snapped it, the worm would come off. So he'd whirl it around and gently throw it out and it would make this big plop when it hit, and then you'd watch it sink and you could see the fish biting on it. Whereas, with a fly, they'd just grab the fly and they're hooked, there was none of this biting action. And always—this was classic—as soon as they put a worm on, they'd dip their fingers in the water to get the slime off.

We could tell. We'd be on the radio with each other, and I'd go, "I've got a whirly." And the other guy would say, "Yeah, he just dipped his fingers three times." So we knew we had him.

Another time, we were watching these two guys in a canoe, fishing with worms, so we got our canoe, put it in the pond, and we paddled all the way across the pond to these guys. Their backs were to us, they were fishing toward shore, and they never heard us; we were just going very quietly. We just came sliding up alongside their canoe, and I said, "Game warden."

The guy whipped around and his rod came flying out of his hands. I grabbed the rod, and he looked at me and he said, "My worst freaking nightmare just came true."

I looked right back at him, and I said, "You're not wrong."

We took the poles and set 'em in the boat. They had no licenses. Fishing with worms. No life jackets in the boat. No money.

So our only option at this point was to take 'em to jail. I think maybe one of 'em had an ID, the other didn't.

So we loaded them into our canoe; we don't handcuff them in a canoe, that would be a bad thing to do. We paddled across the pond and took them up to the truck. The other warden jumped in the back of the truck, I put the two of them in the truck, and we headed out.

The guy that tended the gate—there are a lot of paper company lands or private clubs in the area that are gated—he was an old man, short, very stocky and square with a high-pitched voice. He was always teasing me and I was always teasing him. So I pulled up to the gate with these two guys in the truck. He came running up and he said,

"Guay, are you sneaking people through my gate? There's a guy in the back of the truck."

I said, "These guys are under arrest. They're headed to jail."

He said, "What did they do?"

"Worm fishing."

And he said, "They're going to jail for worm fishing? What the hell ails you?"

"Bud," I said, "these guys are headed to jail."

Then he realized I was serious and he said, "All right. Get through here then."

And off to jail we went. They had to get bailed out, and one of them called his mother and was begging her for money to come bail him out. Because once we get them to jail, they weren't our problem anymore.

All their gear was still there at the pond. They'd gotten flown in but they didn't have the money to get flown out again.

A lot of people think like Bud there at the gate, and echo his question: *They're going to jail for worm fishing? What the hell ails you?* So I'd use the analogy of a flower garden. You've got this great garden in a public park and it's full of beautiful flowers that give pleasure to everyone, and then someone comes along and picks a few. Just a few flowers, and it's just them, so what's the big deal? Until enough people do that so there are no flowers left. Then it's too late. The beauty is gone, there's nothing left for the next people who come along, and you can't bring it back.

It's a fact: because protecting the resource is so important, we sometimes go to great lengths to protect it. Like in this case, for example, that took place on the famous Roach River. It's catch and release only, when it's open to fishing. It's right full of beautiful trout and it is one of the main spawning places for Moosehead Lake. One day, Glenn, one of my officers, called me and said, "You need to come up right now. There are some guys here I think are going to go fish the river."

This was October. It was closed to fishing. So I said, "Okay, I'll be up."

I met Glenn, and he said, "These guys are in the store, buying worms, and they pulled their vehicle down that road that runs alongside the river." I waited and watched and sure enough, they were walking in with their rods and everything. So Glenn went down one side of the river and I went down the other. He got down to where he could see that they were putting out set lines with crawlers on 'em, tying them off to bushes.

When we got close enough, we could see they had a fire; it was really dry, not conditions under which you'd want to be having a fire. They had a dog with them, which made catching them by surprise much harder. We discussed our attack plan. They were in the middle of this little thicket, and sitting there with a fire, and they had all these set lines coming down the river, so there was only one way we could get 'em: to slither down the middle of the river, Navy SEAL-style, to get down there and get to them as quickly as possible.

So we slithered into the water and we started down toward them. We had to go quite a way, and you know, you can't go faster than the water, because then you make noise, and it was deep, and cold and we didn't have waders, just our uniforms. We were just working in, walking along. Finally, we got right into a little bank where we could see the fire and the two guys. We came up out of the water and jumped over that bank and grabbed 'em. That dog went nuts.

One of the guys just looked at us, and he said, "If that dog had barked, all you would have had was this cooler."

And I said, "I know."

He said, "I've got to admit, you guys are bad, slithering through the river."

And I said, "We do what we've gotta do."

After the initial shock, they took it pretty well.

Before the explosion of all the recreational vehicles began to take up so much of our time and shift our focus, we would spend a lot of hours working on protecting these pristine fishing ponds. I would go to a pond with a little lunch and a spotting scope, and spend two or three hours before somebody showed up or I'd move around and find another pond, and watch fishermen for the day. I loved it. That was heaven for me. I had eighty special regulation ponds in my patrol, so I had the pick. I could go in any direction I wanted. One guy. And that was just me, the people on the other side of me had those special regulation ponds, too.

It's hard to explain to people the why and how of some of these regulations, and how flouting the laws can make a long-term difference. But there are bunch of ways that flouting the laws can completely destroy a trout-fishing pond. Take "No Live Fish as Bait" ponds, like Crawford Pond in TAR11 (a township with no organized local government) or Rum Pond in Greenville. I would sit across the pond in spring, watching, and inevitably someone would start putting out live bait like a live shiner. These ponds don't allow you to do that because they don't want the illegal introduction of bait species and the harm that results.

That harm can happen two ways, either when the bait gets off the hook, or when people who are doing illegal fishing dump their bait bucket in the pond at the end of the day. It just takes one time and you end up with bass and pickerel and pike and stuff like that in these pristine trout waters. And then those fish drive out the trout.

Trout are very temperature sensitive; they're also fish that really work the shallows. Bass do the same thing, and bass multiply ten times as fast as trout, so if you have a bass in a particular cove, there will be like seventy or eighty bass in a very short time, which will eat all of the trout's food supply; they just can't compete. It's happening all over the state, and it's kind of an unknown problem—the trout fishing ruined for future generations just because someone decides they don't have to follow the rules.

Quebec, for example, took a really hard stance many years ago, and did away with live bait altogether. Maine said well, we have people who make their living selling bait and catching bait, so we can't do that, we'll just restrict the bodies of water that are vulnerable. And that didn't work. Now the Moose River, out toward Jackman, is full of bass. It's the beginning of the end for bodies of water that interconnect with each other, because once the more invasive species gets in, it affects the whole drainage. So the only thing that's left are these pristine little mountain trout ponds that sit on their own. In my mind, they're the most precious gems the state of Maine has left, and worth serious protection.

With eighty ponds in my patrol area, I had to really prioritize what was important. Ponds that had stocked trout in 'em, I didn't really care about; I was working to protect wild trout. If I had all the time in the world, and all the resources, I'd be protecting all eighty, but I've only got two legs. On an average day in May or June, I'd walk seven or eight miles a day just getting to those ponds and getting into the backcountry, going cross-country on compass bearings to get into some of these places.

We also had the aircraft, and they would be the scouts. The planes would run ahead of you and let you know where the action was, and then you could work your way over.

It can take a lot of patience and persistence to catch poachers, especially those hard-core types for whom breaking the law was part of the fun. That was the case with a group I called the Bluff Mountain Gang. This was a group of people who would go into these remote back ponds that were catch and release only, cut the locks on canoes that were locked to trees there, and use those canoes to fish. They weren't catching and releasing, they were poaching, just grabbing every fish they could. Not even to eat, often just to have the fun of catching them. Then they'd kill them and throw the dead fish back. This gang had a signature. They always left me empty Marlboro cigarette packages, empty Mountain Dew containers, empty worm packages, and there would be blood in the bottom of the boat, so I knew they'd taken fish. When they were done, they'd just leave the canoes floating, to be smashed into the rocks by the wind.

This went on for three years. They were doing a lot of damage to these remote ponds. The problem was that I had thirty ponds that met their criteria and I could only guess which one they would be at on any given day. But with all the damage and filth and destruction, all the harm they were doing, they became my priority.

One of the places they'd go was Mountain View Pond, which is on the Appalachian Trail. One day, I caught a group of people who were fishing there illegally, and in the course of interviewing them—I'd scared 'em enough when I caught 'em that they were kind of rattled and they were just spewing great information—they inadvertently told me who my suspects were, because they said, well, Skippy and his father were the ones who told us to come here and fish, and they told us what day to come.

Then I got a phone call from an informant, out of the blue, and he said, you need to go look at Bluff Pond which is on the top of Bluff Mountain. It's about a forty-five-minute walk straight up to get to it. A gorgeous little pond. So I went up there, and sure enough, I found all the signs—a canoe floating with the cigarette packages, Mountain Dew bottles, and empty worm containers, even though it was a "fly fishing only" pond. So I started working this pond, because once their buddies got caught, they'd changed to a different place.

There was an elderly gentleman who had a camp nearby on First Roach Pond. He lived alone, so I used to stop in and check on him, have some coffee, and see how he was doing. While I was with him, I saw their vehicle go by, headed toward Bluff Pond. I thought *I can't be this lucky.* So I drove up in there and found their vehicle under a canopy of trees, where they'd hidden it so the plane wouldn't spot it.

I hid my truck and slithered up the trail, and I got up there and I watched them worm fishing, littering everywhere. It was disgusting. When they caught a small fish, they didn't even have the decency to take it off the hook, they'd just slap it against the water until the hook came loose, killing the fish. Just true pigs. I watched them fish for several hours. All of them went over the limit. While I was sitting there, I could hear the plane coming. I'd asked the pilot to keep an eye on that pond, so I slipped further back, called the pilot on the radio, and told him to swing wide so he didn't spook them.

When they got to shore, the father of the group went down first. He was the scout. The boys took all their fish—they had two packs, and they hid the fish in them—and then they took out collapsible fly rods, took all their worm containers and threw them into the water or out in the bushes. I let Dad go, and I cut around and set up an ambush on the trail, and when the boys came by, I stepped out and said, "Game warden, hold it."

They were petrified.

I said, "Okay, let's go," and we walked down to the truck. I was a little bit behind them, and when we got there, the dad had a grin from ear to ear, because it was another successful mission. He didn't count how many boys he had. I'll never forget that precious moment.

He was sitting there in the truck, and I walked up to him, put my hand on his arm, and I said, "Mr. O'Day, you're under arrest."

They were running a restaurant on Route 11 on Brownville. I knew they had the scanner on at the restaurant all the time, so I got my radio out because I knew that everybody at his facility would be listening, and I called it in. "Piscataquis, I have three subjects in custody, 1046, and these are their names . . . I have them in custody now. I'll get back to you in a little bit."

This was the culmination of three years of being up at dawn and sitting on ponds all day, freezing, getting wet, eaten alive by bugs—hours and hours of it. It was a beautiful moment. It was a hundred-dollar fine for each of them, plus twenty-five dollars for each fish they had in violation. They had about thirty fish. And I charged them for littering as well, because it was the filthiest thing I've ever seen, what they'd done. But it wasn't the fine. To them, the fine was nothing. It was that their honor had been taken from them. When it went out over scannerland, their big ego balloon just deflated.

I'd caught a whole bunch of their associates because they'd send their friends to go test the waters. To see if I was around. Once the guys came back and said, "Oh, we had a great time," they'd slide right up. They were using other people to see if it was safe to do what they wanted to do.

A little later, we got one of the young fellows, his name was Skippy, with moose meat. That was kind of a precious day, too. We knew he had some moose meat. He'd killed a moose up on the railroad tracks. He was living in a trailer park, kind of at the back of the park. So we set up surveillance, then had somebody call him and say, "Hey, there's a bunch of game wardens coming, they're heading for your house." What they normally do, they'll throw that illegal meat out into the woods. And man, that's just what he did. He came running out and there was moose meat flying, he was throwing it out behind the house. We were off the curtilage of his property. And he brought it right to us.

And we just rose up and said, "Hey, how are you doing this evening? What's this? Moose meat?"

You can tell. Moose meat has a specific smell. You can pick it up pretty quick. It's dark. There's no fat on it. And usually, no one can cut up moose meat without leaving pieces of hair on it. Especially these kinds of guys.

Within six months, that whole family moved out of Maine and was gone.

Before the O'Day family, there was the Eddie Becket gang. We had a special fisheries initiative. The commissioner at the time, Bucky Owen, wanted to find and preserve ponds that could grow five-pound-plus trout so that in the future, a Maine fisherman could take his kid fishing, and that kid could catch a five-pound brookie. He couldn't keep it, but he could photograph it, weigh it, measure it, do all that stuff, and then release it. Ponds that can do that are very rare. You need perfect conditions, perfect feed, and you need time, because it takes four years to grow a trout that size.

Each fisheries division was to pick several ponds that could produce those big brookies and make them "catch and release only." Mountain View Pond was one of the ponds we'd identified. So the fisheries biologist and the brand new commissioner went up there to go fishing for an afternoon. And while they were up there, there were a couple of gentlemen camping and they said, "Jeez, you just missed it, there were three guys here who just left who cut the lock off a canoe, and we watched them fish with worms and then take off and they had a whole pack basket filled with trout."

I had just come in behind Commissioner Owen and the biologist Paul Johnson, and I happened to pull into the Yoke Pond Club. The Yoke Pond Club has canoes that they own chained up at all ponds in this area, TAR11. The Club operates a set of camps in this area, with cook rooms and cabins.

You had to go through the North Maine Woods pay gates to get in there. North Maine Woods organization operates gates and collects fees for many landowners and handles campsites and public access issues. So I scooted right to the gate, and asked about cars that had gone through, and there was no vehicle and occupant account matching the fishermen's description. There was one vehicle that matched, but it didn't have the right number of people in it. I was perplexed.

Two days later, I was coming into Greenville when I got a call from Yoke Pond that said there was a group of people worm fishing at one of the other fly fishing ponds in that same area. I drove like a madman. Took me about forty-five minutes to get there, and I was really hoofing it, and then it was about two miles to hike in, and when I got there, I didn't see anybody.

I thought, *darn, I'm too late*, but I started walking, and as I was walking I made a mistake. Because I was hurrying, I walked out into this open spot. All of a sudden, I heard a voice, and there were two guys walking right toward me, carrying spin rods.

I was wearing camo, and I froze right there, but I was thinking, *oh, this is bad,* because I didn't have them fishing. Unless they had fish with worms inside them, I was in trouble. But then the guy who's coming at me pauses, and he says, "Oh, let's try this rock right here," and they go over to the rock and start fishing.

They never saw me.

I let them fish for a few minutes, and then I stepped onto the rock, and I said, "Game warden. Hold it right there. Don't move." I took the rods, reeled them in myself, and confirmed they were fishing with worms. Then I checked their IDs. They were two guys from Millinocket. One in his sixties, the other a young guy. Then it clicked—these were probably those guys from Mountain View Pond. There's a camp there, near where people park to go into that pond. I looked at this guy. His name was Eddie Becket, and I said, "Two days ago, what were you doing parked at the camp on Crawford Lake? Why was your vehicle parked there? Are you the guys that broke into the camp?"

I didn't know it, but this guy had a two-page rap sheet for breaking into camps. And he goes, "I didn't steal anything from that camp. I went up to Mountain View Pond and we went up there and fished."

I'd sucked 'em right in. "Alright," I said, "who was there?"

And they said, "This other guy . . . we don't know his name, he's the one who fished with worms and took all those fish."

So I wrote them a ticket. Confiscated the fish 'cause they were caught with worms. And then I found out that this guy, Eddie, has a son who's a real bad character, and came up with enough to put him at Mountain View Pond as well. Later, I went up to Millinocket, interviewed the second guy away from Eddie, and got enough to get an arrest warrant for the son.

Then I went and interviewed the son—the kid had a rap sheet just like his father—at East Millinocket PD. They went and got this kid and brought him in for me to talk to. I happened to have my cousin Joel with me that day (he was up fishing for a few days), and I like playing mind games. I find if you're going to interview somebody, the more stress you can cause them, the better. It's harder for them to lie under stress because there are too many things to keep track of. So when I came into the room, I brought Joel with me, and I pointed to the son and I asked Joel, "Do you recognize this man?"

Joel said, "No, I don't."

The whole time I was doing the interview, he stared at Joel. He knew that there were other people at the pond that day who'd seen him, and he thought Joel must be one of them. So I was interviewing him and he was telling me lies, and finally, I started laughing.

He said, "What are you laughing at?"

I said, "Well, your chum kind of said you'd be the fall guy, that you weren't too bright and you'd take the rap for everybody."

And he said, "He did not."

I reached over and got the written statement that the other guy had given and I threw it on the table. He started reading it, and he said, "That asshole! I tell you. I'll tell you how it went down. It was me, my father, and him. And we fished with worms. We killed about thirty-five or forty trout. And we took 'em back to Millinocket. And we laid in the bed of that truck and at the gate my dad gave them a fictitious name of somebody that he knows. The guy at the gate wrote that other guy's name and we were laying in the bed of the truck hiding when we drove through. My dad cut that lock . . ."

And he laid the whole thing out.

It all had to do with playing the psychological game of "who's that guy" and knowing that when the commissioner and the biologist came out, they didn't see a vehicle parked, so I knew it had to be hidden down on that trail by that camp. That was the only place to hide a vehicle. It was a roll of the dice for me, but I hit it. I hit it right dead on the money.

People think that game wardens—fish pigs, we've been called— we're just these guys out there to ruin their day and keep them from doing what they want to do or what they've always done. That we're not really police with interview and interrogation skills, despite our badges, and training, and the ability to arrest. But the truth is that we probably have more face-to-face contact or confrontations with people on a daily basis than most public safety personnel.

We're the invisible little green men who pop out of the bushes and get up in people's faces and ask them hard questions all the time. We're doing it because we want those pristine ponds preserved. We want our grandchildren, and yours, to be able to catch those five-pound brookies. Too many Eddie Beckets or O'Day families, and the whole thing can be destroyed.

CHAPTER TEN

Blind Owls and Others

Not all our fish and wildlife cases involve dealing with people. Sometimes we're dealing with the animals themselves. Like this one case I had where I had to deal with a sick moose. I'd been working ice fishermen all day. It was dark, about 4:30 or 5:00, I'd just gotten back to my vehicle, and the dispatcher called me and said, "You've got a sick moose in the road up near Brookton, and traffic is all backed up, it won't let cars by."

They gave me the complainant's name, and I got to his house and checked in with him. He was a really lonely guy, he'd lost his wife a few years before, and he said, "Oh, yeah, I called that in a few hours ago. That moose is long gone."

I ended up having a cup of coffee with him. Then I went back to the truck and started heading home. I got about a third of the way home and dispatch called again and they said, "Are you there yet? Because there's people waiting and they can't get by that moose."

So I turned around and drove back, and right around the corner from where he lived, there was this whole line of cars. I thought, "Oh, man, this is bad," because I'd sat and talked with the guy for like an hour. Now I was feeling about two inches tall.

I pulled up and got out of the truck and went up to the first vehicle. There was this guy standing by the driver's door. I said, "Where's the moose?" and the guy looked at me and rolled his eyes. He pointed across to the passenger side. I looked, and there was a moose literally leaning on his car. I said, "Yup, that looks like a sick moose all right." So I walked around the car, and gently put my flashlight right on the moose's nose. It didn't even move.

I knew I had to dispatch it. It obviously had brainworm. When a moose has brainworm, one ear will droop down, and this moose had that. There were a couple of guys there, so I said, "Here's what we're going to do. You help me push her down into the ditch and I'll dispatch her there, so these people can start moving, and they won't have to see me kill her."

So we pushed her off the guy's car, and she started running down the road. I knew, from experience, that if I lost this thing and she got away from me, around about three o'clock in the morning, I was going to get another phone call that she was back in the road and I'd have to come back again. So I was running as fast as I can. I had like six guys with me, running to keep up with this moose, and the crowd was thinning the farther we went. Now I had like three guys with me. I was at full pin, running as fast as I could go.

Finally, we got to a corner, she slowed down a little bit, and I pushed her off the road, because I didn't want her to run into oncoming traffic. I got her pointed off the road, and she caught a skidder trail and started really moving.

I was running down this skidder trail, trying to stay in the middle between the two ruts, and she was accelerating away from me. I couldn't keep up with her. Pretty soon I was going to lose her, so I had to make the call. It was pitch black, and I just grabbed my revolver, running full tilt and I went, BOOM! She just flipped right over and flopped down dead.

The guys following me stopped dead in their tracks and they looked at me like I was Wyatt Earp. "WOW! What a shot."

I put my gun back in my holster and I said, "Yeah, we practice that."

I couldn't have done that again in a million years. It was absolutely pure luck. The luckiest shot of my entire life, no doubt about it.

So they were all looking at me like *wow, these guys can really shoot.*

Because moose poaching was so prevalent in the Brookton-Danforth area of Washington County, we always wanted to leave our clientele with a little wisp of mystery. There were these rumors floating around that we would put special bugs in moose meat so we could find out which houses had it and stuff like that. So when I walked up to the moose, these three guys, who were all hanging with me because they wanted the moose meat, were watching. I bent down and I said, "Sometimes, when they put those little bugs on 'em, to monitor, they put it too close to the brain, and this is what happens."

We didn't have a single moose that was poached that fall.

My friend and co-worker, Warden Tom Ward, had received a call the previous evening that an owl had attacked an acquaintance of his. During the altercation, the owl had been shot and killed. Now, shooting owls is a crime, but further investigation had established that this particular owl had attacked several people over the last week, including a state trooper. It was obviously starting to favor humans as its meal of choice and would have to be destroyed.

Driving over to interview Peter Cantara, the shooter, about the owl murder, we knew that enforcement action was not going to happen in this situation, but Tom wanted to make Peter sweat a little. He wanted me to take the lead and act stern and indifferent.

We pulled into Rowe's Garage where Peter worked for his father-in-law, went inside, and asked him for the story.

This is what he said: Peter had just got home after a long day's work and, after parking his truck like he did every night, walked to the front door. As he approached the porch steps, he was suddenly struck from behind. The blow knocked Peter to the ground and stunned him a bit. Looking around, he saw only the clear night sky full of stars and the sound of wind working its way through the large spruce trees around the house.

After a moment, he went in the house to be greeted by his wife, Lisa, who was preparing supper. He started telling her what had just happened and, as he spoke, she noticed blood trickling down the back of his neck. Closer inspection revealed several cuts in his scalp. Lisa thought that he had fallen and bumped his head and was just confused, but Peter was adamant that he had been attacked by a snowball or a fist or something.

As his mind cleared, he realized that in the fray, he had lost his favorite wool hat with the CAT Diesel logo on the front. Now, a man's hat can be his identity, and a good winter hat that signifies your preference in heavy equipment is a very important thing, so Peter decided to go look for the hat, investigate his assault further, and prove he hadn't fallen.

He began scanning the ground for his hat. It should have been right where he hit the ground, but it wasn't there. Neither were there tracks in the snow of an assailant hiding behind the trees. Just as he was about to go back inside, BAM! He was hit from behind once more.

This time, he saw his attacker as it flew up into a big spruce tree, and he ran inside to get his shotgun. Running through the door at lighting speed, he informed his wife about the monster as he grabbed his shotgun. He ran back out the door and sure enough, his nemesis flew out of the tree. Without a second thought, he raised his shotgun. The evening air filled with gentle feathers drifting down to the ground where the great horned owl now lay dead.

Peter then realized a) he had just killed an owl and b) he had done it at night. The neighbors were probably calling the wardens about the shot in the dark. Hence, he decided to call Tom, his friend, to confess his crimes before the neighbors turned him in. Tom's wife, Shari, answered the phone and Peter did what most adult males do when calling a game warden to confess a crime. He gave all the details to the warden's wife, hoping it would bring leniency. Shari told Peter that he was most likely in big trouble and handed the phone to Tom.

Now I was trying as hard as I could to keep a stern face while Peter told the tale as only Peter could do. His fiery black eyes spoke much louder than his words as the story unfolded. Finally, after a moment of silence, Peter looked at me and asked, "What's the fine for shooting an owl?"

I informed him that both state and federal laws were violated. That, combined with night hunting and shooting too close to a dwelling, he was probably looking at a big fine and some serious jail time, maybe five years in prison and a $10,000 fine.

A pale glow now covered his face and I could see nausea setting in. Then Tom broke the silence, "Peter, we're really just here to get the bird to see what's wrong with it. It has been attacking people up and down Route 15. It even attacked a state trooper down the road at the state garage a couple nights ago. Do you have it?"

Peter's color came back when he realized I was not there to take him to jail. Close inspection of the owl showed it was suffering from what appeared to be cataracts. It had lost its night vision so it started hanging around areas with artificial light, attacking anything that moved.

Peter and I became the best of friends, and for many years after that I always made sure a new statue of an owl would be under his Christmas tree. Others joined in after hearing the story and his owl collection is now vast. To this day, his prized CAT Diesel hat has never been found.

About a year later, we had it happen again. I was in the office at headquarters, and a gentleman came in through the door, extremely upset, and he says, "I was walking my Muffy this morning [Muffy was a little white dog] and the next thing I know . . . *whoosh* . . . this owl came down and grabbed her and carried her off. I was running down the road trying to catch her, yelling Muffy, Muffy, and then the owl dropped her and Muffy landed in the road, dead, and then the owl landed in the road to come back and get her and it was as high as my belt buckle."

It was not funny, because he'd lost his really good pet, but the story, the way he was telling it, was humorous.

So about an hour later, at an elderly housing complex right near where this happened, several of the ladies had an owl swoop at them. There was a school right nearby, and the people at the school, who were worried about this owl, complained to the maintenance man. The maintenance man went out and the owl came after him. So they called us and we went down there, Pat Dorian and I—this was just before school let out—and we found that owl in a tree right there in the schoolyard.

We wanted to do this discreetly before the kids got out. Shoot the bird, grab it, and leave with the least amount of fanfare.

Of course, tenderhearted people would think we just ought to catch it and take it away, but that was not going to work. It had cataracts and was going blind and was attacking anything that moved, which was not a good thing to have happening right near a school. A predator bird's talons are sharp and they're contaminated because they're always on dead things. You get attacked by a bird like that, and your chances of getting a serious infection are very high. The other thing about dealing with owls, which I know from first-hand experience, is that should you succeed in catching them, they can turn their head right around and bite you. If you grab them by the back wings where you'd be able to contain most birds, that little head comes whipping around and takes a hunk right out of you.

So Pat shoots the owl—this bird had a wing span of about three feet, and body about eighteen to twenty inches tall—and instead of falling to the ground so we can grab it and get out of there before the kids can see it, it fetches up on a branch, halfway down, just hanging there, dead.

Now we've got to go get a ladder, climb the tree, and grab the owl. Our discreet little owl removal project isn't working. By this time, we've drawn quite a crowd and school's getting out. We finally do retrieve the owl and get out of there, but the story gets into the press and we start getting hate mail for shooting that poor owl. We were getting hate mail for two or three months after that incident. Even the BBC called Pat and interviewed him and asked him if he had to kill animals often.

Owls aren't the only birds that are dangerous to handle, either. Most people would never think it, but the heron, if it's injured, is one of the most dangerous birds in Maine. When they're injured, they'll just curl their head right back, and when you reach down to pick them up, they'll strike. They can strike with enough force that they can pierce your skull. They've actually killed people. They usually shoot for right between the eyes, assuming you're a predator. They hunker right in, tuck their head under their wing and then boom! They'll strike the person who's trying to help them. That bill is sharp; they pierce fish with it. A lot of people, thinking they're going to help this poor little animal, get hurt picking them up. I have seen a couple of people who had big bruises on their arms as a result. It looked like someone took a hammer and hit 'em in the arm. You'd never think of it, seeing this big old bird that's laying there, hurt, but it's better to use a noose pole or a blanket. Or call a warden.

People call us for all kinds of animal problems, including attacking raccoons and monsters that eat their cat food, as these stories illustrate. One Sunday night early in my career, I got a call from a distressed elderly lady down the street who had a raccoon problem. She got my number because it was the same as the previous game warden, and she was in desperate need of a game warden. Being one to never leave a damsel in distress, I stepped out into the evening air, just beaming at this chance to make the world a safer place.

She had mentioned that every time she tried to go outside, this giant monster raccoon would chase her back into the house. Now, having been trained at the academy to face adversity and challenges of which I could never have dreamed, I was feeling rather invincible. When I stepped out of my patrol vehicle, an old Dodge truck just beat to snot by its previous warden (rookies get the hand-me-downs), I was ready to do battle.

I started for the front door of this modest little house. Four porch steps led to the door. Halfway there, I heard a growl from the darkness under the porch. With lightning speed, the monster the lady had described burst out from under the porch and bore down on me with a vengeance, a twelve-pound behemoth about to rip me to shreds. The snarling and gnashing of teeth made it very clear it thought I was about to be supper.

There was no time to shoot the beast with my handgun. The only option I had was to jump back in the truck and shut the door. The raccoon missed me by inches, and then circled the truck, biting tires and the metal truck frame.

Feeling a little humbled, I was sitting there trying to figure out plan B when the lady stepped out the front door to tell me that, "Yup, that's the crazy one right there."

As soon as the monster saw her, he went after her. She slammed the door shut and yelled through it, "That's the mean one."

I reached for my trusty .22-caliber Remington Nylon 66 rifle, slid a round in the chamber, and opened the window of my truck, taking careful aim at Coonzilla. He was sitting at the base of the porch steps so he could grab whoever moved first. After letting the adrenalin surge pass, I fired one shot. He went down, turned back into a twelve-pound raccoon again. Moments passed. Neither one of us dared step out.

After not seeing any movement for quite some time, I ventured forth and so did she, and she explained the reason for the raccoon's foul mood. The raccoon had been feasting on her cat food that she kept on the porch, until she brought it inside. Evidently, Coonzilla did not think that was a good idea. After speaking to the lady for a few minutes more, I drove home, taking Coonzilla along for burial, thinking maybe this job was going to be tougher than I thought.

We're the animal experts, I guess, because when people don't know what to do about an animal, any animal, they call us. That's why, on a dismal, rainy October afternoon in Greenville, my second patrol area, I'd stopped by the office to drop off some paperwork when the secretary informed me that I'd arrived just in time. An elderly lady had just called to report that something was eating the cat food that she put out on her porch for her cats and she thought whatever it was lived under an old hutch on the back of the porch.

Another officer happened to be at the office as well, so we went up Blair Hill Road to investigate. Upon our arrival, we walked up onto the narrow porch and observed the empty cat food plates on the floor and saw a big hutch.

A very tiny lady came to the door when we knocked and told us that she was sure something was living behind the hutch, saying that even if she closed the porch door, the food would disappear.

Now the porch was just wide enough to walk in single file, so me being closest to the hutch, I grabbed a broom leaning up against the back wall and started working it under the open face at the hutch's fancy base. In its day, it would have been a beauty, but now it was used to store garden tools, gloves, mittens, and the like.

I made a couple sweeps under the hutch and a few empty cat food cans rolled out. About my third sweep, the broom handle stopped and wouldn't move. Repositioning myself to get better leverage, I tried pulling the handle towards me. When it finally started to move, I saw two little feet gripping the other end. For a second, I found it entertaining. Then my brain started to run through all the animals in Maine that have front feet like that and I realized that this thing was about to go real bad.

I yelled, "SKUNK!"

But it was too late. Tom, my partner, was leaning in over my shoulder, trying to figure out what in the world the animal was when the wall of spray came shooting out at point-blank range. The mist quickly covered us and the burning sensation in our eyes and nostrils called for an immediate retreat. It was so potent it would make a great mace.

Just as quickly, the inner door of the house slammed shut and movement could be heard from inside as the scent began to penetrate the walls of the house. After letting the cloud clear for a few minutes, I went back to tell the lady that we would return with a live trap to remove the skunk and to apologize for the smell. Skunks in live traps have to be covered with a blanket to keep from spraying. Even they don't like their own smell.

At this time, my family and I lived on Pritham Avenue, the main drag in Greenville, and I discovered why it's not a good idea to live where people can watch you strip down to your skivvies because your wife won't let you or your clothes come in the house.

You quickly find out that after a few minutes, even if you can't smell the smell anymore, others can. Once you have been sprayed, there's nothing you can do. It contaminates everything. You have to wash and air out outside. For weeks after, the scent lingers and when it gets damp the smell comes back—in your vehicle, on your clothes, on your boots. No one wants to ride with you or be near you on damp days. My wife left my my clothes on the porch for two weeks, and then washed them and they were fine. After apprehending the suspect, I took the lady some moose meat as a peace offering.

Of all the animal adventures I've ever had, this one was probably the scariest. It was with Daryl Gordon again. He had a territory called Nicatous Lake, which is near the Moosehorn National Wildlife Refuge, near Calais. There's a stream near there that, when they're spawning, almost runs black with smelts, so it's a closed run.

We were going in there to check on people illegally dipping smelts. We had to hide our vehicle because we knew the bad guys would come looking for a warden vehicle. They know that we're going to hide the truck and walk in, so they drive around and look for the vehicle before they do something bad. The moon was just coming up, we'd ditched our truck, we had our packs on, and we were going to sit on that brook for the night. Like always, Daryl and I had a relationship where we didn't have to talk, so we're walking along the brook and he elbows me, and I could see a man on the other side.

There was a ledge that came down over there, and the point kind of came out into the water. Out on that point, there was a man bent over, picking smelts out of the brook. The smelts were running so thick you could pick them by hand. You didn't even need a net.

We watched for a second or two in the moonlight and we could see the outline: he was bent right over, scooping them up. All of a sudden we both started running for him, we're maybe thirty feet away from him, we're just getting into the water, and we're going to run across the brook and muckle onto the guy before he can run. So we're running at him, full tilt. When we're very close, we turn our flashlights on, because game wardens don't move with their flashlights on until they're right on someone—that makes it easier not to get shot at. And we realize it's *not* a person. My brain is sorting through the things it could be, connecting color and form and proximity, and click! It's a BEAR that's hunkered down there, eating smelts. A great big bear. We've got it pinned against a ledge and we're running right at it.

The bear's eyes get huge. There's water flying everywhere. Total panic sets in. The quickest way out was to break off to the side and hope I picked the right side. Daryl and I spin off, I go left and he goes right. That bear just went straight up the ledge and it was gone. It was a very emotional moment.

Now, when a bear gets really angry, it slaps a tree. If you've ever heard it, it's a very distinct thing, sounds kind of like smacking a tree really hard with a broom. For the next three nights, while we were working there, every so often we'd hear, "Pow!" and a little while later, "Pow!"

We were caught so cold, because in our minds, 100 percent that was a man.

PART III

ON- AND OFF-ROAD TRAFFIC COP

CHAPTER ELEVEN

Chasing Those Infernal Machines

People don't realize it, but in addition to our duties protecting Maine's fish and wildlife resources, wardens have all the powers of other law officers. That includes the blue lights in our vehicles, the ability to make traffic stops, and the training and duty to police all of the off-road recreational vehicles in the woods and on Maine's inland lakes and rivers. In the early 1990s, we began to see an explosion of recreational vehicle use with a resulting impact on fishing, hunting, the peacefulness of the wilderness—and on us to police the off-road population and deal with all the OUIs (operating under the influence), accidents, and drownings.

Over time, as the whole recreational vehicle thing became popular, it really changed—I might almost say destroyed—a great job. In the wintertime, when I was first a game warden, I could patrol ice fishermen all day. I was kind of a free bird. I didn't have to check in on the radio every few minutes or be completely connected to any emergency. Then the use of ATVs, Jet Skis, and snowmobiles exploded, and dealing with them became a large part of the job. It totally changed things. Snowmobilers were the biggest accident crowd. As their popularity increased, on the weekends it wasn't that you *might* have an accident, it was that you were *going* to have several.

We no longer could go sit on a point and watch fishermen all day because there'd be an accident to get to. We became more snow traffic police than everything else, with little time for fish and game enforcement.

The whole transition to the snowmobile and the ATV pretty much turned the quiet woods of Maine into the wild west. Suddenly, people had immediate access to very remote areas without any effort whatsoever. Places that would have taken an entire day to hike into, people could now access in fifteen or twenty minutes. It just concentrated people into these remote areas where we didn't have enough manpower. From a preservation of fish and wildlife resources standpoint, the game changed dramatically. We went from finding the vehicle that was parked at a trailhead, and going up and working that pond or ponds for the day, to realizing that now we had fifteen places we needed to be.

We were always racing behind, and they were so mobile, we would just get in and they would leave. In the course of a day, poachers could hit multiple areas, so now we went from focusing on protecting high quality fishing areas that we knew the fishermen were visiting to racing around trying to keep up with them. They could be at Bluff Pond, they could be at Second West Branch, they could be at Six Roach, all in the course of a day. It seriously hamstrung us as far as being able to keep up with protecting the resource.

The same thing happened with snowmobiles. Ice fishing completely changed. That had been growing, as the snowmobile population increased, but then what happened to us, in the wintertime, was that we went from patrolling ice fishermen and preventing the illegal hunting of moose and deer to dealing with the lost, the injured, and the drunk, often in the middle of the woods in the middle of the night. A snowmobile could run into a tree in the middle of nowhere, then we would have to do the rescue missions to get them out of there and investigate the accidents. Alcohol and drug use was extremely prevalent in this crowd at the time, so we had to deal with OUIs on snowmobiles.

All that rescue work and accident investigation was tapping resources which we would normally be putting into other wildlife issues.

Days we wanted to spend protecting the resources, we were tied up investigating accidents, hauling injured people, and looking for missing people who'd gone for rides and hadn't come back. We'd spend hours and hours looking for them. In a very short time, we got stretched until we were unable to keep up with it. It was like trying to shovel the tide with a spoon, and it overwhelmed us.

Later, as a sergeant in Greenville, knowing there was a snowmobile accident every single weekend, and to allow some of the men under me to go out and work fishermen, I would assign one warden to snow-mobiles, on call, on alert, waiting, so the other guys could get out there and enforce fishing. That worked really well. Sometimes the accidents were so big or so serious it would tie everybody up, but at least it gave us a chance to do some enforcement.

I can still remember the day back in the early '90s when the tide turned. Tommy Ward and I had gone on snowmobiles way up north, and we'd been off the radio all day because we were patrolling. We were doing what game wardens were supposed to do, and when we got back into radio range, we got the dickens from our sergeant because there'd been a guy who'd driven a sled into the open water in Rockwood and he'd drowned and they couldn't find us to respond. To me, as someone who'd become a warden to protect fish and wildlife resources, that was the beginning of the end. We were no longer the guys who could go out and do what we'd signed up to, and it just got worse and worse every year.

To keep up with the population we were policing, we had to have these off-road vehicles, too, because we had to get to the spots where these things happened. We had great toys, which made that part of the job really fun, but chasing accidents took up much of our time. More often than not, a warden would just get to where he wanted to be to do some enforcement work and he'd get a call: someone had had an accident heading up to Kokadjo, and the warden would have to go get a rescue boggan and get the medical people in there to deal with them and get the people out.

To give an idea of the scope of this, on a busy weekend like a school vacation or holiday weekend, we're talking four or five thousand snowmobiles coming through this area. When we'd stop 'em, like we did when we did trail checks, we had to be really careful, because we'd back up a line of sleds, and some guy would come flying around the corner where everybody's stopped, and run into somebody. As soon as we started seeing a line build up, we'd have to stop and let 'em go.

Primarily, we were doing registration checks that might lead to detecting intoxication, because alcohol use was a huge problem in this population. The challenge we faced was how to figure that out when someone was wearing a helmet and you couldn't really see his face. We got pretty good at spotting it by talking to them and observing their reactions. And we could also tell the crowd we were dealing with by the sled they drove and their attitude when they pulled in.

Consistently, the worst crowd were lobstermen up from the coast, because they were off season and they had money to burn and we were the police and were infringing on their fun. So they didn't like us. Over the years, those have been the guys I've butted heads with the hardest.

I've talked about some of the hunters we've tangled with, and the crazy chases they lead us on. Now imagine that on a snowmobile. Probably the most dangerous thing that we did, bar none, was snowmobile checks at night. Here's the scenario: Guy leaves the bar. He's been drinking. He heads down the trail and runs into a warden checkpoint. He knows he's drunk. He has two options—he can stop and submit or he can squeeze the throttle and drive through the middle of the pack, and if he gets through, he probably gets free because there are a million trails he can go on. Add alcohol to that decision-making process and the fact that the guy is sitting on a snowmobile that can go over a hundred miles an hour and can get to the fifty-mile-an-hour range in just a few seconds. He's waiting in a group, he's next, and that little switch in his head flips and he just blasts it.

That is a very dangerous situation because there's a risk he's gonna hit you or someone else. You've got this guy with clouded judgment on a machine that can accelerate rapidly, and you're on foot. Next thing you know, you're dealing with sleds just missing you by inches at full speed. And then the chase is on. It's seriously dangerous stuff, and I've had it happen numerous times. We usually kept a sled on the ground, ready to go, just for those situations.

Here's what you don't want to have happen as a game warden: You're riding on a trail fifteen or twenty miles from the nearest road, and you encounter a drunk on a snowmobile and you arrest him. Now what are you going to do with him? You can put him behind you, where he has complete access to your sidearm. You can put him in front of you, where he can headbutt you and take your snowmobile. You can lay him on his side and sit on him, but that isn't gonna work very well on a twenty mile ride. You can't risk his life or injure him, because once you arrest him, he's yours. You've also got his sled to deal with. Quite simply, you can't grab them there, so you don't check a snow-mobiler where you can't deal with the issue. You learn, very quickly, just like with trigger-happy hunters or other dangerous enforcement situations, that there's a time and place for everything. We learned to set up our stops at bottleneck points where we could walk them out to a road.

When the whole snowmobiling thing transitioned to the size that it did, we went from dealing with snowmobile accidents to taking a look at what was causing the majority of the problems and saying okay, OUI is the big factor, so we put a real big push on to curb the OUIs. I don't remember the exact statistic we came up with, but it was like at that time of night, 85 percent of the people we were checking had been drinking and 60 percent were intoxicated. Really high numbers. So we started doing a lot of these OUI checks and we would schedule them from one to three a.m.

It worked. When we were in downtown Jackman about three or four years into this process, at one in the morning, when the bars let out, we'd see guys walking down the street with their helmets tucked under their arms, heading back to camp. We knew we had turned the corner. It wasn't just that we needed fewer enforcement efforts, the number of fatal accidents dropped dramatically.

There was also plenty of search and rescue work for lost or injured people. The whole Greenville area, it's just a maze of snowmobile trails in the winter. Greenville is a hub for something like twelve hundred miles of trails. I had a group of snowmobilers that rented snowmobiles up in Kokadjo. Three guys from Florida who had never been on snowmobiles before rented snowmobiles and took off for the day. Toward the end of the day, one of 'em came back to Kokadjo and said that in the process of riding around he'd gotten separated from his two buddies. The rental place called us and said, "We think we have a couple of lost snowmobilers."

The first place we always started to look for missing snowmobilers was at the local bar. Sure enough, one of the missing guys was there. I said to him, "You all set?" And he said, "Yeah . . . I'm fine, I'm at the bar."

And I said, "What about your buddy? Is he with you?"

And he said, "Yup. Uh . . . no. I lost him. I don't know where he is. But he's going to be all right."

So I said to him, "Well, when you got to Greenville, how much gas did you have left?

And he said, "Oh, I had no gas left, so I pulled in here and decided to have a drink."

So I was riding around on the snowmobile trails and all of a sudden I came to a snowmobile that had gone off the trail and sank on its side in the woods. There were the tracks of a running man going up the snowmobile trail, so I started following the tracks. About every fifty yards, there was a snow angel, where he'd fallen down. Finally, I came around the corner and there he was. His eyes were as big as saucers. He'd completely flipped out. So I got him on my sled, and he said, "There's no way out of here."

I said, "What do you mean?"

He said, "I have been on every trail. Everything goes in circles. There is no way out of here." He was just really wigging out.

I said, "Listen to me. There is a way out of here and I'm going to get you there." He was quite hypothermic by this time because they'd come from Florida and they didn't have snowmobile suits or any sort of suitable winter gear. They just had semi-adequate stuff. I had the ambulance waiting at the end of the road to pick him up.

He was so sure there was no way out, I had to convince him. I said, "You've got to trust me. You've got to trust me. I'm going to have you in a nice warm ambulance here in just a little bit. You've got to believe me."

We were going along, and I'll never forget this as long as I live: I had him in front of me 'cause he wasn't able to hang on, and this little tiny voice said, "Are we almost there yet?"

I said, "We'll be there soon. We'll be there soon. You're going to be warm in a minute."

And he just said, "Thank you. Thank you."

Oh my word. That poor guy. I can guarantee you he's never been back to Maine.

Hypothermia is a really common problem, because its effects are subtle and people have lost it long before they know they're in trouble. A real quick way to tell is to watch somebody walk. We call it the hypothermia shuffle, where the blood is now beginning to pull to the core and their gait turns into this rigid shuffle, kind of like Frankenstein. They move almost in slow motion, and they kind of walk with their head down. When you see that, when you recognize that they're in that phase, they're in trouble. I've seen it a lot, over my career. And usually, at that phase, they're in total denial. They've gotten past the point of being cold and are just getting numb to everything, and they're just in that kind of state where they shuffle along until they just fall down. That's classic.

You can also usually tell by talking to them, because when they're in that state, they're slow in responding. There's always a lag when you ask them a question. It's like it goes in, it has to be processed, and you can tell that theirs is not a normal response.

The maze of trails is one problem for snowmobilers. Then there's the lake. Moosehead Lake is a huge body of water, with rocks that stick up, islands, and open spots. Over the years, we've had an awful lot of snowmobile crashes out on the lake, or people who've gone into open water. It's a forty-mile-long lake, with numerous spots where it never freezes. People come up here and go out snowmobiling, and they just don't know about that.

What happens to a lot of people is that when they get lost on the lake, they decide to find their way back by following the shore, which is something that works on most lakes. It's often the smart thing to do, but not on the west side of Moosehead, because that's where all the rivers come in. There are three rivers that come in, with open water at each point. What people trying to follow the shore end up doing is driving right into that open water. They come around a point and the next thing they know, they're in the water.

We had a couple from Pennsylvania, a couple years ago, who rented a camp and went snowmobiling and they never came back. The people they'd rented the camp from called it in. We had no idea where to start looking. The lake is huge, and if they weren't on the lake there are hundreds of miles of snowmobile trails. So we just put the plane up and started flying the open water points, because we knew from experience that's where you start. If they were wearing helmets, they'd float. We couldn't see it from the fixed wing, but a helicopter that got right down low could see their black helmets. So we got the airboat, which can go on the water or on the ice, and went out and brought them in.

Getting someone out of open water on a frozen lake in the middle of winter is no small undertaking. These situations require a large team of people to make the recovery. You need airboat operators, divers, a spare watercraft for emergencies in case your airboat quits, and a plane overhead to act as a spotter. Any sensible person on an airboat carries two logs to drive the boat up on so it doesn't freeze into the ice. These are huge, dangerous team operations. Complex rescue operations like these are one of the reasons that wardens are such a close-knit group, because we have to work well together and be ready for anything to go wrong.

It's not just open water that poses a risk for inexperienced snowmobilers on the lake. There are also rocks and pressure ridges, those hard-to-see places where the ice has buckled. We had this one snowmobile crash, in the middle of the night, involving a couple on a sled going seventy, eighty miles an hour along the lake. They hit a pressure ridge, and that sled went about a hundred and thirty-five to a hundred and fifty feet in the air before it came back into contact with the ice.

They were just splattered all over the ice. She had survived for a little while, you could see that from the way her body had melted into the ice, because it still had body heat, and he didn't.

Another time I had a guy, out on the lake at night, who ran into an ice fishing shack at a hundred miles per hour. The ice shack that he ran into was one he had helped put there. He had consumed a lot of alcohol and was out riding with his buddies. He went zipping across this lake, and he was going so fast, at the point of impact, that the skis weren't touching the ground for a long distance. He had a modified speedometer like they have in cars that actually left us a tick mark, the needle of the speedometer leaving a mark so that we could tell the speed at point of impact. We were able to ship it to the crime lab and they could interpret it. I think he was going a hundred and one miles an hour when he hit.

That was a phenomenal scene. It looked like that shack had been hit by a missile. It just blew out in an arc. And in the facewall where he hit there was a perfect outline of him going through it, just like in a cartoon. He hit that ice shack so hard that the roof of the shack fell down on the four wooden blocks that were holding it up. He was about seventy-five feet away, wearing a hunk of the floor caught around his neck.

A buddy he was riding with, who was also intoxicated, ran home, called anonymously, said "Hey, there's a dead guy out on the lake," and hung up the phone. Forgetting, of course, that we had the phone number he'd called from.

With these types of scenes, we had a very short window of opportunity to document it and do the recovery. Because of weather conditions and wind and snow, it's a fast changing kind of thing. More often than not, we had to look at the scene, catalogue it, and try to put it together without the luxury of time. And these things generally happened at night, so sometimes you had to get what you could, right then and there, in the dark. Photographing the tracks and point of impact and the debris field. Taking the measurements. We would do the best we could with what we had at night, knowing that by morning we might have six inches of new snow or the wind might have blown the snow right over everything.

We'd document it right there and then try to get back in the morning.

So yeah, our dual mission is protecting fish and wildlife, and doing search and rescue. And much of our day-to-day, depending on the season, is off-road traffic cop. Except for the mobility they give poachers and people who get themselves lost in the wilderness, ATVs are less of a problem than snowmobiles. They do have an affinity for mud, though, which means mud season, which used to be a quieter season, now puts different demands on us.

I do have this one ATV story. My sergeant, Dan Tourtelotte, and I were going into Spencer Bay, a camping area on the northeast side of Moosehead Lake. As we were going along, we met an ATV coming at us. We put our blue lights on to stop and check the registration and make sure the operator wasn't under the influence. The subject stopped, and as I was getting out of the vehicle on the passenger side, he pulled up alongside the driver's door so the driver couldn't get the door open. We could see it was a kid, and before I could get to him, he took off on a rip and a tear, and the chase was on.

We found fresh spin marks where he'd turned down a little side road, so I bailed out and went in on foot, and the sarge kept running the roads. We had radios and were talking. That little trail made a loop that took it back to the main road and toward the campsites, in the opposite direction from where he'd come, so we figured he was heading back to the campsites. Sarge picked me up on the road, and as we were coming along, we met a pickup truck.

When that kid made the turn onto the road that would loop him around us, we could see where the bike had ripped into the alders really bad, almost crashed, and left a bunch of scarred up trees and stuff. So when we met this pickup, we stopped and got out to ask them if they'd seen the four-wheeler. I'd just had a millisecond to look at the kid who was on the bike. Now, I walked up to the pickup, and the driver's got a big spot of blood dripping down his eyebrow. I looked at him for a second, and I just said, "YOU!"

He immediately started crying. Just bawling his eyes out. And all I said was, "You."

I said, "Get out of that truck."

And he said, "I'm sorry I ran on you. I almost killed myself in the alders." He fills in all the blanks in about six seconds. "I hid my bike. It's in the campsite. I hid it out behind the tents." It was a priceless moment. Other than failing to stop for a public safety officer, the bike was unregistered. Big whoop. Fifty dollar fine. For that he almost killed himself.

Of course, since we had to have snowmobiles of our own to keep up with this population, we did find them very effective for getting out on the lakes and checking ice fishermen. Because my dogs, once I started using dogs, were trained to find fish, one of my training challenges became teaching my dog to ride with me on a snowmobile. It took a lot of slow trips around my yard with the dog perched in front of me between my arms to get Reba comfortable enough to take her with me on the trail. Even harder to teach her to wear a hat to protect her ears in cold weather.

But there were plenty of occasions where I'd get off the sled to check fishermen's licenses and chat with them about whether they were having any luck, and a little brown dog would be trotting around, finding their hidden fish and bringing them grief. Reba could find fish in the snow and under the ice, and her nose was so keen that she would only dig up game fish.

I remember this one party on Moosehead. I'd just pulled into the landing and fishermen were coming back to their vehicle. I was checking their licenses and the dog found a whole bunch of illegal fish tucked into a snowbank next to their vehicle. They took the usual line—that those were not their fish. But the dog could follow their boot tracks right to the spot where the fish were hidden. One thing I always noticed was that when the dog was about to find their hidden fish, the fishermen would turn away because they knew they were guilty.

PART IV

THESE ARE THE BIG WOODS

CHAPTER TWELVE

A World Both Beautiful and Deadly

As I've said, my work as a warden falls into several different areas, and one of the major ones is our search and rescue stuff. A lot of that work comes from people underestimating what they're getting into up here in the Maine woods. They may be outdoorsy; they may be comfortable with hiking and being outside; but often they aren't prepared for what they're going to find up here. It's a warden's joke that what is known as the Kokadjo Triangle, roughly outlined by Greenville, Rockwood, and Pittston Farm, is really the "Triangle of Death" because it's where so many bad things happen.

In my career, I've carried, conservatively, over two hundred bodies out of those woods up there. I think it's probably closer to three hundred fatalities. We also call it "The Lemming Zone," because it's where people go to jump off. They get into this wilderness environment they're not prepared for and bad things happen. And that's what I dealt with, day in and day out.

Most people, when they read about the wardens doing a rescue in the paper, they have no clue what's involved. The hours, the planning, the complexity, the physical demands, the massive scale of some rescue operations, and the risks to the wardens themselves. It's just what the wardens do.

Statistically, when people are missing in the woods, you have to find them in the first three days or there's a 90 percent probability that they've perished, particularly in the fall with the rain and chilly conditions. That's not a lot of time when you're dealing with a wilderness area, and it takes some of that time to assemble personnel and organize a search, so your first attack has to be your best one and you better give it the most you have. Sometimes, even with your best efforts, you may have to stop and regroup, or go home and get more gear and regroup. But the key is always the first three days.

The importance of a fast, well-coordinated rescue effort is what gave rise to the idea of the overhead management team—a management team of wardens each with a specific area of expertise—because it lets us bring together the best experience and the best heads who know how the various pieces fit together. It also prevents us from burning all the resources we have in the first day. The overhead team utilizes the incident command system used by firefighters and law enforcement. It breaks the task down into manageable pieces (for example, logistics, planning, operations, finance). Each branch has its own specific function and tasks, and each branch answers to the incident commander who ties all the efforts together. The planning division sets up mapping, assigns search areas, decides on what resources are needed. Operations checks in search teams, then takes those designated search assignments and briefs the teams and sends them out, then debriefs them when they return, creating an ongoing record of the areas that have been searched.

In my area, the Greenville area, I had the Hundred-Mile Wilderness section of the Appalachian Trail, the longest stretch of uninterrupted wilderness along the trail, and Gulf Hagas, which are both areas where the hiking and the natural beauty attract people, but which can pose dangers even to the experienced hiker.

From the jump off point on Route 15 up through to Mount Katahdin there's very little cell phone coverage, and that's where hikers' family members panic because they haven't heard from their loved ones for a week or more. We tell them there's no cell phone coverage in there. It doesn't mean there's something wrong, it's just the way it is on the Appalachian Trail. I used to get a lot of those calls.

Usually, there's nothing to worry about, but it's a very rough piece of trail that results in lots of injured people. In an average summer, I'd probably rescue sixteen, seventeen, eighteen people on the trail. Get a few days of rain and everything turns really slippery, until it's just as if there's grease on the rocks. That's when you start getting broken ankles or they've blistered up their feet so badly they've gotten infections.

I used to carry a pair of crutches in my truck because, if someone got injured, there were basically two choices—I could organize fifteen or twenty guys to try and carry them, or I could just brace their foot up and then hand them a pair of crutches and help them hobble out. People shake their heads when they hear that number—fifteen to twenty people—but those carry-outs involve a huge amount of manpower. When you're doing a carryout with a stretcher, that stretcher is traveling over the trail so those who are doing the carrying are always walking off the trail. It's brutal, the carry-out scenario. It's about the most physically challenging thing you can do. People express disbelief at the numbers, but it's a fact that to go a mile on rough trail takes a minimum of fifteen men. It's painstakingly slow and difficult, and going that mile can take hours.

To get that many people, we usually call on forestry, the local fire departments, and other local law enforcement groups. We've got a pretty good working relationship with all the fire departments around and they've always been super. We've had some injured people in Gulf Hagas where we've carried them, literally, all night long to get 'em out of there. That's a whole night of strenuous effort for a whole lot of people. Totally exhausting, and we don't get to choose the conditions. When you get to a steep section, where you kinda all line up and just pass the stretcher down, if you don't have enough people, you start seriously running the risk of injuring the rescuers.

These days, you can use headlamps, but back then, we carried these big, heavy Mag-Lite flashlights, which meant carrying the stretcher with one hand and that light in the other. We'd organize it with a scout going in front to spot obstacles and troubleshoot for the carryout team, six on the stretcher, and others walking behind, and rotate the order of their positions so they wouldn't get too tired. It worked like a well-oiled machine, but it took hours and hours carrying someone in shock and pain.

Some of these situations, where we had to get them up a mountain to get to a helicopter because it was shorter, we had to carry them uphill. That's the worst. Downhill is bad enough, but when you're climbing steep terrain uphill with someone on a stretcher, it's a long process.

Probably the most spectacular, and deadly, place I've ever had to do rescues is Gulf Hagas. Located about twenty miles outside of Greenville, Gulf Hagas is a dramatic seven-mile gorge sometimes called Maine's Grand Canyon. The Pleasant River runs through it in a series of waterfalls. The trail runs along the edge of the gorge with drops of a hundred feet or more to the water. The Appalachian Trail connects to the Gulf Hagas trail system. It is a dangerous place. It is absolutely gorgeous, but I've carried more people out of there, alive and dead, than anywhere in any patrol sector I've ever worked.

I had a lady a few summers ago, a fairly big woman, who fell and broke her ankle at about the halfway point, about three miles in. Not a situation where we could give her crutches and help her hobble out. It was such a bad break her foot was pointing exactly the wrong way. We had the rescue team and paramedics and all coming in, and, I'm not exaggerating, we could hear her screaming half a mile away, that poor girl. When we got there I said to her, "You go right on and scream all you want, you poor thing."

I could see right away that getting her out of there was going to be a problem. She was a big, heavy person, and even though there were fifteen or twenty of us, I knew we couldn't carry her the three and a half miles out. It would have been too dangerous for the rescuers, and given her size and where she was, the process would have taken at least ten hours. Given the extent of her injury, that might have put her at risk of losing her foot. The situation called for warden ingenuity. I remembered an old landing zone we'd put in years ago, one that we'd kind of forgotten about. It was pretty grown up, so a forest ranger and I, we ran up there—we had just handsaws—but we made a hole big enough to get a chopper in and we were able to get her out of there. Even that short carry was painful—steep ledges, the trail too narrow to walk. In some places we had to line up and pass the victim along steep spots. Under those circumstances a crew can average a mile every two hours.

One Gulf Hagas fatality happened right around the first of the year. Another one that could have killed all of us—because, though people don't realize it, there are often serious risks to the rescuers as well. This one really had me scrambling to find a way to get the victim out of there. We had gotten freezing rain overnight so everything was coated with ice, and then we had a light dusting of snow on top of it. By morning, the whole world was like a glass bottle lightly coated with snow. Absolutely the worst conditions for people or vehicles. Then the call came in that there was a seriously injured man who'd fallen into the gorge.

He had hiked in with his daughter. She was going away, maybe on a Peace Corps mission, and they wanted to do one more hike together before she left the country. So they went up the trail, and at the height of land, he slipped and fell and slid right over a cliff and down into the gorge.

His daughter had found her way down to where he was. I don't know how she did that without hurting herself. At that point, he was conscious, and he told her not to leave him, but to stay with him, so she did, but after a while, he told her to go and get help.

She was just an amazing girl. She found her way out and got back to her vehicle. You couldn't drive a vehicle in those conditions. There was no salt, no sand, it was like skating down a mountain. But somehow she made it out to the parking lot, to civilization, where she could get a phone signal, and called us. I had four officers available. I sent two of them in via the Katahdin Iron Works Road, and the rest of us went in from the Greenville side, knowing that the last two miles of the route to the parking lot that they had left from was down a mountain. Even with chains on the vehicles, I figured we had a 50 percent chance that we might make it in, and a 50 percent chance that the guys from the other side might make it.

I got on the phone with the National Guard, trying to get a helicopter in there, because under those conditions, even with crampons, there was no way we could have gotten him out of there, it was just too treacherous. I had started the process as soon as I was enroute. The first officer to get in there, to meet up with the daughter, was Mike Morrison. He found the victim. Just a few minutes after I got there, the helicopter arrived, lowered a medic, and called the man deceased.

Now I had a serious problem. The National Guard would not retrieve a body; their protocol was to only deal with live people. The usual practice with a death situation was to bring the medical examiner to the body, something that would be just impossible under these conditions, and getting the victim out of there ourselves would have been unbelievably labor-intensive even if we could have done it. Under those conditions, it would have been too dangerous. And we couldn't just leave him there until conditions improved.

I had only one shot at getting him out of there, and that was if I could get permission from the medical examiner to move the body, and convince the National Guard to put him in the stretcher while it was already there.

I had to move fast, before that helicopter left, so I got on the phone with Dr. Margaret Griswold, who was the medical examiner at the time. I had dealt with her often because I had a lot of fatalities, and I said, "Margaret, you have to trust me. I'm in a very serious situation and I need you to give me permission to move the body without all the information you usually need, because otherwise other people could get hurt or even die in this thing."

She asked me a couple of brief questions and I outlined it for her. I said a guy had gone off a cliff in Gulf Hagas and everything was glare ice and my only hope for getting him out was hovering right over me. She said go ahead, and to call as soon as I got things squared away. Because of the circumstances, the Guard bent protocol. They put him in the Stokes basket and lifted him, and took him over to the gatehouse and landed in a field there. They unloaded him and we had a hearse come and get him from there.

But now, we wardens were still there. We couldn't get out. We had gotten in, but now we couldn't get out. We couldn't keep our vehicles on the road. I hadn't been able to reach Dr. Griswold from the parking lot. While I was trying to get to a point with cell phone service where I could call her, I had to make an S-turn, with very steep banks and a bridge. When I tried to make the turn, I slid. If I'd gone off just another few feet, I would have rolled the truck and gone into the abyss.

I was stuck in a hole, and I couldn't move, because if I moved, I'd roll the truck down the bank. All of the details with Dr. Griswold and the National Guard were negotiated while I was sitting there on this slippery slope, praying the truck would stay put, staring into the abyss, and explaining the whole circumstance of this death to the medical examiner. And all the time that we were sorting all this out, that poor girl was waiting down in the parking lot.

I don't know how she got out of there to contact us. By rights, she should have ended up in the river. Everybody had to stay there until they could get a sand truck in to sand the road. The sand truck hooked on to me and pulled me out onto the road. Then every one of us went out the Katahdin Iron Works Road, and we had to drive all the way around to Greenville, twenty miles or so on slow, rough road. We got the call on that around noontime, and I think I got home around midnight.

It got so that every time I got a call to Gulf Hagas, I braced for the worst and the worst was what that place kept serving up. We had three young men who went for a hike in, I want to say, June. Two brothers and friend for whom this hike was a yearly thing. They got beyond Stair Falls, where there's a whole series of little pools, and it was their tradition that they would jump in and swim in this particular hole. The water was unusually high that year, and it was very cold, but they were determined to swim. The first one jumped into the pool, and he never came back up.

His brother, who was in the navy at the time, got really concerned, so he jumped in, and he never came back up, either. The third man was standing there, and he didn't know what to do. He looked downstream, and after a while, he saw one of the brothers come out and wash up against a rock. He went and tried to rescue the guy he could see. He was unsuccessful at reviving him, so he ran for help.

He had to have run about two miles to get to his vehicle, and then to get out to the gate, where he could call for help, would be about ten miles.

We got the call fairly late in the day, and we went in. Pat Dorian was there, and I was there—we had about four or five officers—and we went down and searched all the shoreline on both sides of the gorge, in case someone had gotten out, but we couldn't see anything.

We were able to get the first body out that night. There were eighty- to one-hundred-and-fifty-foot cliffs on the sides along there, but there were places where you could work your way down. We used a Stokes, and were able to get the first guy out that night. But there was still another guy missing in the pool.

The next day, we went back to look for him. This time there were fifteen of us. We had to cut a trail—and the Appalachian Trail folks were really cranked about this—from a woods road down through to the Gulf Hagas trail, and we had to pack in all the gear for our dive team: tanks, and weights, a canoe, all the gear, and all these ropes. We started at seven in the morning and I don't think we got a diver in the water until after noontime. I think we had two divers, maybe three, because you always have a spotter as well. They were on ropes, for safety. So they went down, and the guy was caught in a cross-current, kind of off to the side, tucked under some rocks.

When we looked at the dynamics of what had happened, the only thing we could figure out was that where the water came pouring over the rocks into that pool, it got completely aerated. It didn't have enough density for them to push themselves out, but they were still trapped by the weight of the falling water that held them in place. They literally drowned in water that was half air—when they dove in, it was like diving into feathers, nothing to push against to save themselves—and then they got caught in that undertow. Looking at it from the surface, you never could have seen that in a million years.

Gulf Hagas. No signs. No ropes. No rangers. If you brought children in there, you could lose them at any second. And I've pulled so many bodies out of there. So many bodies.

I had a guy who got about halfway into the gorge, halfway up the trail, and he had a heart attack and died. He was about three and a half miles in. So we raced in there. At the time, we didn't know if he was dead. This was a fairly good-sized gentleman, and harsh as it seems, often the first question you asked, when you got a call from Gulf Hagas, was how big the person was, to know how many people you needed to organize the carry out.

The medics came in with us, did everything they could, and declared that he was dead. As usual, it was late in the day, that's when these things happened, so now we had to pack the guy out in the dark, which added another element to the process. He was a very big man, nearly three hundred pounds, and we're organizing this painstaking process of getting him out of there.

I know when people read about these events in the papers, they'll see the numbers of people we call in to help us with extractions on these things, and they'll shake their heads and not believe it. But when you're dealing with a gorge, or a location deep into wilderness, no roads and rough trail, it takes just a huge amount of manpower to get the victims—or the bodies—out.

We were also dealing with the family members who were with him, and they didn't want to leave. For their sake, and ours, we try to get the family to go down to the parking lot and wait. We try to have an officer to be with them, do the interview with them, get their statements, and keep them in the loop about what's going on. We sympathize, because we know what the family is going through, but it's a huge added stress on personnel doing the carryout if they also have to deal with the anxiety and distress of family members every step of the way.

I'll say this over and over again, because it just keeps happening. People who come up here for some fun and recreation too often have no idea how dangerous places can be. It's a pretty day and they're out in nature, having fun, and in a split second, someone can be dead or severely injured. Then we get the call and we have to go in and deal with that.

We had another incident at Moxie Falls, kind of near The Forks, Route 201. An absolutely beautiful, very scenic area. One late summer day, this couple, for whatever reason, were playing right at the top of the falls. According to the girlfriend, he stepped into the water, right at the top, the edge of the falls, where the current is funneling. He lost his balance, she grabbed him, and they both went right over the falls. At least a sixty foot drop onto rocks.

According to her, they both bounced against the wall and then she landed on him at the bottom. There were some people who saw them go over, and worked their way down to the bottom and helped them out immediately. She was injured, but he was deceased.

We could get her out by taking her downstream where we could walk her up to an ambulance, so we got her out of there fairly quickly. Now we had to get him out. Imagine a giant hole, straight down into the ground; we had to get a rappel team in. We had to find a team with that expertise—a group from the Sappi paper mill in Fairfield, 'cause they were trained in rappelling for high angle work they did on some of their structures.

So now we have to put the guy in the Stokes, wrap him in tight, and hoist him up the face, and then hoist him up through a notch to get him on the trail. At that point, the National Guard was coming because they didn't know he was deceased, and through Pat Dorian's connections, he convinced them that they had to take the man out of there. We would have had to carry him about a mile and a half, he was a big guy, and it would have taken us three hours or more.

When the chopper came in to do the rescue, it was a Black Hawk. I looked at all the people around me, and I said, "Listen, we've got to get all this gear out of here, because when that thing lands all your gear is going to blow over the edge, and it's all going to go back into this gorge. And we've got to get these people out of here, way down off the top. We only want four people, five people max, when this thing hovers over us, because all these trees are going to blow down. "

Now they're all looking at me like I'm an idiot, like I'm overexaggerating this thing. They think it's no big deal because of what they've seen on TV. It took a lot of convincing, and the rescue team had carried a lot of gear in. All the rope, all the gear they'd used to pull him up was sitting on the trail, and I told them, "You've got to get it out of here or it's going to go down in the hole again." I tried warning them three or four times: you've got to get farther back. And they didn't believe me.

Finally, I just said, "Move it."

When that helicopter came over and it stopped to hover, it just started raining trees. I'm talking eight-to-ten-inch spruce trees. It pulled them right to the center. By the time the medic got down, half the trees in a thirty-yard radius had blown down, and by the time the stretcher got down, me and the medic were the last two left. Everyone else had run because of all the trees coming down.

With helicopters, the other thing you have to be really careful of is a lowered cable. You cannot physically grab that cable when it's coming down to you or you'll get a shock you'll never forget, because it builds static electricity with the rotor wash. You've got to let it hit the ground. And don't be standing in the water and grab that cable, either.

The most difficult and dangerous rescues in Gulf Hagas are in the wintertime. Like the time we got a call from the owner, Bud Fackelman, that a couple who were staying at Little Lyford Pond Camps had gone cross-country skiing and never come back. It was dark by then. Dead of winter. It was twenty below that night. He had called so late because he'd gone out looking for them. He'd gotten to the head of the gorge and he could see from their tracks that instead of following the trail along the edge above the gorge—almost impossible anyway—they'd gone right down the gorge because it was frozen over.

Frozen over, it might have looked safe enough, but they were actually skiing over boulders and a river and waterfalls, total treachery underfoot that they couldn't even see. It was a death sentence, going that way.

So Tom Ward and I got in there—we took the track at about seven at night, on snowshoes—and we immediately knew we couldn't follow them. We couldn't travel down there in the gorge. It was way too dangerous. What we decided to do was follow the trail up above, periodically going out and looking over the edge to check for their tracks. The snow was unbelievably deep and overhanging the edge. Even in daylight we wouldn't have been able to tell what was edge and what was false. What we had to do was tie ourselves off, one person on belay, and the other work his way out to the edge—a risky business on snowshoes. At the edge, we'd run the light down to see if their track was still there. Then we'd untie and keep tracking our way along.

It was slow, hard, exhausting work. We finally found them at Screw Augur Falls, four miles in and six hours later, at about one in the morning, both of them still alive, which was a miracle. We'd been almost positive from the start—knowing what was below where they were skiing—that they were gone. They'd both fallen through the ice into the water. They were hypothermic. She had good Gore-Tex outerwear, so she'd been more protected. He was in really bad shape, incoherent.

It was deep powder snow and we were soaking wet from it falling on us and melting. As soon as we stopped in that cold weather, it soaked right into us. We knew we had to get a fire going right away or they, and we, were done. We gave them our coats and started working on making a fire immediately. It was not a good place to make a fire; we had to range pretty far to find wood, but we got it started.

We were able to get a radio call out and say, "We've found them. You've got to come to us."

So another team, about five people, came in from the other side—the Katahdin Iron Works side, where there was a shorter walk in from the road. We'd started at the worst end, following their tracks, and now we had two miles farther to go to get out. From the other end, they could get a snowmobile in about half way, so we only had to hike out with them about a mile. But they did have to walk out, because we couldn't carry them while we were wearing snowshoes.

That team brought them warm, dry clothes, food and thermoses of hot tea and stuff, and snowshoes to walk out on. While we'd waited, we'd kept the fire going to keep them warm and gradually got him warm enough to move, though it was still with a hypothermic shuffle. At five a.m., we finally got them out. We walked them out to sleds and snowmobiled them back to the camps.

So rescuing that couple was just another day in Gulf Hagas. But there are so many such days. Spring, summer, fall, winter. People get in there and it's absolutely gorgeous, and they don't see that it's also amazingly dangerous.

CHAPTER THIRTEEN

Matches, Hatchet, and Dryer Lint

Hypothermia is often what gets people in the woods and it's a stealthy killer. It very nearly got that young couple in Gulf Hagas. If we hadn't found them that night, he would likely have been gone in the morning. I've talked about the hypothermic shuffle—this is what happens first. Then they begin to have trouble communicating, and then they get tired and want to stop. But it's a process that goes from being normal to slowing down to this shuffle to going very quiet and they just get into the rhythmic shuffle. Then there's hypothermic thinking. This is when things start getting very cloudy in their thought processes, and this can be a killer because people start making bad decisions and making their situations much worse. Instead of stopping and making a fire, they continue on; instead of turning around and getting back into the car where there's heat, they leave the car. This is the hinge point that usually causes their demise—the point where they stop thinking clearly.

The key to survival is that you've got to spot it early on when it's happening to you. In reality, people deny that they're in a desperate situation until they're past the point where they can function. It can be really bad. I've been there. I'm supposed to be kind of an expert, but I let it sneak up on me. That's what it does. Fortunately, I was close enough to a vehicle to reach it. Here's what happened.

There was a schoolgirl here in town who had an asthma attack and died. Her dad was away hunting, camping way up on the north end of Moosehead Lake. It was October and it had snowed during the night, heavy wet snow on every branch that had pulled the alders and small trees right down into the road. It was pretty important that I find her dad, so I went up there, roaming around, trying to figure out where he was.

I got to a road that led down to a campsite on Moosehead Lake, where I suspected he might be. I couldn't drive in because the trees were all down in the road, so I parked my truck and started walking. By now, it was probably in the forties and warming up, so I put on a light rain jacket because I had to push through all the snow. What I didn't realize, because I was bent on my mission of finding that man, was that that snow was falling off the trees and sticking to my jacket, and it was sucking out my body heat because I didn't have enough layers on. I got down to really close to where I wanted to be, and I went to zip my coat up, and my hands couldn't do it.

I realized right away that I was in big trouble. If I couldn't use my hands, I was already past that point where I could make a fire. I tried to think it through. But I was hypothermic and already sliding into the fog. I thought, everything I've walked through I've already knocked the snow off, so I might be able to backtrack. I might be able to get back to the truck without it having too much more of an effect on me. I was able to do that. Then it took me literally five minutes of fumbling to get the truck door unlocked. I started it up, turned on the heater, curled up into a ball, and stayed there for about two hours. I couldn't even move. I just lay there and thought, *Well, that was a really brilliant move.* I had come so close.

It can happen to anybody at any time. The circumstances being what they were—needing to get to this guy fast—I pushed harder. And because it wasn't like a cold blast of air or wind hitting me, but just gobs of snow landing on me and sucking away my body heat, I wasn't noticing that I was getting cold. It happened very gradually. I didn't see it coming until I couldn't use my hands and I'd gone into that full shiver. Usually, by the time you get into the full shiver, you're in trouble. And if you don't recognize that as trouble, then you're *really* in trouble.

It's not just places like Gulf Hagas, of course, that get our attention. We're constantly going into the woods to pull out lost hunters. We had a kid from Pennsylvania come up here. He'd never been hunting before. He was with his friend's uncles, a group of adults and these two teenagers. It was just one of those things, these people came up here to go hunting, and they didn't have clue what they were getting into. I think they had the mental picture of rural hunting. With rural hunting, there's the expectation that wherever you come out of the woods you'll soon come to a road or a house so there's no place where you're going to wander around for days and days before you are found. That's not true up here.

This is the big woods, where you can go for hours and not find a road. And they just turned these kids loose on their own. They just all went in separate directions, and then he didn't come back. It snowed and he was dressed like a typical high school kid would be; he was not dressed for wet. He got into trouble in the first ten minutes, got all turned around on these woods roads. It was just before dark when they finally figured out he was missing. I was in charge of that search. What we did was try to run logging roads, looking at the fresh snow and trying to pick up his track. And of course we're doing this in the dark.

I think we found him at about one in the morning. Glen Feeney ended up finding him on a woods road, walking toward Canada, up almost to the Canadian border. When we found him, he was in serious hypothermia. He wouldn't have made it through the night. He was trying to make a fire and his fingers were so cold he couldn't use them anymore. A bad, bad situation. When we got him into base camp, the more he warmed up, the more he was shivering. When we tried to give him something hot to drink, he was shaking so violently he couldn't hold a cup. He was done.

The people he was with were like, "Oh, he's okay, he's fine," but the second I saw that, I put him in an ambulance. The people he was with weren't competent to care for him. Oh my goodness, that poor kid.

Knowing how to deal in a situation like that—getting lost in the woods or going through the ice and getting hypothermic—it's something a lot of people don't understand. One thing that was ingrained in me from the time I was nine years old was to always be respectful of the water. And always have the equipment you need to make a fire—an ax, matches, basic essentials to keep yourself alive if something goes wrong. I often suggest carrying dryer lint because it's light and great stuff to use to get a fire started. Carrying the right equipment has saved me numerous times. Because if I end up in a scenario like the Gulf Hagas search where we found those lost skiers, if we couldn't have made a fire, we would have watched those people die, because they were done, the husband in particular. We literally had to have a fire going right away. Within an hour, he would have been gone, because once the progression starts, it increases in speed.

For me, being able to make a fire in any circumstances, in any environment, is most essential, and it's something that not even all wardens know how to do. When I became a sergeant, I had a brand new section, and I had three very new officers, not from my generation, who didn't necessarily have that deep background in woods skills and hadn't grown up in the kind of environment that I did. After I'd been on several operations with them, I recognized that they were lacking in some basic survival skills, so we had a meeting one day, and I gave them a scenario. I said, "Okay, I want you to grab all the stuff that you feel you need to have, we're going to go check beaver traps."

The two senior guys grabbed an ax, grabbed their pack with extra clothes, extra mittens. Matches. Everything. The rookies grabbed their summons books and their snowshoes, and they were good to go. We went down to the beaver flowage behind my house. It was about ten below zero that morning. I said, "Here's the deal. You walked out on the flowage and fell through the ice. Now, using the equipment you have with you, you'd better do something quick or you aren't going to make it back to the truck."

The two senior guys had fires going in about three minutes. The rookies looked at me blankly.

I guess you'd put this under the heading of "warden lore," but it's important. It's easy to make a fire when you're warm and comfortable, but when you're shivering so badly that you can't even unzip your coat, how are you going get the match to light? You have literally less than two or three minutes to get yourself together and get some heat coming your way, or you're done. When I'm training rookie wardens, it's something I concentrate on.

What you do is get underneath a dense fir or spruce tree. Spruce is better because of the tiny limbs. You gather all those little sticks, break them up and make a big pile. And then you get bigger sticks, looking underneath the tree spread where they're dry. And you light your fire only when you have enough wood to keep it going for five or ten minutes. What people do is they light their fire and then run off to get more fuel and boom, it's gone out. You have to have enough bigger wood to keep it going for a while. Put on some bigger stuff that will burn long enough to let you go and get more fuel. I have a special waterproof container to carry matches, and I carry hurricane matches, which are matches that won't blow out in the wind, it's almost like a firecracker when you ignite them. You can get 'em at any outdoor supply store. They also carry waterproof matches. And I carry a couple of Bic lighters in every coat that I wear in the wintertime.

Those rookies spent the rest of the winter practicing making fires. They still remind me of that to this day. And they thank me.

I could take you for a ride in my truck, and the roads around Greenville would literally be a map of fish and game enforcement, off-road traffic enforcement, and disasters of every sort. Emergencies can happen at any time and we have to be prepared to drop anything else we might be doing and respond. We have a lot of plane crashes up here because so many people get into the more remote areas by floatplane.

We had one accident that happened down at the end of Horseshoe Pond Road. It was a beautiful day in September. Another officer,

Sergeant Dan Menard, and I were heading down into Greenville when a call came on the radio that there had been a plane crash at Horseshoe Pond. Our pilot had heard the traffic and zipped over there and sure enough, there was a plane that had just gone down. So Dan and I drove in as fast as we could, parked the truck, and started running, because we could only drive in so far in this country.

We ran about a mile and half, and when we got to the plane, it was still burning. The pilot had broken his wrist, but he'd still managed to get two of his three passengers out, though both were badly burned. The other one was still inside the burning plane but it was completely engulfed in flame. He was obviously deceased.

One of the victims was lying right beside part of the wing, right by the fuselage, and the other was off toward the nose of the plane. For both of them, all their clothing had been completely burned off. Normally, you don't move somebody who has been in a violent crash, but in this case, this thing was happening fast, and there was a very real risk that the plane would explode, so we had to move them.

They were semi-conscious. We got them back a little ways off from the plane and started calling for help. Forest rangers and a whole bunch of wardens came in, and we tried to figure out the best and fastest way to get these guys out of there because they needed to get to a hospital ASAP and carrying them out would have taken hours. We had often used National Guard helicopters, but all of the hoisting helicopters had gone to Iraq.

It was decided that our pilot would land on the pond. It was a shallow, rocky pond so he was limited in where he could land. He could only get to about twenty-five yards from the nearest shoreline. And it was about a hundred yards down to the pond. We couldn't carry them around the pond, because we'd be running a shoreline with boulders and swamps. It would have taken hours and hours and in their condition these guys did not have that kind of time.

In the end, we had to carry the guys, one in a Stokes, the other on a spine board, right through the water, over these boulders and rocks, slide 'em up over the strut of the airplane and load them into the plane one at a time. Then the pilot could fly them to the hospital in

Greenville where they'd be triaged and flown out. We didn't stop to shed gear because those guys had to be gotten out right then if they were going to have any chance. So we went right into the water, gunbelt, radios, uniform, everything still on, walking out into the water until it was chest high.

We had to do it twice. And one of the things I remember, the kind of thing that stays in your mind forever, is this: I'm on the side by the spine board, down by the guy's elbow, and as I'm loading him in, his arm and mine butt, and his skin just peels right off against mine. I'm left there, standing chest high in a cold pond in my uniform and boots, and all I can smell is the scent of burned flesh. It's one of those pungent, nasty smells that you'll never forget.

Our pilot, Charlie Later, did an amazing job, because that pond is really hard to get in and out of. That's why their plane crashed. So we get 'em out. They fly one of 'em to Lewiston, to the burn center, and the other one to Boston.

Then we had to deal with the body—that is, wait for the plane to stop burning and get him out. We do that, and put him in a canoe and paddle him along the shoreline. There was no hurry for him. We finally got him to where we could put him in a vehicle.

Later that evening, hours later, I'd just gotten home. I was still wet, my clothes, my gunbelt, my radio, everything, since there was no time to pitch gear off at the scene. I was cold and miserable, and I was taking everything off, dying to shower and get that burned flesh smell off me, and I got a call from dispatch. They wanted me to talk to the people at the hospital down in Boston. So Boston called me, and I talked with the people in the ER who were dealing with one of the victims. They wanted to know the name of the person they were treating.

I told them—it's one of these three gentlemen. And I gave them the names I had. And they said, well, we need to know who *this* man is. I said, "I don't know," because all of his clothing was burned off his body. And the pilot of the plane only spoke with them briefly when he was flying them back to Greenville. The pilot knew their names, but not who was who. They weren't associates or friends. So we didn't know who survived and who burned in the plane. He wasn't identifiable.

I said, "I'm sorry but I don't know who you have."

The only way we were going to know was the family had to go look and figure out who's who. Which they ended up doing, and it finally was resolved.

But that lady on the other end of the phone was so curt and nasty to me. She was quite put out because we didn't know the person's name. And I couldn't tell her: *Lady, you have no idea what I just went through. I drove at top speed down dirt roads. I ran a mile and a half through the woods. I pulled these guys away from a burning plane. We carried them to the lakeshore, we walked them through the water out to a plane and then we had to go back, secure the body, load it into a canoe, and paddle it across the lake,* because she wouldn't understand. Because the kind of work we do—the conditions, the intensity, the reality—isn't something most people have any experience with.

It didn't matter to her that even after I got clean and warm, I still had more time ahead of me taking care of my gear. My handgun had to be dried out, shells replaced, leather gear slowly dried out and polished, my portable radio, mace, and handcuffs all had to be inspected and oiled or cleaned and dried.

She couldn't fathom that the reason I didn't take their ID and identify them was because their clothes were all burned off and the plane burned up. She was filling in a form that had no place for the reality of the experience. I was just putting a wrinkle in her day.

Sadly, both of these guys perished three days later because the flames had seared the inside of their lungs. But they lived long enough to see family members, and for their families to see them. And sometimes that's the bittersweet end of these rescue operations—that you're only buying them time. But that time can be quite precious.

PART V

TRAINING DOGS FOR EVIDENCE, SEARCH AND RESCUE, AND CADAVER WORK

This book is dedicated to the gentlemen below.

Daryl Gordon

Rick Stone

Rookie Game Warden Roger Guay.

Roger with his son, Justin, and Reba, prior to a tracking session.

Reba, left, and Rader, right, on the move.

Rader ready to work.

Reba with her evidence of over-limit brook trout.

More over-limit brook trout, K9 recovery.

Reba with a pile of apples placed as illegal bait for deer.

Equipment seized at a fly-fishing-only pond. Note the blue dishes for live worms.

Snow-covered moose bones from illegal moose kill recovered by dogs.

Illegal moose kill, shot and left.

Snowmobile patrol, overlooking Mount Katahdin.

Roger with Warden Pilot Daryl Gordon, checking ice fishing activity.

Roger and Maggie conducting a water training session.

Roger training Saba.

Roger on duty
with Rader and
Reba.

Roger evaluates a
map in the search
for a missing
Rhode Island man.

Search team after finding Maria Tanasichuk's body. Back: Warden Tom Jacobs, Warden Roger Guay with Reba, MESARD volunteer Michele Fluery; Middle: Specialist Deborah Palman with Anna and Alex, MESARD volunteer Spencer Fuller with Gabe; Front: Warden Kevin Adam, Lieutenant Pat Dorian.

Roger and his colleagues search for human remains in a cold case.

Baxter Park Search

Poles used by cult members to carry boxes to site.

Investigators removing box from ground.

Baxter State Park burial ground.

FEMA vet inspects Rader after a day of work in New Orleans.

Far right, front, Warden Wayde Carter with K9 Buddy and Roger with K9 Rader.

Roger with K9 Rader and Wayde Carter with K9 Buddy in front of the breach of the levee in the Ninth Ward.

Roger and Rader searching inside a building in New Orleans.

Rader looking for shell casings on a deer case.

Roger and Rader on Saba Island on a private search for missing New Jersey man.

Warden Tom Jacobs with K9 Dutchess (background) and Roger with K9 Rader (foreground) at a K9 demo during a sportsman's show.

Roger and K9 Rader talking to a church youth group about K9s and how they work within the Maine Warden Service.

Roger with his wife, Jolyne, at his retirement party.

Roger, wearing his uniform for the
last time, walks his daughter, Jenna,
down the aisle.

CHAPTER FOURTEEN

Going to the Dogs

After about six years as a warden, I got my first working dog, Reba. I'd been working search and rescue in the field and on the incident command team. I'd done some cases with Deb Palman, one of our remaining K-9 handlers, and knew how her dog had helped us on some important cases. But I kept seeing dogs that were not successful at searches over and over again. Knowing how useful dogs could be, I thought, *this can't be right.* That piqued my interest and I began to take a serious look at how our dogs were being trained. I realized that our dogs were not working well for two reasons. First, because of the limitations in their training—a lot of our K-9 training was in a box, doing the same things in the same place and at the same time. We were not stressing and challenging the dogs with new people and new obstacles.

I was also seeing deficits in the level of their training. The warden service dogs at that point were trained for evidence, physical protection (bite work), and tracking and trailing. They were more like standard police patrol dogs, and they weren't acquiring the necessary capabilities to be an asset to our work. They weren't trained do specialty evidence searches like finding shell casings and fish and game.

They weren't trained for important search and rescue capabilities like hasty searches, clearing a block, or picking up a scent from the wind rather than following every step—this last an important and effective skill in search and rescue because of the high likelihood of contamination issues at the initial scenes.

When I decided to get a K-9, they were phasing out the warden service K-9 program because it wasn't doing what game wardens needed. I believe Deb Palman was the last K-9 officer in the program. So when I asked to get a dog, the warden service said no. I decided to go ahead and get a dog anyway. They weren't paying for shots or dog food or anything. I did it on my own because I believed dogs could be a real asset in our work.

Getting a good dog begins right from the moment you choose your puppy. You know, you look at things like: Are they really timid? Are they comfortable with who they are? Do they look you in the eye or are they always looking away? Do they have ball drive? Are they willing to chase a ball and play? And, if you pick them up and hold them, do they fight you or are they willing to let you hold 'em? Those are some of the little signs. Reba was my first dog. She was just eight weeks old when we started.

I partnered with Deb Palman, and I also started learning on my own. I read a couple books. And I used my kids. They were at just the perfect age so I could say, "Jump on your bike and go down the road (we lived on a dead end dirt road), take the trail that goes up . . . " and they would leave tracks for me. They were eight, nine, or ten, so they would do that for me without any big fuss. I started working Reba that way—on searching for missing people—and then started on the other stuff, evidence searches and cadaver work.

I got connected with Mel Graves, who was a retired state police K-9 trainer and handler, and he helped me really learn and get on track. I had to undo a lot of the training I'd started, but Reba was a good enough dog that she could handle that.

What really helped to revive the warden service K-9 program was the successes that Deb, her dog Anna, Reba, and I started having retrieving evidence and putting together successful hunting prosecutions. Then another warden, Wayde Carter, also got a dog. Seeing how dogs like these could be an asset in our work, the warden service (spurred on by Sergeant Pat Dorian, who was in charge of search and rescue, and Sergeant Dan Tourtelotte) got behind the program. They revamped the training process, raised the training bar, and the program took off.

As we got better at training and understanding what our dogs could do, we started using them for search and rescue operations and deploying the dogs so that they could be effective on searches. In particular, we started learning the best times to use dogs to maximize their efficiency—trying to bring them in and use them before the scenes get contaminated by ground searchers or many people milling around.

Among the things we learned was the effectiveness of using dogs at night, when other searchers were out of the woods. It sounds strange, given how leery people are about being out at night, especially in the woods, but when you're the dog person, the night is your friend. You just go where your dog goes. Everything may be slower, but you can be more effective, and you can go all night without your dog being distracted by other people or other people's scents.

One of the hardest parts of training, and you'll hear handlers say this all the time, is this: Trust your dog. *Trust your dog.* You have to learn to do this and it can take years. I can train a dog in three or four months and make him a pretty decent dog. It's gonna take me a year or more, probably longer, to train the handler, because the handler will always want to override the dog. The dog is willing to do its part. It's the human part that doesn't conform. If I think that a body is over there, and the dog thinks it's somewhere else, I'll force the dog to go over there.

It's not until you learn to trust your dog that the two of you can work together as a team. Usually, that happens after you've been humiliated. Through that, as a handler, you learn to start trusting your dog. And that's where you start getting that connection, that deep bond at the level where you read the dog and the dog reads you. That's where the dog handler's challenge lies.

I had the biggest piece of humble pie handed to me by my dog one day. I was a new sergeant up in the Houlton area in Aroostook County.

We got a call about a missing three-year-old; two or three hours had passed and I was first to the scene. It's kind of a rural neighborhood, and the neighbors were saying to the distraught mother, "Well, yeah, I saw a sow bear and three cubs yesterday, hanging right around. She looked pretty hungry." You know, just winding that poor mom right into a frenzy.

I got there and I talked to her. She told me her husband worked nights and she worked days, and they were having coffee together and the little tyke was playing on his tricycle just off the porch. And they got talking and when they turned around he was gone. They searched for a while, and then called us.

I asked, "Where was he last?" She told me the story and I started the dog. Now, by this time, we had quite an audience. So Reba and I went right around the house, and there was a snowmobile sitting up on blocks. Reba went right to the snowmobile and started digging at it, saying: Right here, right here, right here. I put my hand on top of the seat, I reached up under the cover, and there was nothing there. But my dog would not leave.

Now I was stressing because there were all these people watching me, and she just kept hitting on that snowmobile and hitting on it, so I literally dragged her off, physically dragged her off and I said, track, track. Finally, she got upset with me, and said in eloquent canine body language, *fine, you want to go for a walk, we'll go for a walk.* So I knew I was tracking searchers now. I was tracking the parents.

Now, by this time, since I was the guy in charge, I had to get some resources coming, so I went back to the truck. There was a state trooper there and we were going over a quick plan, and this little tyke came walking around the corner of the house, soaking wet and in his little footie pajamas. He went right to his mother and she scooped him up and said, "Coleman, where have you been?"

And he said, "I was sleeping in Daddy's snowmobile."

He was up between the handlebars and the windshield so I missed him when I reached in. That poor dog did everything but write me a note, right? From that point on, I learned to trust my dog. It doesn't matter what I think; my job as a handler is to remember my dog is trained to do this. I put the dog in the necessary search mode, I give the search commands, and I keep the dog from getting hurt, but I let the dog do what it needs to do. It's hard. It sounds easy, but it is very hard.

So that was my piece of humble pie.

The rescue or recovery of persons lost or deceased in Maine woods on inland waters is a mandatory part of our job. Under Maine law, the Maine Warden Service has statutory authority in MRSA Title 12 Sec. 10105:

Whenever the commissioner receives notification that any person has gone into the woodlands or onto the inland waters of the State on a hunting, fishing or other trip and has become lost, stranded or drowned, the commissioner shall exercise the authority to take reasonable steps to ensure the safe and timely recovery of that person.

The amount of search and rescue work the job involves somewhat depends on what part of the state you're in. Greenville was a search and rescue hub, a hot zone all the time, even before the explosion of ATVs, snowmobiles, and personal watercraft. We always had lost hikers and hunters, especially in the fall. So almost from the first, once I had Reba, she was with me in the truck because of the likelihood of getting called somewhere in the state for a search.

Every dog has a distinct personality. Reba was a chocolate lab, and she was a real take-charge K-9. She always wanted to be in the front. Because we spent so much time together from when she was eight weeks old, the special bond that develops between a dog and a handler was especially strong in this case. It got to the point where I barely had to give her direction. That dog could read my mind.

She was also a "leaner." She'd just kind of lean up against people. At search scenes, people used to find it comforting to have this nice dog leaning against them. In the truck, in tight quarters, it could get more uncomfortable when she'd lean against someone I was interviewing. She did it there because the person was in what she regarded as "her" place, and she wanted them to get out of the way.

Because I was doing a lot of homicide stuff, or searches where we suspected that the subject was deceased, and situations where there would be people around and we would be discussing stuff that we didn't necessarily want anyone to hear, one thing I quickly realized was that I had to develop commands for the dogs that wouldn't give away what I was saying. For the warden service dogs, trainers like Michelle Merrifield and I would start our dogs with the word "locate." That way, if there were family members around, they didn't necessarily click to the thought: *Oh, you're going in to look for my nephew and you think he's dead.*

We'd do the same thing for finding fish. You didn't want to be standing around a bunch of fishermen and say to the dog, "Find the fish," because they would start doing evasive things, and dropping food to distract the dogs, so I just developed my own words. I'd say, "Catch 'em," and the dog would be searching while I was talking to the people and checking their licenses and all, and they wouldn't know what the dog was doing. They're thinking, "Cute doggie," and all of a sudden the dog would stop, indicate, and lay down. Then you'd discuss that.

Human scent is a big thing, and the advantage is that at many of these crime scenes, there would be cigarette butts. You could go in with a metal detector but you wouldn't find the cigarette or a candy wrapper. So our dogs could find subtle little things that with traditional methods we wouldn't find.

Different trainers might evolve different commands. For my dogs, the command for live search was "track," for evidence was "gun," for fish it was "catch 'em," and for cadaver it was "locate." Some trainers use "find Fred" or "find friend" for cadaver searches. For a deer or a moose, I was usually alone so I would just name the animal.

CHAPTER FIFTEEN

Canine-Style CSI

One arena in which our dogs turned out to be very valuable was in searching for evidence. Imagine looking at a five-hundred-square-yard clear-cut and trying to find a shell casing from an illegal moose kill. It could take days to find, and, more often than not, it wouldn't be found at all. Most metal detectors have only an eight- or nine-inch disk to search with, so covering an area of any size is hard to do. A trained K-9, on the other hand, will find the casing if they get to within twelve to twenty feet, and can do it while running. Dogs can also track the humans involved to reconstruct the scene as well as locate the evidence they left behind.

Training dogs to find evidence means training them to find anything with human scent, gun powder, brass, or any combination thereof. They all go into the same category. When I'm directing the dogs to look for evidence, that cue is "find gun." On that command, the dogs will basically go and find combinations of, or singly, any of those items. This ability sometimes led to very important information in our poaching cases. If the dog can locate them for us, we can examine the casing and the projectile and match them to the gun that fired them.

With more recent technology, we can also do forensics with shotguns, like matching the plastic cup that holds all the shot (called the wad) to the shotgun that fired it, because as it comes out the barrel, the barrel leaves marks on the wad.

I found that a shell was the best thing to start a pup on, because they naturally learn to find things you throw like balls and sticks and often use their nose when they can't see it with their eyes. For example, that shell gets thrown and when the pup runs to it, you give them the ball. Gradually that gets expanded to teaching them to lay down to indicate their find, and then they get the ball. Teaching it in little increments, they make an easy transition to learning to indicate a find. Then I gradually shift to harder finds and soon they are good to go.

I would begin with human scent, because that was easiest for them. But since sometimes due to weather or the passage of time, human scent might be gone from the shell or other evidence, I had to teach them to look for the smell of brass. Still later, when we wanted them to look for those shotgun wads, I taught them to look for the scent of gunpowder. All under the command "gun."

Over the years, with the help of my dogs, I have recovered hundreds of shell casings, shotgun wads, money, pagers, rifles, handguns, fly rod pieces, and glasses.

Reba, and later my second dog, Rader, worked wildlife investigations all over the state. Rader, whose official name was Fish and Game Rader, was Reba's son and he grew up under mom's enormous shadow. Rader always wanted to take the lead and had to wait for five frustrating, impatient years for his mom to retire before he could be the lead dog on the team. Rader was a very strong dog, all power; if he couldn't get over something, he would go through it. He was also very vocal, and would howl continuously if I left him in the truck and took Reba. I used to call him my "truck locator beacon," because I could hear him fussing from a mile away at searches. Rader was a very stubborn fellow who loved mud holes, Kongs, and tennis balls. He would on occasion run away to visit the girls in the neighborhood.

Something I learned from Reba, then Rader, and from the dogs that came after them was that every trainer-canine relationship is individual and unique. They learn to read us, and we need to learn to read them and figure out how best to work with who they are.

These are some of the memorable cases where my dogs made valuable evidence finds. A small Houlton convenience store was robbed just before dark. The suspect, who was wearing a mask, had his hand in his pocket and demanded the money from the register. When he got the money, he then ran out the door just as a police cruiser drove by, causing his wheelman to panic and drive off, so the robber ran for the woods. Realizing that very soon he would be sought after, he decided to bury the money and throw away his facemask, then pop out of the woods free and clear. As he stepped into the field, police nabbed him and kept him there. But the police still needed to find the money and the mask to establish he was the robber, and asked for our help.

Reba and I started the track from the store and off we went through the woods. Every once in a while, Reba would lay down and paw the ground and money would boil up. We tracked the robber to the point where the police had arrested him very easily, then backtracked to locate my portable radio that I had dropped on the way in. She found the radio as well as his mask, which he'd tossed up in a tree, and the rest of the money.

One significant case involved two Canadian brothers up near Dole Pond. One brother had shot the other twice, thinking his brother was a deer. This case was a challenge in every possible way, and ultimately we could never have had a successful prosecution without the evidence the dog turned up. It began with a call from the Sainte-Aurélie gate, next to the customs station, that someone had just gone through the gate who had been shot while hunting and the ambulance was supposed to meet them in Sainte-Aurélie and take the wounded man to the hospital. The incident had happened in Maine, but by the time we heard about it, both the wounded man and the shooter—his brother—were back in Canada.

I was in Greenville, an hour and a half away, and by the time I got up there, the shooter, his victim, their car, their weapons, their clothing—everything that I would need as witnesses and evidence in the case had gone back over the border. Because I'm bilingual, I went to the hospital to find out what happened and interviewed the shooter in French. I was on pretty shaky ground, since I had no jurisdiction in Canada, but my job was to investigate this hunting accident.

The victim, who was shot twice and badly injured, was in surgery. I interviewed the brother and he admitted he was the shooter. Then he told me the story. They'd been driving down the road and they'd seen an albino doe on the edge of the woods. The victim had a doe permit; the shooter didn't. They pursued it into the woods. One brother (the shooter) looped around on a ridge so he could look down; the other brother followed the deer. From the ridge, he looked down and saw something white moving, which he assumed was the deer. He was using a 7mm Magnum, which shoots a huge bullet. He fired, and what he believed to be the deer went down.

A few seconds later, the deer got up. He shot again and his brother yelled, "Why are you trying to kill me?" It was warm that day and the brother was wearing a white tee shirt 'cause they'd pitched off all their hunting clothes.

He told me that while they were waiting for the ambulance, he wigged out and smashed his gun to pieces. At this point, we didn't have a location for where this happened. So I left another warden at the hospital to retrieve the bullets (in Canada, where we had no jurisdiction), and I got the shooter to agree to take me back to the where they'd left the car when he jumped into the ambulance with his brother, and then back across the border to the scene. I had to get the evidence. Depending on whether the wounded brother died, this could be manslaughter. At the least, it was a clear case of shooting an unidentified target.

We got to the car and I collected what I needed—smashed up gun, ammunition, etc.—and threw it in my truck. But as we were crossing the bridge, heading for the border, the shooter's older brother came along and stopped us, and advised the shooter that he shouldn't come to Maine with me or he would get arrested.

So now we were standing by the road, still in Canada, arguing about what to do, the whole conversation in French, and Bill Chandler, the warden I left behind to collect the evidence came along. What I wanted him to do was switch trucks with me, so at least he could get back into

Maine with the evidence, but I couldn't tell him that because the older brother also speaks English. So I said, "Bill, you need to go back and get your lunch now," and he just looked at me like I was crazy. Finally, he got it. We swapped trucks, and I stayed behind to see if I could negotiate bringing the shooter back to show me where the incident took place.

So we talked and we talked there by the side of the road with the traffic roaring past. Finally, we agreed that I'd get the DA to fax a letter to the shooter stating he wouldn't be arrested if he came into the states to show us the shooting scene. Back and forth on the phone and the letter got faxed to me at the local store. Doing my crime scene investigation and paperwork from an office that consisted of a cell phone and pickup truck.

Now all of this was taking a lot of time. Pretty soon we were going to run out of daylight and there was a big storm coming. I had to get to the scene before the snow came. Once he had the letter, we jumped in the truck and crossed the border, with the older brother following in his car. I got my own truck, and the shooter directed us to this skidder trail. Two wardens, two trucks. He pointed out the spot where they saw the deer, we spilled out to investigate, and the shooter jumped in with his brother and booked it back to Canada.

There was a big blood spot in the road. I got Reba out, and she backtracked from the blood spot and pretty soon we started finding stuff they'd dropped. Then we found the point where the brother got shot. It was just gross, with human fat and muscle, bits of his clothes, and all this blood. It looked like hamburger exploded into the trees.

The dog had done a good job, but we still needed to find where the shooter was standing and the spent shells. I put the dog in "gun" mode and off we went. We ended up on the skidder trail on top of the ridge a hundred and fifty yards away and Reba found one casing that matched the gun. But only one. It was getting dark. The clock was ticking. Reba searched and searched and much as we looked, we couldn't find that second shell.

We decided to come back in the morning and try again, if the storm hadn't socked in. When we went back in the morning, the only place left to search was this little puddle. I took a stick and measured and it was a foot deep. The second shell was at the bottom of that. When he'd recovered enough, I went back to Canada and interviewed the victim and charged the brother. He pled guilty and lost his license for life. With a storm coming, we had no time for a lengthy search. Without Reba finding the locations of those two brothers, and the shell casing evidence, we couldn't have made our case.

Another example involves finding the handgun from a home invasion. The subjects in this case had just broken into a home in Abbot and stolen everything they could lay their hands on. The family wasn't home, and the subjects used a gun to kill the family dogs. Both dogs were very old and did not pose any threat. A neighbor saw the unfamiliar vehicle in the yard and called it in. By the time the officers responded, the vehicle had left the scene. When the responding officer met the suspects' vehicle, the suspects sped off and a chase ensued which lasted for miles and ended up with a foot chase in a different county.

At the end of that chase, the police had the suspects in custody, but they didn't have the gun that was used to kill the dogs. The sheriff's department felt it was most likely thrown from the car near the spot where they first met the suspects on the highway. I searched with both Reba and Rader that day, covering about a mile of roadside over the course of a three-hour search, and Rader found the .22 Colt replica in tall grass near several houses with kids. The gun was loaded with six rounds. Ballistics matched the gun to the killing of the dogs.

In this case, finding the gun was critical for prosecuting the case. It also meant that a loaded firearm wasn't left lying near a yard where curious children might have found it.

As time went on, and we begin to have successes, warden K-9s started getting more calls from local police, Maine State Police, and even from the state fire marshal's office. Just like a police officer or a warden gears up before going to work, our dogs get the signal that they're going to work when we put on their harness and give them the signal or cue to tell them what they're looking for. At night, or if the terrain is thick, I'll also put on a bell. I can tell how the search is going from the sound of that bell. If a dog is getting close to a find, that ringing will get more intense. Then, when they've made a find, or something needs to be checked out, the bell will stop ringing. Often, for night work, I'll also clip on a glow stick to help me keep track of them. The majority of the work is done off lead, unless we're physically tracking a person or working next to a busy road.

Rader found another handgun from a crime scene in Little Moose Township. A night hunter had shot at a decoy bird after dark, and when the wardens tried to apprehend him, he sped away in his car. When he was finally stopped a few miles down the road, there was no gun in the car.

I started working the dogs right at the point where he sped off. I didn't even have my gear together when I realized that Rader was not moving. He usually ran around the truck as I was getting ready and this time he was gone. I realized that he must be indicating on the evidence, so I walked down the road a few yards and found him laying by a loaded handgun, wagging his tail and waiting for his reward.

One of Rader's most unusual searches was for a drug dart used to tranquilize a moose. A sick moose had been hanging around a small field in Bingham that the neighborhood kids used for a ball field. When the state biologist attempted to remove the moose by using the dart, the first shot missed and landed somewhere in the grass. Those darts are extremely dangerous. They are charged to inject the tranquilizer upon full penetration of the needle into the moose, and carry a dose which would kill a human instantly. If a kid found the dart and fooled with it, it could be fatal.

After carefully interviewing the biologist, I searched the area where the dart should have been without success. The whole time, Rader wanted to go way down the field, far off course from where the incident took place. Finally, after exhausting the high probability area, I let him run to where he had been trying to get to for hours. He immediately charged down the field, lay down, and put his nose on the dart buried in the grass. The dart was still charged with the tranquilizer and eventually would have been found by a child. This was one of the many lessons I've had over the years about listening to my dogs.

Sometimes, when we're doing evidence searches, it's absolutely the things that the dogs will find that let us put the whole story together.

Like with a bunch of postmen in a hunting camp in Parkman. I believe these men were from Connecticut. Another warden had contacted me and he'd said, "I've got a bunch of deer hanging at this camp, and I've got information that they've killed them all illegally. Could you come down? I may need you and the dog."

We pulled into this camp, and they had five deer hanging on the game pole. A game pole is a pole hung horizontally with pulleys or rope set up to hang deer or moose to cool and store them out of reach of animals that will eat the game

We started interviewing them. One guy was obviously the camp leader, and after talking to him a few minutes, it was pretty clear that he was being evasive. As we were talking, these gentlemen, who had been drinking—there were at least five of them—were getting mad. They had this thing they used to crush beer cans, and as the interview progressed, they started really pounding those cans.

Eventually, the leader decided that he was going to take it upon himself to show us where everything happened. We were particularly interested in the last two deer, a doe and a lamb (what we call a yearling here in Maine). The tag book showed that they were shot at the same time, and experience has shown us that when that happens, more likely than not they were shot by the same person. One person shot both and another person tagged one of them.

He took us to the scene. Mike Eaton was in one vehicle and I was in the other with the dogs. We pulled in and the guy from Connecticut said, "What's the dog for?"

I said, "Oh, you'll see."

So he tells us this great story about how Uncle Joe was over here to the right, and he was over here on the other side, and the deer came running through, and Joe fired and he fired. It was a great story. I took the dog out, and boom, we found six 7mm shell casings together, where the guy said he fired, and the deer paunches from where they'd gutted the deer were lying right side-by-side. Then we worked the other area, where Uncle Joe was standing and we found nothing. Now we know we're looking for a 7mm rifle, so we go back to the camp to interview the actual shooters.

We'd asked, before we went out, what rifles each of them carried. Only one had a 7mm Mag. Sometimes it got complicated when a couple guys had the same gun, but this time there was only one. We said we needed to see the other rifles. We checked them all, all the guns in the camp. I look at the .30-30 that supposedly shot the little lamb and the barrel was all rusted. No way was that gun used to killed that deer. When a bullet goes out the barrel, it cleans the barrel of any rust or anything, and this one is all full of dust, rust, and gunk. That gun hadn't been fired in ten years. He was the camp cook and drunk. He never left camp.

So we snapped the two rifles up, and now these guys were going ballistic. In the morning, we went to all the places where those other deer had been killed. We traced that down, the dog tracked where they dragged the deer out, and the dog found the casings. We ran trajectory lines, we recovered casings, and we could see where trees were clipped by the bullets. We ended up putting this tremendous case together. Ultimately, the story was that one guy had shot two deer, with another guy tagging one of them. And the other three? They were killed as part of a deer drive.

Maine law regarding deer drives at the time was:

Unlawfully driving deer. A person may not participate in a hunt for deer during which an organized or planned effort is made to drive deer except that a group of 3 or fewer persons may hunt together as long as they do not use noisemaking devices.

The guy that we charged for shooting the two said, "I will see you in court. I'm going to fight this to the end." We just said, "Yeah, that's no problem." So the day that we went to go to court, he was there. He read the report, and said, "Hell, you got me. You and that stinking dog."

That was Reba. I said, "Yeah. That little lab has put a lot of people in jail, my friend." It cost him a thousand dollars and three days in jail. And they forfeited the guns.

Sometimes, between the dogs and our knowledge of human nature, we can do some pretty good big woods CSI. That was definitely the case with what we called the "Rockwood Doe Mystery." A gentleman called in to Warden Mike Favreau that he'd found a dead doe. He'd been hunting that morning and heard a shot across a clear-cut. He hunted his way in that direction and found a large dead doe. Mike gave me a call, said, can I give him a hand, see if I can find the shell casing, all that. So I got there with Reba. The doe was fresh. She'd obviously been shot within just a few hours. I took Reba, started working around the area where the doe was, and she doesn't find anything.

Well, Reba had this great ability to track. I didn't have to tell her to do it, she'd just do it. The next thing I know, she was tracking across the clear-cut. She took me to this big tree seat about three hundred yards away, and boom, she spun around the bottom and lay down, poking her nose, and there's a shell casing, a .308 that I recognized as very old military-grade ammo. It was a very unusual round, had a unique marking, stuff that not everyone was going to have.

Now I remembered that the hunter who'd called us had said he was on that side of the clear cut when he heard the shot, and he'd walked that way toward the doe. I collected the casing. I knew the caliber of the gun carried by the complainant, and I said, "Mike, what are the chances he's the shooter?"

He goes, "You know, you're right."

This guy was waiting down the road, and so we went out to him and we said, "Hey, can we check your ammunition?"

He said, "Sure, sure . . ." So we took a look at his ammo and that's what it was.

We had him and he knew it, so he gave it up and told us what happened. He thought it was a buck. He fired, and killed it, and being a conscientious hunter, he didn't want to leave it to rot, so he made up this fictitious report so the deer wouldn't go to waste. But the little brown dog beat him, so he confessed.

As I noted earlier, one of the skills that makes dogs valuable to the warden service is their ability to help us investigate poaching. That ability isn't limited to deer and moose. I've been telling you stories of how we use dogs to catch game violations. But our dogs can also find fish. Fisherman are often the most surprised when the adversary that brings them grief is a dog. Reba was especially good at that, as in this case. Warden Rick Clowry was watching a guy fishing on a beaver flowage, and saw him catch well over his limit. The guy had been fishing a while before Rick got there, and the guy had a stick, like people do—a forked stick that was filled with trout. When the guy turned to leave, Rick went around him to intercept him and missed him. What Rick didn't know was that there were two other guys who'd been fishing who'd seen the warden truck. They were hanging around the truck, and when this guy popped out to the road where his buddies were, they said, "Hey, the warden's here," so he turned and ran back into the woods.

When Rick finally caught him, he had just his legal limit of fish. Now this guy was known to us as a real big time jerk, as some people are, so we didn't want to let it go. Rick called me, wanting to know if I could help him locate the rest of those fish. I couldn't make it over there that night, but I went first thing in the morning. I was walking along with Reba, and she was working, working, working, because we didn't know exactly where he'd gone back into the woods, and all of a sudden, she was jumping. Not laying down like she was showing me something hidden on the ground, but jumping.

I stood there for the longest time, looking, I couldn't see it. Finally, after about thirty seconds with my dog looking at me like I was a pretty dumb human, I realized that just above my head there was a tree limb, and on that limb those fish on the stick were all laying there. A dozen trout. So I pulled them off, and gave her a reward, and she started working again, finding more trout. Individual trout now. He'd been throwing 'em as he went and ran out of time, so he just threw the rest of them up there on the branch

I can't remember how many trout we had there, but it was a lot. I have a picture of her somewhere with the fish. It was a great overlimit case. And without the dog, we'd have never found them, and that guy would have gotten away

Another time, we did a road check up near Millinocket off the Golden Road. We usually did road checks there on Memorial Day weekend. Just set up a checkpoint along the road, stop people, and ask a few questions. Well, this old, ratty camper came along, garbage bags covering the windows, with three guys, kind of a rough-looking bunch. We asked them to show us their fish. It's voluntary, but most people cooperate. The guy went into the camper, went into the refrigerator, and came out with his limit of fish, and he was shaking like a leaf, like something was wrong. So I just took Rader and walked by the camper door. He was trained to find fish just like Reba was, and boom, he hit on the door, saying, *There's more fish in here.*

I asked the guy, "Is it okay if I put the dog in the camper?" and he said, "Oh, yeah, no problem."

So the dog went in and he hopped on the bed—there was a bed right by the door—and started digging into this sleeping bag. I was thinking, "What the heck?" so I reached into the sleeping bag. I could feel something ice cold, and I pulled out a five-inch trout. The man knew it was in there, and when he pulled out the fish from the refrigerator, he spun around and stuck it in the sleeping bag before he showed us the legal fish.

As soon as I stepped out with that short fish, everyone turned around and looked away. Another one caught by the clever brown labs.

CHAPTER SIXTEEN

On the Scent of the Lost

Of course, my dogs weave in and out of so many of these stories, because they've been an invaluable resource not just in evidence searches and catching illegal hunters and fishermen. They've been an incredible asset in our other primary job—search and rescue. Reba and Rader, and later Maggie and Saba, have located many missing people, both alive and dead, in these big woods, like the missing ninety-eight-year-old man.

What happened was, this guy had gone out to his camp alone, to a place where there was no cell phone coverage. He'd just purchased a brand new four-wheeler, and his daughter, who was in her seventies, said, "I want you to leave a note if you go anywhere away from the camp."

He'd gone over the weekend and when Monday came, he hadn't returned like he was supposed to, so she sent a friend over to check and sure enough, he'd left a note two days prior, saying he was going up to this brook, he was going to go look for some beaver flowages for next year's fishing. So the district warden from The Forks and the guy who'd checked the camp looked around. After a while, they found the four-wheeler way off in the woods with his lunch, a .22 pistol, and a little daypack—what you would normally take into the woods with you if you were an experienced outdoorsman, but there was no sign of him.

By this time, it was night. These things always happen at night. I got there about one or two o'clock in the morning. We had a huge wilderness area to cover, but we couldn't wait for morning. He'd already been gone for two to three days and that three-day rule weighed heavily on us, especially since it had been raining hard and the temperatures were in the forty- to fifty-degree range. So we—Warden Skip Bates and Reba and I—started in. I tried to do tracks from the wheeler, but the rain and dark made it impossible. We had to trust the dog and follow.

We started making a loop, up and around, hoping we'd pick up something. We tramped for hours and couldn't find any sign of him. When it began to get light, we had a helicopter come in and do a buzz. Then our plane came in. Still nothing. This was real wilderness with few roads. We finally found some of his footprints at this bog, so we started working that area, looping back toward the wheeler. When we came back toward the wheeler, we found this little branch brook that kind of teed into the main river that the wheeler was parked at. When we got to that, I noticed just this little thing—a dead birch tree stub, there was only about six to eight inches left standing—that had been knocked over.

It was a fresh break—the broken tree part had splayed out and hadn't been displaced by much rain. Right out of the blue—it was divine intervention, I guess, which is something I truly believe in because I've been guided more than once—I looked at it and I turned to the dog, and I said, "Track."

Boom, she started tracking. When she was on track, you knew it. Her whole body showed it. So she was going along, we were going along, and we came to this kind of a blow down, just masses of old dead, downed fir trees, a tangled thicket of limbs to clamber over. It was chest high and daunting, but Reba didn't hesitate, she just muddled her way right through that. From the way she attacked that, I knew she was tracking because otherwise she would have gone around instead of pushing her way through.

Beyond that blow down, the grass was laid right out like someone had dragged a deer. We started going faster; she was right on track now, not casting about for scent. The closer the dog gets, the stronger the scent is, the harder they push, and the more excited they become because they know they're getting close. You can actually feel that intensity.

We went another quarter of a mile along, following a stream, and all of a sudden, I saw the dog sitting down. And she was sitting right by the guy. He was laid right out. That flattened trail we'd been following was him crawling. I was sure he was dead. All of a sudden, just as we were getting to him, he lets out a snort. The dog jumped. We jumped.

Immediately the mission changed from locating him to saving his life. This guy needed to have his inner core warmed up. He was very, very close to the end, and when they're at that stage, even moving them can kill them because their systems are so fragile. Then there was the gentleman's age. What we had to do right away was warm him up, and we didn't have a lot of resources. We were seriously in the middle of nowhere. We looked around. There had been a logging camp there sometime in the past and we found some old bottles. We started a fire, put some water in the bottles and put them around the fire to heat them up. Then we put them in his groin and under his armpits, trying to get him a little bit of heat.

The irony of it was that he was lying on a little pack that had everything in it he needed to survive. He was an experienced woodsman and he knew how to prepare. He had matches and food. Most of the time, people aren't that well prepared, but he'd spent his life going into these woods. We figured that most likely what happened was that the rain had cooled his core temperature down, and hypothermia had gotten him before he could do what he needed to do to survive.

I called in on the radio and I said, "I need a helicopter right now."

Before all the helicopters went away to war, the National Guard was really good about airlifts, and I knew that the only way we were going to get him out of there was with a helicopter and a hoist. It would have been at least three miles to the vehicle or the nearest road. The way these streams came down and then split, this was a big valley, a drainage area at the base of a couple mountains. There were no roads in there at all, just a huge tract of land.

Even if we could have organized one, he wouldn't have survived a carry out. When I called, the response was they were going to be at least three or four hours. I called back, and said, "I've got to get this guy out of here right now. He's right at the end. He doesn't have hours. We're talking minutes."

So they said all right, we're coming.

Finally, the chopper came. The pilot was over our heads and we were trying to talk him in to where we needed him, and he said, "How did you ever find this guy?" Because there were no roads. It was just solid woods. We'd been searching from one a.m., and now it was mid-morning.

They loaded him and took him to the hospital. At the hospital, they found a note in his pocket, basically his dying words. He'd written: **LOST TWO DAYS. CAN'T FIND MY WAY AND I CAN'T WALK ANYMORE.** And he'd dated it.

He got to the hospital, and he came right back, but because his system was shut down so long, his blood was toxic because his liver wasn't able to detox the deoxygenated blood. He died the next day.

Very sad, after all he'd survived, but at least he got to talk to his daughter. He had a nice, long conversation with her and then he went into a coma and died. That was a classic case of hypothermia. He had everything that he needed to save him, but when he realized it, he was too late.

We would never have found him without Reba. When I think of that search, I have to wonder why, when I've walked past thousands of trees that have fallen over and thousands of broken stumps and never said "Track," for some reason, I caught that out of the corner of my eye, put her in track mode, and she was on it.

There's something to this divine intervention thing. It's impossible to explain, but it happens. When you're in this business, you learn there is something like a sixth sense that comes into play where, just like in this case, you do something out of the ordinary that lets you find that person or that thing. It's this subtle feeling that I get. I've had it happen so many times where I'm walking through the woods, on a search, and I kind of get that feeling, like *All right. I'm here.* All of a sudden, everything heightens and boom! I find 'em. It's one of those unexplainable things that makes me understand maybe I'm not totally in control. Maybe I'm just a little pawn in a much bigger thing and I'm being guided to do what needs to be done.

Finding that man, still alive at that age, was a wonderful thing. It was sad that he died, but at least it gave his family a chance to say goodbye, and some closure. It would be so much worse if he was never found and they were always left wondering what had happened.

And there are a lot of times when we're successful and we do have a good result. Like with the little lost boy. We got a call one day that a three-year-old had walked off. In this country, in the spring, small children have the ability to walk on the crust of the snow, while adults can't. I've had it happen multiple times. We got to the house and talked with his mom and learned that the family puppy had wandered off and the little boy had followed it. She was able to follow the boy's tracks up this little ravine behind the house. It was a really cold day, windy and miserable, and the mom had gotten up to the height of land and lost the tracks at kind of a little snowmobile trail intersection.

One of the things we have to be aware of, when we're using tracking dogs, is that fear scent overrides everything. When we're tracking somebody scared, the scent signature is different and the dogs key in on that. They'll lock right in on it. It's almost like they're chasing a scared rabbit. So I knew I couldn't put the dog in the track mode right from the house. The mom's fear scent totally overpowered her little boy's, and she'd walked right up his tracks and completely destroyed my ability to follow him.

It was getting late in the afternoon. It got dark early, and this little kid had now been missing for several hours. I knew he'd gotten wet in a small brook when he was working his way up the hill. Night coming, a cold wind, and a small, wet child. It was an awful combination.

I went up to the height of land with my dog. I wanted to start him right there, just blind start him, but I couldn't risk it. Time was too tight. I had only one chance to make the right decision. The warden I had with me, Glenn Annis, was an expert tracker, so I said, "Glenn, I'm going to stay right here with the dog. You make some circles and see if you can find a place to start him."

The crust was so hard at best you might see a little corner of a heel or something.

He started making a loop. Glenn was off to my left, and the helicopter I'd called in was overhead, and then I could just hear the faintest something. I called in and I said, "Can you just get the helicopter to back off for a minute. I think I heard something."

With age, my hearing abilities had started to change ever so slightly, and it was one dial below where I could hear. The wind was howling, and in between the gusts, I could just kinda hear it. I said, "Glenn, do you hear it?" and he goes, "Nope." My instinct said just keep going straight. So I said, "hold up." I put the dog in a down stay and started going straight. I went about two or three hundred yards. All of a sudden I saw the puppy, and the little boy was with him. The dog was running around and the little boy had these big tears running down his face, he was just crying and crying. I ran over and scooped him up. "Are you okay?"

And he said, "I'm okay. I'm good. I'm okay."

And I got on the radio and I said, "We got him."

What greater thing in life could you do?

So we were carrying the little boy out, and now he had his composure back, and he looked at me, and he said, "No deer sign around here. They'll never kill a deer out back here, I guess." And he was just this little bitty thing. My partner, Glenn, was holding him at that point, and he looked at Glenn and he said, "My dad's in jail, you know."

He was so cute, and I'll never forget those big, big tears coming down his cheeks. He was scared right to death, the poor little bugger. It was just such a heartbreaker.

We got him home, back with his mom. Of course, the story never ends when you find 'em. Saving a life or writing up a violation or dealing with the family; there's always a reason, there's always circumstances that come into play, you know. The home life where this little kid was living looked extremely rough. When I went inside the trailer to get an article of clothing to start the dog on, it was just like being inside a dumpster.

We called the Department of Health and Human Services because of the circumstances, and because things about her behavior were making us suspicious, and found out DHHS was looking for her for not taking care of this little boy, and she was in hiding. I think they ended up taking him into state custody shortly after that.

My dogs are good, but there were some real challenges on that search. Most dogs aren't trained to find little children that size. There's a difference between searching for an adult and searching for a child. With a child, especially a small child, there's much less scent. Then there was the fact that the mom had been all over, and she had fear scent, and by looking around, she'd covered that whole area with fear scent, which is compelling to the dogs. Not that a dog can't work with fear scent, can't work through it, but it's another obstacle to deal with. It's always going to be the case with a missing child that there will be fear scent. So it could take several attempts with really, really good tracking dogs to pin that down.

The tendency would be for the dog to pick up mom's fear scent as the strongest, most compelling thing. It helps if you use a scent article of that child, and you start the dog exactly where the child was last seen. But to get the best possible result, you'd work that scene with at least two or even three tracking dogs, one at a time, and bring the scent article to them, and let them track and see where each dog goes. And if, after a few minutes, I can see the dog is tracking mom, then I'd bring another dog in, and see if one of them can get beyond that pool of fear scent. Then you're good. But that fear scent is a huge distraction.

Goldie Jordan was sixty-seven, and she had a compulsive walking disorder where she would have to walk for hours every day to keep herself calm. She had a routine, where she would walk down a woods road to a certain spot where she had a marker set out, then she would turn around and walk back. But this particular time, she'd gone out walking and she hadn't come back. She was last seen by some guys on an ATV, walking down the road, a little beyond the spot where she was supposed to turn around and head back.

This search took place way up in northeastern Maine, in the Caribou area. There must have been thirty or forty game wardens there, plus twice that many volunteers. The search had gone on for a while. I'd worked daylight to dark three days running. I had blisters on my feet so bad it wasn't even funny. Reba and I were completely cooked.

We were the dog handlers on this particular one, and were working basically all the daylight hours, sleeping, then heading back out at daylight the next day. The night of the third day, my feet were a mess of blisters and I was totally exhausted. We all were—exhausted to the point where we couldn't recharge our batteries any more, sleep just didn't do it.

By day four, we'd gotten some misinformation that an elderly lady who kind of matched her description had been seen walking down a road about five or six miles to the north, and that had kind of shifted the search in that direction. But—and this was an example of that spidey sense, or sixth sense coming in—I had this feeling that some of the blocks we'd already covered needed to be searched again.

So the search is going on. It's now focused five miles away. I had done one assignment and I'd come back to the command post, and I said to Kevin Adam, who was our mapping expert on the overhead team, "Kevin, I want to do this area again. I've got a feeling about it. So don't give me an assignment for a little bit, just let me go work over here."

I went back out to that block I'd had the feeling about. The wind was perfect that morning. It was blowing the right way so the dog and I could come into it.

I should explain. When you're doing a search, you organize the search area by blocks. A block can be a piece that's encompassed by roads. It could be a block where a road is on one side and a river comes around. It has some kind of physical boundaries that demark where you are. And when you get to those boundaries, you know you've cleared your block. When we're doing a large search, we will record the areas searched with GPS units, and then upload the data at the command center so that our mapping experts can keep track of what terrain has been covered and what remains to be searched.

In this case, this particular block had already been searched, but I just had a strong feeling that was pulling me back out there. So Reba and I were coming into the wind, in an area where there was an old dump, and I found a golf ball. A brand new golf ball sitting in the woods, so I picked it up and I looked at it, and as I looked up, Reba was coming toward me with that look she had that said, "I got her." Reba and I, it was like we had this Vulcan mind meld going. She came up, spun on a dime, and said, with her body language, "Come on, Roger. You've gotta follow me."

So I started following her, going through real thick growth, and we were going along, and going along with no sign of Goldie. We kind of popped into an opening, and Reba went on a little bit more. All the time, she's stopping and waiting for me, which was not her normal habit. She was making sure she was keeping me in sight and that I was still following her. Eventually we came to this berm and I could see something white. Goldie was said to be wearing a white sweatshirt, and as Reba was going in past it, I was thinking, *There she is.* I got there, and it was a piece of a washing machine. And while I was looking that over, Reba was getting more and more frantic, like she was saying, "Stay with me here, okay?"

So I kept following her, and sure enough, we came into this thicket, and popped out into another small opening and boom, there was Goldie.

She was laying out on her back, and I thought, *She's gone*, because of how long she'd been missing and the weather and all. I got to her and I said her name and touched her on the arm. And she stirred. She woke up. She sat up. I said, "Goldie . . . you want some water?"

She nodded her head, and patted the dog, and that's when I calmly called on the radio and said, "I found her." And the whole world came running.

The thing with Goldie was that if her glasses fell off, she couldn't see a thing. What she'd immediately do was drop to the ground on all fours and paw around, trying to find her glasses. What had happened was where the ATV gentlemen had seen her, there was kind of a fork in the road, and she'd gone beyond the end of it. When she turned around to go back, she took the wrong little road, an old road where the dump used to be, and it was completely overgrown. When she got to the top of the hill, she could see the road she wanted to be on, so she started walking overland, and she fell and lost her glasses.

For almost four days, she was on the ground, crawling around on her hands and knees, trying to find her glasses. On the side of that berm where the old dump was, there were these big burdock plants, with the big leaves, the elephant ears, and she had spent all that time on her hands and knees underneath these giant burdock plants, these huge leaves, completely obscured, while we were literally on top of her.

People walked past her. Helicopters flew over her.

It goes back to that gut feeling again. Totally out of character for me. Not anything I would normally do. But something was telling me to go back to this one spot. On the way home, people were doing high fives and beeping and yelling. They saw the dog in the truck and wow. It doesn't get any better than that. It just doesn't.

That was a good experience.

Many people don't realize how many different skills our dogs can acquire. One of those is the ability to locate cadaver scent in water. This came into play when we had a drowning accident at Buttermilk Pond, and involved my third dog, an intense, demanding K-9 named Maggie (more often called Crazy Maggie).

When we first heard about the situation, it was night. This would have been mid-to-late November. Four men were staying at a camp on the lake, hunting, and were going across the lake with an apple pie to see some people who had a camp on the other side when their boat capsized. Basically, the boat was overloaded, and it must have tipped or something and took on water and swamped. Two guys made it to shore and two guys didn't. The four guys had been close friends since kindergarten, so this was a really tragic event for them.

We went in that night to run the shoreline in case those guys had made it to shore. Maggie hit right away at the edge of the lake, so I marked the spot. I put the ribbon up and kept searching. I knew what she'd hit on. Dan Carroll was with me, and it was clear as day. She was barking, going down to the water, spinning, coming back, and going down again. Trying to get her reward. The trouble is that you can't give the reward until you can confirm it, otherwise you could be making a big mistake, building in bad habits, so I praised her as much as I could, but I didn't feel comfortable giving her a reward. So the search went on all the next day.

The divers found the stronger swimmer of the two about halfway from where the boat had gone down. They searched for the other guy between where they found the stronger swimmer and where the boat went down for hours and hours and they couldn't find him.

The thing is, with divers doing water searches where you've got depth, you might be too high or too low when you make your sweep. I had told the head diver, before they went out that morning, "Look, I put a ribbon up where the dog hit." The head diver had forgotten what I'd told him, so they searched for hours and hours, but then he looked over and saw the ribbon. They paddled over, and when they got to the ribbon, they looked down and they could see him right there within eight feet of the shoreline. Maggie had been right dead on the money.

Sometimes, it's not the lost person who needs help, or evidence that needs to be located, it's the warden himself who needs the dog's help, as this story illustrates.

To catch a poacher, everything has to fall into place. You have to be in the right place at the right time and all the stars have to line up so that you can see the violation happen and you can be in the right spot to intercept the violators before they can ditch the evidence on you. Sometimes things can go to hell in a handbasket just when you think you've got it in the bag.

This happened on a beautiful mid-summer day. Glenn Annis, Reba, and I were headed up to Yoke Pond country to see what kind of trouble we could find up there. On our way in, we found a vehicle parked by what used to be the trailhead to Alligator and Seventh Roach Ponds. We checked the hood for engine warmth and it was stone cold, meaning they'd either gotten there very early or they were camping. I dropped Glenn off to take the trail where they went in, while I would go around from the Yoke Pond side of the mountain where I would have an ideal vantage point to watch them and Glenn could make the apprehension—easy Wardening 101. After dropping Glenn off, I drove around to Yoke Pond, ditched my truck, and speed-hiked into Alligator Pond, where I located our party fishing, two guys and a girl.

Both Alligator and Seventh Roach Ponds are considered remote ponds and trophy waters and have these special regulations to protect the trout from being overfished. They have a slot limit there to control the number and size of the fish that can be kept. A fisherman is allowed to take only one large fish over fourteen inches and one fish between twelve inches and under fourteen inches. That way the large breeder fish are protected, because, to fishermen, bigger is always better. The regulations also prohibit the use of any kind of bait. Fishermen must use artificial lures. This reduces the catch rates by making it more challenging for the angler.

As I watched the three in the canoe with my spotting scope, I could see that the young lady was not fishing at all. She was lost in a book. The bow man was fishing with a spinner and using worms as was the stern man. With my spotting scope, I could watch from half a mile away and see their activities like I was sitting right beside them. I watched them for a bit, then decided to check in with Glenn to see if he could see what I was seeing. I dug out my portable radio and tried to call him but got no response. I thought maybe he had turned it off because they had trolled close to him and he'd forgotten to turn it back on. He was on the right side of the pond to make the apprehension when they got ready to leave.

That was important, because I could see their activity, but I was not in position to grab them before they left. I watched them catch and keep every fish they caught, five in all and all over the fourteen-inch slot limit. By law, three of these fish should have been released and none of them should have been caught using worms.

Finally, they started getting ready to leave. The men took the spinners and bait hooks off their rods, dumped the secret stash of worms in the pond, and put legal lures on their rods in case they got checked on the trail heading out.

This was the moment when Glenn would step out at the landing and give them the bad news. The canoe made its way to the landing, though, and no moment of truth came. Two poachers were walking away. I kept trying Glenn on the radio and got no response. I was a half a mile away across the pond and my day's work was just walking away from me. My only hope was to grab one of the canoes stashed on my side of the pond and try to catch them before they made it to their vehicle.

Reba hopped into her spot up front and braced herself for the mad dash that was coming. By this time, they had a good ten-minute head start on me, so every second counted. From the pond back to the vehicles was about a mile down the mountain. I dragged my canoe up on shore, headed down the trail, and ran smack into a brick wall. Logging activity had completely changed the landscape. The old trail I knew was gone. It would have taken me hours to find and stay on what was once the trail. By then, my quarry would be long gone.

My heart sank. My chance of getting these guys was slipping away. I had my GPS, but using it would slow me down and the poachers had the edge because they had found their way in and knew the way out through the logged out portion of the trail.

Then it hit me. I had Reba! I looked at her, said "Track," and she went to work. Would she get what I needed her to do without her normal cues? No problem. Sensing my urgency, she shot off, nose to the ground. All I could do was follow and believe she would get the job done.

We popped out onto the road to find Glenn and the fishermen standing at their vehicle. I could see by the look on Glenn's face that he was at a stalemate with these guys and was very relieved to see me. I was completely out of breath. As soon as I could talk, Glenn and I had a quick briefing. He had gotten turned round in the cut and never made it to the pond. His portable radio was dead and he had no way to let me know.

The two fisherman who had been snowballing Glenn were now horrified as I explained that the young lady had never fished and that they had five large trout, all caught on worms, putting each one of them in line for a fistful of summonses.

Without the little brown dog's help, I would have been lost on the trail and those poachers would have won.

Finding evidence to put the scenes and cases together. Finding hidden fish and game so we can stop poaching. Weapons searches to help law enforcement. All of that is critical to the job and shows what an asset our dogs can be. For me, though, it is being able to find lost people that's most gratifying.

Here's the thing all this has taught me. I can't build things. I have no gifts when it comes to doing anything creative. But I can find people. I've seen it happen way too many times, like on that search for Goldie Jordan. Or seeing the broken stump in the middle of nowhere while looking for that ninety-eight-year-old man. I get that feeling, before I make the find, and it just directs me into the place I need to be. At the end of the day, as I drive home, I wonder—did I do that, or was that something else? It happens so often that I always wonder: Did I see something so subtle that my unconscious got it and I didn't? Did some unseen hand turn me and point my eyes toward the clue or did it just fall on me?

PART VI

THESE WOODS ARE FULL OF BODIES

CHAPTER SEVENTEEN

The Arm Bone's Connected to the Homicide

One significant thing led to us getting our dogs into the cadaver realm. We realized that some of our lost person searches were unsuccessful because the people we were looking for were already deceased. Our dogs were trained for live searches. We were seeing a pattern of search and rescue situations where dogs had walked right past a body and wouldn't go near it. A lot of dogs have a natural aversion to dead humans. They sense the badness of it, and it creeps them out. In part, I think, they get this from their handlers' negative reactions. For that reason—even with dogs that were only going to be doing live searches, tracking, trailing, or air scent—we decided we needed to expose them to cadaver scent as part of their training, so we could observe and be aware of their behaviors when cadaver scent was present.

Something I'm acutely aware of, from spending so many years in the woods, is the science of searching. In our world, we did it every day, day in and day out, whether it was for a lost person or a poached animal or a shell casing. We were always looking for something. That's where our skills were. Once we had dogs that were trained in cadaver searching as well as search and rescue, we began to be drawn into another realm: assisting public safety organizations with finding the bodies of homicide victims.

One of the first things I realized, when we started getting called in to assist with homicides, in the Amy St. Laurent case, the Carol Caswell case, and some of these other high profile cases we got involved with, was that we brought a different set of skills and a different set of questions to the cases than the police did. We quickly saw that we had this whole different approach to locating things outdoors that nobody in other arenas of law enforcement really paid attention to.

We had developed strategies, outdoors-specific methodologies, that helped us find that little square spot on the ground that everyone was looking for. We realized that for our assistance on these searches for other law enforcement agencies to be effective, we had to educate the people we were working with about what we really needed to know and what information they might not think was relevant but was often critical to our success. Sometimes that could be a slow, painstaking process, because what we needed to know was so far outside the realm of their normal investigative techniques. It also often became a case of shifting their thinking about what was relevant and important.

Frequently, when we were called in to help other law enforcement agencies, they weren't anticipating that we would arrive and start interviewing them. But that's often what we had to do. Before we could use the dogs effectively or design a coherent search, we needed to know the answers to these behavioral questions that we had. They weren't anticipating the process. They acted like they'd seen too many of those old prison escape movies were the farmer comes out with baying bloodhounds to track the convicts. They thought we were going to come in and walk the dogs and go home. In reality, our process is far more complex and scientific than that.

If we were coming in to help law enforcement find a body somewhere in the woods, we'd arrive with our computers and our mapping programs and our expertise, and we'd start learning about their suspect. We'd say okay, we need to know what the suspect does, we need to know where his world is—is he a hunter, a fisherman, what types of outdoor activities does he do? How comfortable is he in the woods? How familiar is he with the area? We'd ask what they'd learned from their interviews so we could build a timeline and figure out how much time he had to dispose of a body, whether that had happened during the day or at night. It would matter, for example, if they could tie their suspect to a shovel, so we might be looking at a buried body. Or whether the incident happened in the winter, and the body might be frozen and not giving off scent.

Once we got them past the fundamental public safety instinct to share as little as possible and they started to see how this worked, they'd buy into it. Then our value to their case, and how we could use the information they'd shared, would start to really click.

Carol Caswell Search

Very early on in Reba's cadaver training, in April of 1998, we got a call from the state police; they had information about a missing woman from New Hampshire who had been buried somewhere off the interstate in Lincoln, Maine. A man named "Mickey" had been with the suspect in the case when they hid the body. Now he was in jail in Maine on an OUI, so they interviewed him and he started talking about leaving the interstate, driving down a side road, and burying this body.

At this point, Carol Caswell had been missing since August of 1996.

By the time the state police contacted us, they'd already spent five or six days looking for the body. That winter, I had started tuning Reba up for cadaver search—up to that point, she had not really been trained for cadaver—and I was waiting for the snow to melt in Aroostook County to go and look for a missing man named Bob Smith. Then, in April, this call came.

Pat Dorian and I met up in Lincoln. When we got there, and got their information—the suspects had driven up there with the body, gotten off the interstate, and buried her—one of the key things we focused on was that this Maine kid, Mickey, had said he'd gotten all scratched up going into the burial site. This statement was insignificant to the investigators but, being game wardens and very familiar with different types of vegetation and where it grows, it *was* significant to us.

We went down to the area where they'd been searching and drove the road. There was only one place where you could turn a car around, and gee whiz, it was full of black raspberry bushes. So I took the dog in, and, I am not exaggerating, within five minutes, I had the burial site.

But this was now a pretty old burial, so this is what happened. The dog hit, indicating that she had made a find, and I went over. I knew, the way she acted, something was there. So the investigators took a shovel and dug around and they didn't find anything. So they said, "Nope. She's not there."

Now, I knew my dog, and I was saying, "This is it." But they kept searching. I brought the dog in again, and this time, she went a little bit beyond that grave. She was getting a little bit flustered. She was basically saying to me: *Roger, how many times are you gonna make me do this?* And she kicked the leaves a little bit and I could see bone. It was the arm bone, and it had evidence of an old break in it. As soon as I saw that, I knew what was going on and why we weren't finding a body. I knew that a bear had been there and dug her out of the grave.

When bears have been at a body, their habit is to grab a piece and move a few feet away. Bears like to eat kind of lying down. So they'll grab a piece, go a few feet away, and sit down where they can keep an eye on any other bear coming in. Then they'll consume it, and they'll go get some more. The thing about bears is that they crush bone to get the marrow out. When they're done, there's not a lot left besides bone fragments. They tend to leave bone fragments in a fifteen- to thirty-foot circle around the site. So all the bone fragments would be spread out like that from the gravesite.

Once I found that bone, everybody came back to that spot and when they dug a little deeper in the original hole, they found her hair and teeth. Then they searched the whole area. That bone that Reba and I found had major significance because she had broken her arm as a child and it had the mark of that break right on it. That case kind of kicked us into the homicide world.

One thing I should note about using the dogs for cadaver searches is that it's not a simple matter of bringing in the dogs and turning them loose. When you're going to do a cadaver search, and you know that's what you're doing, the dogs will know by the commands you give them, and the collar and the bell. When I put the bell on them, they know what they're going to do. To increase our chances of success, if I'm going to be working a cold case or an old case, I always start them out with a find. I try to keep scent samples the vintage of the cadaver around that time or that age, if I can. And then I'll do a couple of training finds before I go on the actual search, dialing them into the level of cadaver that we're looking for.

So often, people outside of the public safety realm have no idea what goes on with us. It's the unusual world—the warden's world, the public safety world, the things we've seen and the conflicts and confrontations we've had—clashing with the real world. Let me give you an example of this. A Hartland woman, Vella Gogan, killed her husband while he was sleeping. She shot him in the ear with a .22. Then she shot him in the other ear. (At trial, she would claim self-defense and a history of domestic abuse but was ultimately found guilty.) She dragged him to the truck and drove about twenty miles to his hunting camp. She completely dismembered him—she was a part-time butcher—put him in military duffle bags, drove the truck into the woods, and she hid each piece, thirteen or more, phenomenally well, over a pretty large area.

I've been dealing with people who hide stuff my whole career, and I've always been able to pick it out, but even to me this scene was just amazing. I was out there with the state police, searching. The dog would hit. That was Reba, and she was so good, and so reliable that I'd just tell the detective who was with me, "Take a picture."

He'd say, "There's nothing there," and we'd take a stick and poke around and there it would be.

I think we'd found everything but the hands that one night. It was getting dark. It was September, a clear, clear night with crisp fall air, and I was in the woods pulling out all these body parts. And I vividly remember—the things that stick in your mind, you know—at one point I turned around and the medical examiner was walking out of the woods with this human thigh in his hands.

So I got done there, and that night my wife and I went to a dinner party. We're having pork roast with a whole group of people, and I was really hungry but I couldn't eat that roast because, chopped off, it looked exactly like that thigh I'd just seen. I was sitting there thinking that I really couldn't discuss what I'd just gone through with all these people at the dinner party, and saying, "I'll have a little more salad."

My wife was giving me that, *What's wrong with you, you love this stuff!* look, and I was thinking: *Not tonight dear. I can't do it.* Here I was at this party, acting normal, and two hours before, I'd been picking body parts out of the woods.

One thing we learned, from working homicides where the perpetrators had hidden bodies in the woods, was that when people hid bodies, or something they'd stolen, they'd hide things where they could monitor them. Often, they did this subconsciously. They just had this need to hide them in ways that they could find the spot again to ensure that it hadn't been disturbed.

Part of that is due to the fact that a lot of these people who kill and hide bodies are control freaks of one sort or another, because that's the personality trait that got them to the point where they were thinking: okay, this person isn't controllable anymore, so now my only option is to destroy them. And once they have a body on their hands, they have to do something with it. Those types of people have to have that element of control throughout the process. Consciously, they might not even know they're doing it.

So when we go out on a search looking for where someone has hidden a body, we put ourselves into their mindset, to help us find it. Part of our preparation for the search will be understanding that perpetrator and the circumstances under which the body was hidden.

CHAPTER EIGHTEEN

Amy and Maria Put Us on the Map

Two cases that really got us into the homicide world—and made the warden service a go-to agency for helping to find bodies in the woods—were the Amy St. Laurent case, in Portland, and the Maria Tanasichuk case up in Miramichi, New Brunswick. In both cases, it was Lieutenant Pat Dorian who got us involved, and in both of those cases, the bodies might never have been found, and the cases never successfully prosecuted, if we hadn't brought our search and rescue expertise and our cadaver dogs into the searches.

Amy St. Laurent Search

Twenty-five-year-old Amy St. Laurent disappeared in October 2001 after a night she'd spent showing a friend from Florida the club scene in Portland's Old Port area. At the end of the evening, she and her friend got separated, and Amy was never seen alive again. As the weeks stretched on without her being found, and winter approached with all the complications he knew that would bring to finding a body that was outdoors, Lieutenant Dorian grew increasingly troubled by the pain he knew her family, and public safety personnel, were feeling.

As hunting season grew to a close, he offered the wardens' mapping and planning expertise to the Portland and Maine State Police. Pat Dorian, Kevin Adam, Joel Wilkinson, and I met with them at the Portland police department, and later spent part of the evening driving around, examining our highest probability sites at night to assess them for mapping and structuring the search.

On a Saturday in December, with a snowstorm headed our way, wardens, local police, and volunteers from Maine search and rescue groups assembled to conduct an intensive, day-long search for Amy's body in the areas we'd identified as high probability spots. Because of the value of using dual resources—both searchers' eyes on the ground and cadaver dogs—areas were searched using both, with some of the higher probability areas saved for later in the day, when it would be warmer and the air would be better for carrying scent.

Late in the afternoon, with the smell of the oncoming snow in the air, a searcher noticed a tree branch buried in the ground. Closer inspection showed the sod had been cut and removed, then replaced and sprinkled with pine needles. Our plan had been for this area to be searched earlier in the day with a dog before the ground searchers came in, but there had been a mix-up in the paperwork and another area was searched instead.

I had been up in a chopper, viewing high probability areas from the air, and when we'd flown over this particular piece, which was very near the suspect's house, I'd made an X on the map. So when the ground searchers found that branch, I was called to bring in Reba to see if she could confirm the presence of a body. Before she hit on the suspected gravesite, Reba hit hard on another spot under some trees. Her reaction was something I had never seen before. Her hackles went right up on the back of her neck and she went into full alert mode. She then moved to the gravesite and dug once or twice with her paws in the soft soil before she lay down. One of the case detectives, Portland detective Danny Young, got a trowel and dug down about twenty inches until he hit gray sweatshirt material. Amy had been wearing a gray sweatshirt the night she disappeared.

The fact that Reba had had a significant hit on a different spot first became important at trial because it confirmed what detectives had learned from the suspect's confession to his mother—that he had killed Amy and left her lying on the ground under the trees for a few days, then returned later to bury her.

Maria Tanasichuk Search

In 2003, Pat Dorian's sympathy for stymied investigators, and his belief in our cadaver dogs as an extremely valuable resource for homicide investigations, led us across the border into Canada and another case involving a missing homicide victim. The police in the small city of Miramichi, New Brunswick, were certain they had a homicide on their hands when a local woman was reported missing by her husband in January, but despite their best efforts, they had been unable to locate her body in the immense woods surrounding the city. Eventually, they had concluded that their only hope was cadaver dogs. They couldn't locate that resource in Canada, and their inquiries across the US border led them to Pat Dorian and the Maine Warden Service.

As happens so often when we're working with other law enforcement agencies, they were initially very guarded with the information they were sharing. They just wanted us to take the dogs and go look around an industrial park area that was close to their suspect's house and matched the timeline they'd developed. They didn't understand the process that we were bringing to them, the kind of information we needed to help them find her.

Well, we went up there twice, and by the end of that first trip, they could see what we were doing and they could see the process. But that first search effort didn't work out well because there was still snow in the woods and it was probable that the victim's body was still frozen. Dogs work on scent, and when you have those conditions, windless days and pockets of snow, it just holds all that scent right in, and nothing is moving.

Actually, everything about that trip was a challenge. We didn't have the mapping programs that we needed—we had to create those on the ground. The weather conditions were awful. It was hot and the woods were full of water and the mosquitoes were terrible. We had this one detective, Brian Cummings, who wanted to walk with us. He was determined to keep up. He was wearing waders, and there we were, typical warden style, walking ten, twelve miles a day. After that first day, he was somewhat chafed. But he was determined to find Maria and stayed with us throughout the search.

And what we learned—we didn't know this at first, it was something we learned from spending so much time with them—was that part of what was driving them to find this missing woman, Maria Tanasichuk, was because they'd had a relationship with her. They'd gotten close to her after her son was killed, and they wanted to give her family closure and all that. But more important, we learned that the husband who'd reported her missing was a real bad guy, probably had killed a couple other people, and during the investigation, when he couldn't get the investigators to back off, he had threatened the officers' families. So finding Maria and getting her husband David locked up were really important to these officers.

It was pretty discouraging when, at the end of three days of searching, we didn't find her. We'd driven those hundreds of miles up there, spent all that time, our handlers and Maine Search and Rescue Dogs (MESARD) volunteers with their dogs. And the Miramichi police had such high hopes. I think they were pretty heartbroken when we left without finding Maria. This was in May. We knew that we were going to have to go back, but it was a real challenge, with Maine's tourist season underway and heavy demands on our search and rescue expertise, to go back that second time. And Pat Dorian was the one who made that happen.

Those guys, they were at their wits' end, they'd done everything they could do, and we were saying, we need a mapping program, and we need to sit down and interview you guys, and we kinda need to know who this guy was and what he did with his time, what his interests were. During our initial search, we completely missed that their suspect, David Tanasichuk, was into bear hunting. That didn't come out until the second time, and it gave us a lot more information about where to search. So we went back a second time, in late June, because

Pat, whose faith in our ability to conduct successful searches and in the talents of our dogs, had made the Maine wardens' search and rescue capability so strong, and he wasn't going to give up on finding that body. Because the area was full of hungry bear emerging from hibernation, we were racing the clock, trying to find her before the bear did, because, like in the Carol Caswell case, they needed her body to establish cause of death, and if the bear got to her, that might well have been impossible.

It was so hot that second time that we had to do our searches in the early morning, then rest the dogs, and go back out in the late afternoon. And because we knew his stomping grounds, and because of our mapping program, we were able to study our maps and identify an area that hadn't been thoroughly searched on our first visit. So Pat sent Debbie Palman and her dog, Alex, in to clear that section.

Yeah, it was funny. We were shutting down, packing up, and getting ready to head back home, and Debbie Palman came on the radio, and she said, "I found her." And she was really excited, which was not Debbie at all.

And I said, "What?"

And Debbie said, louder, "I FOUND HER!"

"Where are you?" I asked.

And she told me, and we all zoomed over there on two wheels.

He'd covered the body with brush and packed it with snow. She was in her winter clothes. And that body gave them so much information for their case. They were able to match bullets from her skull to a gun they'd found. And the reason her husband could never come clean and just say he'd lost it and shot her? Because it wasn't a single shot he might have fired in anger, it was an ambush and execution.

I never expected to be working in the world of homicide. We wardens are out there trying to protect fish and wildlife resources for future generations, and fulfilling our mission to find people who are lost in the woods and waterways; but sometimes, with these homicide cases, our expertise—knowing how to map and search thoroughly, how to read the woods, how to do a suspect profile to identify the best search areas, and having the special resource of our trained cadaver dogs—can provide so much value to investigators and to the victims' families.

There was a homicide case that took place in Canaan. Cheryl Murdoch had found the love of her life, Shannon Atwood, in Maine. She'd called her mother and said, "I'm coming home to pick up my stuff. I'm moving to Maine. This guy is so awesome." Well, she never made it home. After a little time passed, her mother got worried and started calling. She called the boyfriend and he told her, "Oh yeah, we got in a tiff and she left."

Her mother called the state police, because it was not like her daughter to be out of touch with her family, so they started investigating. About a month after she went missing, they called me to bring a dog in to search. They'd learned that on the night they could last account for Cheryl being alive, her boyfriend had called an old girlfriend and had a rambling, incoherent, hour-long conversation with her in which he was so distraught she thought he was suicidal. She got him to tell her that he was camping about three miles from his house at a campsite in the woods. She said that he wasn't making any sense, because he was talking about being in the military and how he'd had to kill women and children and he was going to hell for what he'd done. And he'd never been in the military.

The investigators were thinking that this campsite where he was staying was going be a high priority, so they called me to come down and search with the dog. On my way in to meet them, I took the wrong road, just short of the entrance to the campground. It went in about half a mile and dead-ended. When I turned around and came out, I saw a blue tarp out in the woods, and I thought, "Oh yeah, got to come back and search this area," because I can't tell you how many times we find what we're looking for wrapped in a blue tarp.

I found the campground. We searched the whole area and the dog did pick up a couple of spots where we thought there was some blood. They checked the spots with luminol and they tested positive, but we didn't find Cheryl. We were getting ready to pack up, and I said,

"Let's go check that other road 'cause there's a blue tarp there." I had worked with these detectives before, so they were willing to go along with my hunch.

We parked at the entrance, and we started working the road. Rader was roaming, working wind currents, and I was following his lead. About halfway down, we saw the tarp. We went over to it and opened it, and it was all old bones—moose and deer bones that someone had for a coyote bait or something. It wasn't anything. We continued on toward the end of the road. Rader was working and his bell was going *ding, ding, ding,* and as I got to the end of the road, the bell stopped.

Now Rader had this glitch. In a search like this, cadaver dogs are trained to stay with the body and alert by downing and barking if they can't see you. It had happened a couple of times with him, where, if he could see me, he wouldn't bark, he'd just lie down. The problem was that this was late summer. Things were turning brown and he was a brown dog, so he was hard to see. I knew not to call him, because if I called him, I'd literally call him off the find. I'd had this happen with a firearm. That would screw things up, because he might not take me back there.

I was standing there, looking for my dog, and the detectives were looking at me like "So?"

I started walking in to where I'd last heard his bell. When I got in about twenty-five yards, I could see him. He was lying there and he was all excited. His legs were going and his tail was quivering. I literally walked up to him, and I looked down and all around, and I didn't see anything. I said, "Rader, what is wrong with you?"

And he was going, "Give me the ball, give me the ball," because his reward was play, not food. Finally, he got frustrated with me, and he poked with his nose. I looked down and I realized that I was seeing the tip of a hiking boot sticking out of a deep rut that was covered with brush.

I went, "Holy crap! There's the body." And I hollered over to the detectives, "I've got her. She's right here."

The detective, who was still standing in the road, said, "Yeah, right. Tell me another one."

And I said, "Listen, I've got the body. It's right here."

He said, "Don't be pulling my leg."

I said, "Gentlemen, I have a body. Right here. You might want to come see this."

He came and looked more closely and said, "Holy shit. She's right here."

You know, you train for days and weeks and months, and the dog's doing exactly what it's supposed to do, and you're too dumb to notice it. Not until Rader got frustrated and started poking did I wake up and see that shoe. *Stupid handler*, he was saying, *can you please pay attention?* Yet another lesson about remembering to trust my dog.

Something that lingers about this search, that question I come back to again and again: Was taking that turn down the wrong road just an accident, or was something or someone guiding me to that spot?

This was probably Atwood's second homicide. His wife, Shirley Moon Atwood, also disappeared. We've looked and looked for her, but she has never been found.

Early on, during the Cheryl Murdoch investigation, Kevin Adam and I met a guy from England, Mark Harrison, at a conference in Virginia. He was, at the time, in charge of missing and abducted people in England. One difference between the United States and England is that they have one law enforcement entity, so their statistical data goes into one source vs. all these different jurisdictions we have here. So I called him when we were looking for Atwood's other victim, the wife who's never been found.

I picked his brain on that, and he told me that the wife would have been Atwood's first homicide, and he felt strongly that Atwood wouldn't have put as much effort into her. You know, as they do it, each time they do it, they get a little better at it. He told me that one of the places that he felt very strongly about was the water. I think it was like 63 percent of the victims end up in water. This guy, Atwood, had a canoe, and there was a big stream right out behind his house. Police did dive it at the time, but they didn't really dive it. They did dive by the bridge but they didn't go upstream. They did do dogs, but at the time they didn't have water certified dogs.

I think it's possible, depending on many variables like silt depth, water temps, current, and fish and crayfish consumption of flesh, that a good water certified dog might still be able to locate that body. There's no clear line as to when the scent trail would fade away. It's one of those cases that lingers; one of those bodies I'd really like to find.

CHAPTER NINETEEN

Buried Babies in Baxter State Park

I've been involved in three major searches where the outcomes—the ability to locate a missing victim's body and the implications of that find for a successful prosecution—had incredibly serious hopes from public safety organizations riding on them. I've written about the search for twenty-five-year-old Amy St. Laurent, and the search for Maria Tanasichuk way up in Miramichi, New Brunswick. But the search for two babies buried by Massachusetts cult members was the longest and most time-consuming of my career.

The story of our yearlong search (from 1999 to 2000) for two babies buried in Baxter State Park, a two-hundred-thousand-acre Maine park, is almost a book in itself. The challenges of vast terrain, Maine weather, a well-hidden burial site, and an inability to get good information from the police agencies all complicated the lengthiest and most difficult search I was ever engaged in.

This case pretty much brought together every skill I'd honed over the years: using the techniques the warden service had developed for organized wilderness searching; using our mapping skills to identify high probability areas and tracking what had been searched and eliminated; coordinating teams of handlers and cadaver dogs; applying interview skills to get useful data about timing, equipment, and geography from child witnesses (and later, from a member of the burial party) so we could imagine their process and do a more intelligent search; applying knowledge of how people behave in the woods; the importance of patience, persistence, and teamwork in formulating a methodical approach to an enormous task; the value of assessing and eliminating possibilities over the course of a search; and the importance of being able to "read" the woods and know what it is saying.

Over the course of that year, I made twenty-three trips up to the park with my dogs.

It started for me when Lieutenant Pat Dorian called in the middle of the night and said, "We've got to go to Baxter Park." He was mumbling, because he was tired, and he was saying that we had to go because there were some babies buried up there. This case initially came to us from Massachusetts; the Bristol County DA's office and the Massachusetts State Police got in touch with the Maine State Police. From them, the call went to Pat Dorian, and Pat called me. The Massachusetts authorities had been investigating a cult group down in Attleboro, Massachusetts, because they'd received information that two babies born to members of the group had died and had been brought up to Maine and buried in Baxter Park.

Finding those babies was a very significant thing for Massachusetts authorities. Two cult members' children had simply "disappeared" from a small cult sometimes called "The Body" in the Attleboro area. According to detailed records kept by the cult members, one of the babies had been stillborn or died at a birth without medical attention; the other child was slowly starved to death. The story of little Samuel Robidoux was heartbreaking. One of the cult members, Michelle Mingo, sister-in-law of Samuel's mother Karen, and sister of his father, Jacques, claimed to have had a vision in which Karen's faith and vanity needed to be tested. She was to only drink almond milk, and the baby, who had begun eating food, was only allowed to nurse and not to be given any solid food. Karen Robidoux was pregnant again and the nursing was unsuccessful, yet cult members sat around, diligently recording the events as tests of their faith, as baby Samuel cried in desperate hunger until he weakened and finally died.

They had then wrapped his body, put it in a basket, and stored it in the cellar. Later, when another baby died or was stillborn during a home birth, that baby's body was wrapped and stored as well. The babies' bodies were brought to Maine when the cult came to celebrate what they called the Feast of Tabernacles. According to information gathered by Massachusetts investigators, the cult members had stayed at a local campground and buried the babies somewhere in the park. That had taken place earlier in the fall. Now, cult members, including the cult leader Roland Robidoux; Samuel's mother, Karen Robidoux; Samuel's father, Jacques Robidoux; and his sister, Michelle Mingo, were in jail and their children had been taken away and placed in state custody. Authorities needed to locate the missing babies as part of a successful prosecution.

We ended up meeting with the Massachusetts folks the next day, along with Maine State Police. I believe that it was November 17, 1999. Initially, the Massachusetts people were under the impression that this park was like a city park. Instead, it was a park as big as a city. They showed up with this file that said they had information that two babies were buried somewhere in the park; could we help them? This was pretty late in the fall, the height of hunting season, with winter arriving soon, and we were very busy.

We sat down with them and did what we always do—conducted an interview from a warden's point of view, looking for the details that would help us design a search. From that initial interview, we learned that this cult group had stayed at a campground near the park entrance. Massachusetts police had conducted interviews with some of the children who had been taken away from the group, and the children remembered the wooden boxes the babies were in, and they remembered some of the men of the group lashing those to carrying poles. They also told us that other members of the group had dropped this burial party off at the Trout Brook campground, at the beginning of what we identified from their descriptions as the Freeze Out Trail, a rough twenty-three-mile wilderness trail on the east side of Baxter Park.

The Massachusetts police were telling us that according to the information they'd developed, there would be a significant burial site with crosses and so forth. We were looking at it from this perspective: people don't come into the Maine woods and go through elaborate planning to bury bodies and then make it so other people can find them. They do, on the other hand, as I discussed earlier in this book, often take steps to ensure that *they* can find the burial site again.

What their information was telling us was that this would not be a "walk in the park." Assuming that their information was correct and we could limit our search efforts to this part of the park, our search area would involve a rough, sometimes almost mountainous, twenty-three-mile wilderness loop trail with no road access other than at the beginning and the end, and no shortcuts to reach the middle sections of the trail. They had no idea what that would entail.

Also, the Massachusetts State Police detectives—and I totally understand it, I've been there, I've seen it with every agency—they weren't forthcoming with all of the information, which made it very difficult for us. They were telling us what they thought these cult people would do, and we were experienced enough to know that we were almost certainly missing some important pieces of information. Still, winter weather was coming soon and they had an urgent need to find those babies, so we went to work with what we had.

We assembled teams of handlers, warden service K-9s, and MES-ARD (Maine Search and Rescue Dogs) volunteers with their dogs, and starting working at the beginning of the trail, where the burial party was believed to have been dropped off. Initially, we cleared the area by the campground. Then we started working our way up the trail. I knew, after getting some background on these people, that they weren't woodsy people at all. They were farmers but they weren't woodsy people, and so when I was assessing how to design a search— because searching the whole length of the trail thoroughly would have taken a vast amount of time and many, many teams of dogs and handlers—I was figuring that they would need a really good physical feature to reference so they could get back there if they wanted to find those bodies again.

As an overhead commander, responsible for organizing the search, supervising the mapping, and designating the blocks to be covered, I quickly determined, because of the dense forest we would be searching in, that using cadaver dogs would be our best bet. Even at that, given the conditions and the small size of the bodies we were looking for, I estimated our probability of success at about 30 percent, and that was if the gravesite was visible, as the Massachusetts police had predicted. If they were buried and the burial site was disguised, our probability of success, unless we could get better information, given the small amount of cadaver scent they would give off, was around 5 percent.

So that's how we organized it—a basic search along the trail with more intense searches in places where there were distinctive features. We started from the Trout Brook campground, over a walking bridge, to where there's an old grown-up farm field close to the head of the trail where spruce trees are coming in. That was the first place we looked, but that was obviously way too easy. They wouldn't have had to lash the boxes to poles to carry them such a short distance.

Then we started up the trail. What we were trying to do was a two-hundred- to four-hundred-yard sweep on each side of the trail, with extra concentration around these physical features. There we would expand to a larger area.

During the initial, intense phase of the search, we had five or six teams of dogs and handlers working on this project. Phase one was identifying all the areas that we wanted to clear. We looked at that trail and identified distinctive physical features that someone could easily recognize, like the sawdust pile. There was a rock that we called The Chicken Rock, a rock that if you used your imagination, looked like a bird. It was very distinct, so that was a point that we really covered a lot. And there was one spot where there was a little beaver flowage that the trail came up against.

We did a general search along the trail and these more intense, wider searches around physical features that might have been used by the burial party to locate the bodies again. We searched a wider perimeter around those areas. Using these distinctive features, our teams slowly worked their way up the trail. It was a slow, laborious process that was hampered by the oncoming winter weather and the demands on warden personnel because it was hunting season.

Eventually, we had worked our way so far up the trail that we could no longer come in on foot. We'd searched the first twelve miles of the trail, up to the head end of Matagamon Falls, and we'd reached the point where we couldn't walk in anymore. Wardens are used to walking long distances, but the prospect of twelve miles up and twelve miles back, before we even got to the starting point of the actual search, was unworkable. Besides being completely exhausted ourselves, our dogs would be done. So to continue clearing the trail, we had to go in by boat.

By this time (late November) the lake was beginning to freeze, so the only way we could get the boat in there was to break the ice. We'd drive the boat up on the ice, jumping and breaking it to cut a trail, make our way a little farther along, and do it again. The Massachusetts investigators had been searching with us, but after a day of that, they disappeared. They stayed down in Bangor while we went out and did the searches.

All along the way, we were frustrated by our lack of information, by having to work with their interpretations of how the group had conducted the burial, information from their interviews with the cult member's children, and their interpretations of the cult's behavior and psychology. We were happy to help out, that's what public safety organizations do for each other, but quite frankly, when you're deal-ing with the woods, and people hiding bodies out there, wardens ask different questions and want to know different things from other law enforcement agencies.

Everyone does it—they give us the information they believe is relevant—but it often means we're missing key pieces or small bits of information, like the black raspberry bushes in the Carol Caswell case, that can be of significant value in helping us to design or focus a search. We try to educate them, but keeping things close to the chest is just the way public safety organizations work.

So here's what happened. One day, when those guys headed back home to Massachusetts—they'd come up for a couple days of heavy searching—one of them left his briefcase behind. A briefcase full of information. The officer with me said, "We're going to Bangor right now." And we went down from the park—about ninety miles down the highway—and photocopied everything. It completely changed things. It reaffirmed what we were thinking—that this would be a hidden burial site.

Once we got to read some of the stuff that they were writing in their diaries, including their day-to-day observations recording the terrible way that baby Samuel had died, and how meticulous they were and how they documented everything, we were getting insight into how they were thinking. They were very into elaborate ritual and recorded everything that they were doing. We were certain, after that, that they had somehow recorded the details that would let them locate the burial site again, and in our assessment there would be a significant physical feature that they had used to identify that burial site.

We never told them we had seen their files. We just left the briefcase in Bangor.

In that initial phase, we only got to search intensely—dawn to dark warden intensity—for about a week, with smaller efforts going into December. Then we had to suspend our searches over the winter. Snow and cold made it impossible for the dogs to work because they worked on scenting the air, and frozen bodies don't give off scent. But in those early searches we covered over one hundred and thirty-five miles on foot and logged twelve hours of helicopter searching.

It was May before the conditions were finally good for resuming the search, before things had thawed enough to give off scent. As part of gearing up for that, as spring approached and we knew that we'd be going back out there to search more of the trail, Maine State Police detective Kenny MacMaster and I went down to Massachusetts and arranged to do interviews with some of the children. Kenny insisted that we do that, because—as we'd learned from those "borrowed" notes—some of the things the children had told the Massachusetts police didn't make sense to them, or weren't significant. What we learned, when we spoke to the children, made all the sense in the world to us.

One thing the children described was the preparations the burial party made, which included walking around with a compass and counting their steps. This confirmed for us what we had suspected all along—that the group would have chosen a specific feature, something significant, to mark the starting point where they departed from the trail, and that they would have recorded direction and their paced-off distance so they could find it again. It also affirmed that this was a very planned event, so the selection of the burial site, and, even more significantly, their actions to conceal it, would also have been very deliberate.

We weren't looking for a significant burial site that would be marked with crosses. We were looking for a carefully located and recorded burial site with a marker they could use to find it again, but that was disguised so that no one else would know it was there.

We learned that they had been gone overnight. That they had taken supplies, and carried the babies in wooden boxes lashed to carrying poles. That when they were picked up the following morning, the boxes and poles were gone. The boxes we could presume were buried; the poles might still be discernable.

On our previous searches, we had searched a lean-to near the head of Matagamon Lake, and found where they'd had a campfire. They were the only ones who were in the area at that time, so we knew that's probably where they spent the night.

As time and personnel resources allowed, we resumed our searches of the rest of the trail. There would be search after search after search until finally we reached the other end of the trail. Because of the terrain and the distances farther up the trail, we had to fly in with helicopters and we were landing in really small places. It was scary as hell, we were just nosing in on the corner of these little eddies on a brook, and we'd bail out with our dogs and go search.

We'd searched most of the trail without success—it was like looking for a needle in a haystack (I believe the park and its surrounding sparsely inhabited townships are about the size of Rhode Island)—for almost a year when we got word that one of the cult members, David

Corneau, who was the father of Jeremiah, the baby that died at birth, had agreed to talk with the police. His wife was pregnant, their other children had been taken away from them, and he was hoping they would be allowed to keep this baby, so he was trying to strike a deal.

Then I got a call that he was going to come to Millinocket. It was late at night—ten p.m. or later, before he finally arrived. We had everybody there—the Bristol County DA and some of the DA's investigators, Corneau, his lawyer, an investigator his lawyer brought along, Massachusetts State Police, and Maine State Police. Corneau had stated that he would only speak with one person. Everything rested on that interview. Then I got the word that I was chosen as the guy who would interview him. Just a podunk game warden from Greenville, Maine. No pressure on me, right?

But it worked out beautifully in the sense that anybody else who would have interviewed this guy—and I'm not talking about my skills or anything—he never would have spoken openly with them, because he hated law enforcement as a whole. But he had positive feelings about game wardens because back when he was on a scouting trip as a kid, he'd had contact with game wardens and he thought they were pretty cool.

It also made a big difference, of course, that I was so familiar with that area. When we sat down to talk, I had a topo map of that part of the park, and I set it in front of him and I said, "Can you show me where they are?" because he'd made this deal that he was going to cooperate.

He indicated the whole map, and he said, "It's here."

I said, "That isn't going to work," so I kept talking and talking, and finally, after about an hour and a half, I'd brought him around to trusting me, and understanding what we needed from him, and he put his finger on a specific spot. I think his version of cooperating with them, because of his animosity toward them, was to be as vague as possible and get what he wanted out of the deal but make everybody have to work a lot harder. That's why we started out with a circle the size of the park on the map and then I was able to get him to put his finger on the spot.

As I suspected, with all the pacing and everything the children had described happening, they had taken quite a few steps to do this. It wasn't just a spontaneous "let's go over here." They had thought it through. They had those two plywood boxes, and they lashed 'em to poles, and they carried them twelve miles, and they carried them overnight; that's what the children told us. And they (the children) were left there in the vehicles when they dropped them off—they did this at night—and the children were there when the vehicle came back to pick up the burial party in the morning. So we knew that they'd been gone a night's worth. But again, we had this whole question of how far can you go, especially at night when people's perceptions of distance are distorted, and you're talking solid wilderness and you're looking for something the size of a cushion.

Now I've got a spot that he's indicated, and I'm looking for the details of how we're going to find it. In my mind's eye, I was thinking, *There's got to be a marker. There's got to be a marker.* I was right in my assumption. What ended up being their marker was this big flat rock in the middle of the trail, as big as a table. They had measured off of that.

But what they had really used, I discovered, was the sound of the waterfall. Matagamon Falls. That was their indicator. They had teed off that. They started from that rock in the trail and went as far as they could hear the falls and ended up right on a knoll. If they'd gone down the backside of that knoll, they couldn't hear the falls, you could only hear the falls from the top, and so that was as far as they dared go. I knew they wouldn't randomly strike off; they'd have to have something to use as reference to come back. I was thinking a physical feature, I wasn't thinking sound. It ended up being two things: that rock and the sound of the falls.

What he had told me exactly dovetailed with what the children told me about them going out with a compass and counting their steps, details the Massachusetts State Police had failed to share. It was irrelevant to them, but it was significant to us. They had had a specific place that they would come to, a marker—and they'd paced off from there.

Corneau described it to me. They took a compass line, and they went from point A (the rock) and they paced so many paces to a big tree, and then they paced over to another big pine tree, and that's where they buried them. It was just a little pine hummock, with that big pine on it, and they buried them at the base of that big pine. But they always stayed within earshot of the falls. Once we talked about the falls, it made all the sense in the world. He'd gone there as a kid, as a boy scout, and they'd canoed up this lake, and they'd stopped and swam in the falls here. That was the connection to the area and why they'd chosen it.

The reason he was late coming to this meeting, was that they (the four who'd buried the babies) had hidden the compass bearings and the directions to where the bodies were somewhere in the park, written on a piece of paper. He had spent the day looking for it, and couldn't find it.

I was beyond nervous going into that interview. A year of work. The horrible death of little Samuel, and a homicide investigation hanging on this. A roomful of bigwigs and experienced police detectives. I remember saying all that to Kenny MacMaster, and Kenny told me to go ahead, I'd be fine. He looked at me and he said, "It's gotta be you, you know every inch of that place now."

And I said: "Yeah, but this is the million-dollar question."

He said, "You're good. You'll do it. You'll be fine."

I was really stressing out; it was pretty unnerving for me, a major big deal interview and a whole room full of people waiting for me to get the answer. I knew what was riding on this. I'd read the diaries. I knew what these people had done. I'd testified before the grand jury about the search operation we'd conducted. I knew how much finding these babies meant to Paul Walsh, the DA and his investigators, and to the Massachusetts State Police.

And the thing was, if Corneau had sat down with them, it wouldn't have been meaningful. It had to be me, or it had to be a warden, someone who'd been on the ground and who knew that terrain and who knew the questions to ask. Someone who knew the locators. And second of all, it helped to have a warden's expertise to sit with a map like we did, and keep working him through the story until he finally came up with the data that was relevant. The waterfall. The compass bearings. The pine knoll. I had to be patient, and persistent. It took a long time to get to the point where he actually gave me a location. But I understood his process—the pacing, the compass bearings, the way they'd prepared. The importance of using a marker as a starting point.

What made the interview go well was that, because I knew the area so well as a result of our searches, I could describe things, like the lean-to where they'd spent the night, and the nature of the trail and the terrain. Never mind the fact that he absolutely hated police but he didn't view game wardens as police. He actually said that to me. "I wouldn't of told those guys, because I hate them with a passion, but you guys, you're all right." So we had a different rapport that allowed us to have this conversation. And when he finally put his finger down on the map, he was—boom!—right on the spot.

I came out of that room, where I'd been talking with this guy for hours, and I said, "I know where we're going, I've got the spot."

They're all waiting for me. The prosecutor, Walsh. A couple detectives from the Massachusetts State Police, Kenny MacMaster, MSP Sergeant Coleman. And I believe there was a detective from Attleboro. That was on October 23, 2000, almost a year from that first phone call asking for our help.

The following day, we went out to the park to see if we could recover the babies.

Somehow, the press had gotten wind of the fact that we were going out that day to look for those babies. The phones were ringing off the hook. I always suspected it was his attorneys who'd leaked it, since the calls started before he even got to Maine. I knew, from the media presence during our previous searches, that it was going to be crazy out there by the park gate. After talking with him all that time, I also knew he was the type of person—very quiet, reserved, a very shy person—that this thing was going to spin him emotionally and he was going to shut down and stop cooperating. My sense, all along, was that at any moment he might stop cooperating. He was really struggling with cooperating with the police when he bore so much animosity toward them.

I've dealt with a lot of people like that over the years, and I knew we had to keep it quiet and calm. We still needed him when we got there to help with the details, where the marker was, how many paces, and in which direction. We had the key but we hadn't opened the door yet. Didn't even know where the lock was, because he might not be right in what he was telling me. He'd given me a dot on the map, but did he really know? So I knew we couldn't bring him in through the gate.

Right there, in the middle of the night, we started planning how the op would go in the morning. I was on the phone with Pat Dorian as soon as I got out of that interview, explaining to him that we had to fly Corneau in because he'd shut down if he had to go through that gauntlet. I mean, I had never seen so much media in my life as I saw there.

We drove to Millinocket. Our pilot picked up me and David Corneau, his lawyer, and another guy, in a float plane and flew us from there to the head of Matagamon Lake, while the others drove in through the media frenzy at the gate. His attorney was adamant that it would just be me flying in with them. It was a complicated event, you understand. An awful lot of people wanted a piece of it—Massachusetts investigators, Paul Walsh, the DA, Maine State Police, crime scene investigators, our medical examiner Dr. David. I'd made arrangements that they would all show up at the gate, and they all had to be taken up the lake from the parking lot by plane because it was twelve miles up the trail. We had so many people involved we had two planes going back and forth that day.

Some of the others were already up at the head of the lake, waiting on the shore when we arrived, and they stayed there while we—David Corneau and I, and his attorney's investigator—went on ahead. We went about half a mile up the trail from the lean-to. When we got to the big flat rock in the trail that they'd used as their marker—it was about three feet in diameter—he took his compass bearing, and he paced and counted his steps to a big pine tree, then he reset his compass, took another bearing, and paced so many steps to this berm on a white pine knoll.

He indicated a big, big pine tree, and he said, "They're buried right there."

I suspect, though I don't know this for a fact, that after we had our meeting, he went back to look for that note. I think he had it that morning, because he wasn't struggling. But I think he remembered it visually as well. These were huge pine trees that were pretty obvious. And he went to the first one, boom, to the second one, boom. Once we had the site, I called in the GPS coordinates, and then everybody started to come in to work the scene.

As I'd suspected, looking at that site, there was nothing to the naked eye that would tell you there was anything there. They'd disguised it well. They'd replaced the pine needles, replaced everything, even dropped a couple dead trees over the top of the site. There were only two things, visually, that you could see if you understood their significance—those poles they'd lashed the boxes to, which were discarded off to one side, and, because they were farmers, every time they hit a rock when they were digging, they threw the rock off to one side, so the rocks were sitting on top of the leaf litter instead of underneath it. There were probably eight or nine rocks thrown off to the side. It was extremely subtle. You had to know the woods real well to spot those things. To know that the rocks wouldn't be on top of the litter and that the poles were abnormal, because they were poles, they weren't just some branches lying there.

This had been a long time coming. There was quite a crowd up there, everyone eager to get started, but no one could dig until the medical examiner, Dr. David, got there. He was coming from Bangor. He was on the third plane trip over. When he got there, he said, "We are not going to dig one shovelful until a K-9 confirms that there are bodies there." So then they had to go and fly Reba in. Adam Gormely, another warden, went to my house and picked up Reba and flew her from Greenville headquarters to Matagamon Lake. Like so many things about this case, that was a departure—both for Reba to be with another warden, and for her to be in a plane.

They flew her in, and she confirmed it. Not an easy job for a cadaver dog. Not much of a scent pool for a small baby, and, as we later learned, when they were unwrapped at the ME's office, they were wrapped in blankets in a basket in a plastic garbage bag in the plywood box. They were buried about four feet deep, which is pretty deep for a wilderness burial site.

While all the digging was going on—a careful, methodical forensic exhumation—supervised by Dr. David from the ME's office, and conducted by a team of Maine State Police and Massachusetts State Police evidence techs and detectives, David Corneau had pretty much been discarded. He and I had moved away from the center of activity.

We were sitting on a log and talking. Just talking. I could sense from him the total anguish he was feeling from the loss of his child. It's hard to describe, but watching him sitting there, while they were digging up his baby, it was like watching a bunch of wolves take down a fawn. From my perspective, watching his private grief and awareness was very intrusive. On my side it was great, it was exciting, watching a year of work come to a close, but at that point, sitting with him, I was in his bubble. I could feel what he was feeling, seeing that whole thing going on. It was very invasive for him.

He and I were just having a quiet conversation and there was one of those defining moments when the weather seemed to match the circumstances. It had been a real cloudy day and it was at that point—where the impact of these events was hitting him—that I recognized the sun had finally come out and it was really getting nice. That weather change mirrored the significance of the day, where clarity was coming for us on the investigative side.

For him, also, there was clarity about this thing, what it was about, and what it meant to the rest of the world. His view of it had been skewed by the cult and their ways of thinking. Now, as this exhumation was happening, the veil was starting to lift away from him and he was able to see it. He'd been pulled down a road into the whole cult belief thing, and all of a sudden, watching them digging up those babies, he was seeing the end result of it.

Kind of a collision of views. There's the perspective of the world, vis-à-vis him, this cult, and those two dead babies, and the reasons for the investigation. My sense, from watching him, was that he had kept himself from realizing all of it all that time, and now it was finally hitting him. It was a very emotional moment for him. He was right on the verge of breaking down.

At that point, in my mind, the investigation was over. Now, in hindsight, for a really good investigator, that would have been the opportunity to get a lot of good information, but we were all so emotionally invested that we were only focused on finding those babies and getting them out of the ground. After the weight of a whole year of searching was lifted, everybody was kind of in a "now we get to breathe a little easier" mode. Except for him. He went in reverse. He'd been calm in his world and now it had flipped. He was going downhill when everybody else was going uphill.

He was sitting there on the log, and right at the moment when they were getting to the top of the boxes, they were probably only twenty yards away, remorse was starting to come into him, and he said, "Am I really such a monster?"

I could see he was asking a whole lot of God questions in his mind. Then he made a comment about faith. I'm trying to think how he said that—it had to do with that monster statement. And it kind of referenced, I think, how he realized that his belief system was really screwed up. As that veil was starting to lift, it was bringing his entire faith system into question.

We didn't exchange a lot of words. I said, "Well, you know, there is somebody up there," and I said, "You're going to get through this." And that was kinda all. It's not typical for guys to have that connection, you know what I mean, but we had that connection for that minute. I could sense what he was feeling and he could sense where I was, and twenty yards away, all of these people were digging up the coffins of these babies.

Once the babies were out of the ground, and those makeshift coffins were put in body bags, they were flown back down the lake to the parking lot and we moved on to the next crisis. Massachusetts State Police were under the assumption that we'd take those two boxes, put them on a plane, fly them down the lake to the parking lot, hand them over, and away they would go to Massachusetts. Then the Maine medical examiners' office and Maine State Police said no, these are bodies in Maine, they go to our facility, this is our investigation, cause of death is *our* responsibility. The Massachusetts police insisted that they *knew* they died in Massachusetts.

There was some serious banging of heads.

The digging was done by a coalition of Massachusetts and Maine police. Everyone was doing the exhumation, but no one had discussed what happened next. So they off-loaded those bodies and the discussion began. When they were taking them out of the airplane after they flew 'em back to the end of the lake, to Trout Brook, that's when Massachusetts State Police said, "We'll take 'em from here, we'll make arrangements."

It wasn't so much a battle between Maine State Police and Massachusetts State Police as it was between Dr. David, from the medical examiner's office, and Paul Walsh, the Bristol County DA. There was twisting and grinding going on. But the medical examiner's van was there waiting to take them right to the crime lab, and in the end, that's where they went. Which turned out—forensically—to be a very good result.

Because they went to the Maine medical examiner's office, Dr. Marcella Sorg ended up being involved—she's the forensic anthropologist who works with the ME's office, and she's the expert on bones. Her role turned out to be absolutely critical to this case. She could testify about the lack of development in the bones and certain aspects of development, how Sam's bones were developing normally and all of sudden they went into this stage where it was obvious that they weren't getting any nutrients or anything. She's an absolutely sweet lady. She's one of the best.

So, in hindsight, considering the collision between the agencies over custody of the bodies, they couldn't have had a better result. Dr. Sorg's a world-renowned expert. She's been all over the world working on mass grave sites and genocides, she has expertise in bones, and that's what they needed to show that this child had been starved to death. She was a star witness when the case went to trial.

In the end, Samuel's father, Jacques Robidoux, was convicted of first degree murder for starving him to death. A good result. And some of the other cult members got lesser convictions.

But in the short term, the day had kind of a funny ending.

After everything was done, after we'd exhumed the bodies and they'd been taken off to the medical examiner's office, we all went to Millinocket to have dinner. The group included Paul Walsh, the district attorney from down in Massachusetts. He seemed to consider himself to be a pretty important person. We were all at this restaurant, and he was getting up and giving the congratulations, and you know, doing this team rah rah thing, which isn't game warden-style. Wardens are quiet about our achievements. We just do our thing and then we go home. Anyway, he was trying to make it like a political statement, and while this was going on, this sweet little French lady was trying to get things ready for our dinner. She was making some noise, and he kinda snapped at her.

A little later on, after the meal was over, she came over with this contraption, all these tubes and stuff, and it went all around and it went a bunch of ways and it kinda ended up right in front of you. She said to him, "Would you like to try our moose call? This is moose country, and everybody that comes here needs to try the moose call." I'd seen it before, and a couple other people caught on to what it was.

Well, he blew, and it went poof, and white flour came out of that thing and his face was all white. She just walked away, and we were rolling on the ground, laughing. She got him back so perfectly. It was unbelievable.

PART VII

DANGERS AND MYSTERIES OF THE WARDEN SERVICE

CHAPTER TWENTY

Outlaws, Boat Crashes, and a Wild West Shootout

Working in the world that I did, where everyone carried guns—not just hunters, but snowmobilers, and boaters, and even people out for a hike—I got used to watching the gun, reading people's body language, doing the assessments that I was trained to do and planning strategies for handling things if they went wrong. But sometimes, the danger was a lot more serious—palpable—and I'd find myself in situations that spun out of control really fast.

Just down the road from my house, right in the middle of Route 15, coming into Greenville, I got into a knock-down drag-out fight one night with two very drunk members of the Iron Horsemen motorcycle gang. It was December. Dark. My friend Jim Turner had just dropped my daughter off after a birthday party, and we were talking in the doorway when we heard a vehicle up on the road, tires screeching. It sounded like it had gone off the road, so we decided to go up and see.

I was in uniform because I'd just had a call from a lady about a raccoon that was causing problems, and my boys loved to help me catch things like raccoons and stuff, so they jumped in the truck with me. I got up to the end of the road, and looking down the hill about two hundred yards, I could see there was debris like clothing and shoes and beer bottles all over the road, and there was a truck crossways in the middle of the road with a blue bubble light flashing on the dashboard. I didn't recognize the vehicle as any of the locals, so I pulled out onto the highway, parked, and started walking down the road to check it out.

There were two guys out of the truck, trying to pick up a tractor trailer tire that had flipped out into the road, and as I approached, I heard one of them saying, "Someone's coming, let's get out of here."

Typical game warden, we don't walk with a flashlight on, it's just a habit we have, so I was really close to them before they realized I was there. They both scrambled to get into the vehicle to leave. Something was wrong with the whole scenario, so I sped up, got to the driver's door, put my flashlight on and told them to hold it. I did a quick visual check for weapons—something that's as natural as breathing. Then I did what we're trained never to do: they were trying to drive away, and I suspected the driver was drunk, so I stuck my hand in through the open driver's window and snapped the keys right out of the truck.

Then I got the driver out and walked him to the back of the vehicle. I was trying to get his ID, and he was so drunk he had no finger dexterity at all. That's one of the first clues to impairment—the inability to use fine motor skills. He was pawing at his wallet, trying to get his driver's license out, and all of a sudden, the passenger also exited the vehicle. He was about 6' 2" or 6' 3" and between three hundred fifty and four hundred pounds, an absolute mountain of man, a biker dude who came right after me, screaming, "Fish pig!"

Meanwhile, my friend Jim, who'd come out ahead of me, was picking stuff out of the road. He heard the hollering start and he came down to me. I was thinking this was not going to go well. My boys were still sitting in the truck, seeing all this, so I told Jim to go up and send them home.

By this time, another friend, Otis Gray, a forest ranger who lived on the other side of the dip, had heard the same thing—screeching tires and things crashing onto the road—so he came down. Now there were two of us, and we had to deal with Godzilla and this other drunk guy, the driver. I put the passenger up against the guardrail, gave Otis my can of Mace, and I said, "If he gets off the guardrail, put him down." Then I—dumb move—put myself between the driver and Godzilla just as the driver went into a drunken defiance thing and said, "Hell no, I'm not giving you my license."

Then I really started talking loud to him, trying to get him focused and compliant, and while I was working on that, the big guy, Godzilla, jumped up and came after me. When I turned to face him, the driver came up behind me, grabbed my coat, and pulled it down, trapping my arms. It's a trick hockey players use that acted like a straight jacket. Now things were really bad. I couldn't use my arms. I knew he had a knife on his hip, I'd spotted it when he got out of the truck, and I knew I needed to get it secured as soon as I could get him cuffed. My gun was exposed. I had my flashlight in my hand and I couldn't drop it to wrestle my way out of the jacket because it could be used against me. I couldn't use my sidearm, because I couldn't see much in the dark so I had no idea where my friend was. If things got worse and I put a couple bullets in the big guy, they were gonna go right through.

A million things started going through my mind as I triaged possibilities. Everything in slow motion. I was flashing back to an exercise at the Academy. One night they took us out and told us to watch a car for violations. A beer can was thrown out the window. They told us to deal with it and when I got to the driver's door, he shot me in the chest as he opened the door. I remember that inhale of my breath and the end of the gun barrel discharging at me. And how everything stopped. Time and space went into super slow motion.

I took my flashlight and I hit the driver in the groin as hard as I could. He didn't go down. I hit him in the stomach, drove it right in. But I couldn't get much power behind it. Confined by my jacket, I had limited arm movement. He had me in a bad spot. Finally, I did a semi-spin and got enough momentum to get my arm free. He kind of rolled back, and I cracked him on the side of the head with my Mag-Lite, because this thing had to end now. As far as I was concerned, I was in a deadly force scenario. So I knocked him down. He hit the ground on the yellow line.

Now, the driver was down but the big guy was just winding up. What made it worse was I couldn't call for backup. All our cell towers for our radio communication were powered by solar panels. We'd had two weeks of really miserable weather and I couldn't get out with the radio.

So it's me, Godzilla, my friend Jim, the plumber, and Otis from forestry. I've got the driver in an arm bar, I've got him on the ground and I'm trying to put handcuffs on him. It's clear this guy has been arrested multiple times, and he puts his second arm out, so I can't pull it in. I can literally feel the tendons in his wrist starting to go. I'm on him with everything I have, but the guy's about twice my size and I'm getting zero pain compliance because he's so intoxicated he's not feeling it. So I was on the ground with this guy, and my friend, Otis, the forest ranger, was keeping the big guy back, and the big guy was starting to go at it with him. So Jim scooped the driver's arm up, helped me get the handcuffs on.

We're all out in the middle of the road in the dark. Now I've got this guy cuffed, literally lying on the yellow line, and he was bleeding like crazy from a big split on his head. And the instant I got that second handcuff on, the big guy went berserk. And I mean berserk. He totally lost it. He's literally chasing me down. This man is huge. Huge. He could squish me like a bug. Then this other forest ranger came driving by and we hollered to him, "Call the sheriff's office on the phone NOW. We need help."

We were in a stand-off with this big guy. We weren't going to try to take him, because we couldn't contain him if we did. I'd only had that one set of cuffs. He was stomping around like *T. rex*, trying to find the keys, and every once in a while, he'd come after us. We'd sprayed him with mace, that old-style mace from back before pepper spray. The trouble with that stuff was, if you sprayed someone who was drunk, it only made them madder.

Finally, it seemed like days—DAYS—or the longest half hour in the history of the world, before we saw blue lights and two sheriff's officers came over the hill. It took two sets of handcuffs, hooked across, to secure this guy. The whole time, these guys were threatening me and my family. They were going to burn my house. Kill my kids. Just oozing total poison. And I was covered with this guy's blood, from our little dance around. Finally, they hauled them off to jail and I went home.

I got cleaned up, and I headed for the sheriff's office, which is where I learned about these guys. About the Iron Horsemen thing. They were truck drivers, which was why they were so concerned about an OUI. Of course, when I got down there to do the paperwork, they were already gone. Turned out Godzilla's wife worked for the bail bondsman, so he bailed the guy for free. No conditions. No anything. They'd just cut these guys loose.

I had a conversation with the bail bondsman. I told him, "Look, these guys have threatened my family and threatened to burn my home, and I can tell you they mean it, because these are really bad guys. And I can tell you right now, if they come near my home, they're leaving in a body bag, and it's your fault, because they're mad drunks right now and you cut them loose."

That next morning, these same two guys, Henry Kidd and Tucker Jacobs, landed at my neighbor's house, asking questions. Which house was mine, what time did I leave to go to work, and stuff about my family. My neighbor didn't know what had happened, and not having a law enforcement mindset, he didn't connect the dots. It was a very challenging time. If you look at the history of these motorcycle guys, they are not nice people and they don't like to be crossed.

It really affected my family. We took that threat very seriously. We rehearsed strategies for what to do if strangers came to the door, and spent that whole Christmas season with a loaded shotgun by the door. But we survived it.

After it went to trial, the defense attorney came up to me, and he said, "If it's any consolation to you, you did a really good job testifying, and my client has his toothbrush in his back pocket and he's kinda figuring he was headed to jail."

Another time, we got a call about a bunch of drunken guys riding around in a boat on Moosehead Lake. The informant was evidently someone who'd gotten into some kind of fight with these guys. So this person called and said these guys had launched their boat from the forestry service ramp on the other side of the lake, and they were coming in, drunk as skunks. So we went down there and waited, and sure enough, when they pulled in, they were exactly that: very drunk. The driver was completely pickled. So we had to deal with him.

At the time, we were using breath kits. We were dealing with the operator, taking him through the testing process, and the other two gentlemen were pulling the boat out of the water and loading it onto the trailer. If I remember, one of them was sober enough to drive. So that process was happening while we were processing the drunk.

We were all standing by the boat as it came out of the water, and all of a sudden, in the middle of a conversation, the drunk spins around, flips open the dash of the boat, and reached for something. Instinctively, I knew that he was not going for the registration, so I grabbed his arm and put him in an arm bar, right away, pinning him so he couldn't move, and spun him away. Once he was subdued, I checked. There was a loaded .45 there, and he was going for it.

If he'd actually gotten his hands on it, he would have gotten shot and killed, probably. Or one of us would have. But he never made it that far. We knew exactly what he was going to do. He never made a verbal threat or anything, but we knew from his body language and everything else. That was a close one. It came within seconds of being a very bad situation. He was just drunk and stupid.

Guns weren't the only dangerous aspect of my world. Having Moosehead Lake in the territory, I got called out on some really dangerous things, like going out on the lake in a thunder and lighting storm and high, high winds, going on a search for a missing boater. In those cases, the person sitting at home, like my wife, Jolyne, has all the anxiety, because I'm out there doing my job and I'm so busy I don't have time to think about whether it's scary. But I've been on some rescues out on the lake so harrowing that when I got out of the boat at the end, I kissed the ground, because I figured I was never going to make it back.

Just to give you a sense of its size, Moosehead is about forty miles long and ten miles wide, and has over four hundred miles of shoreline. Any search on the lake is a big undertaking.

Like this one night. Another warden, Tom Ward, and I went up the lake, in the dark, in a Boston Whaler because someone had seen distress flares. It was a terrible night, thunder, lightning, high winds. We had to turn all our lights off, going up the lake so that we could see the horizon, so we were running in the dark. I had to wrap my arm around the bar on the windshield, just so I could stay in the boat. We were going down so deep between the waves that it was like being on the ocean, and the water was coming over the sides. We got about halfway up the lake, where there's a marker buoy, and as we came by, I put the flashlight out to light it up. After we'd bounced and thrashed for about another ten minutes, I ran the light out again, and there was that same buoy. We hadn't moved an inch, which meant we had to throttle up more, which meant we were going to bounce more. Oh, my word.

We finally made it up to Sugar Island and we saw some activity at the camp on the island, so we pulled in and asked if they'd seen any rescue flares. They promptly admitted that it was fireworks that they'd been setting off. We'd risked our lives because they were playing with illegal fireworks.

We couldn't come back down the lake, and we couldn't turn around because we'd get swamped, so we pulled into the state park and called down to headquarters and had someone drive up and get us.

Another time, we had a couple with a baby who had rented a boat and never came back. It was the same conditions—we had a huge thunderstorm, and we were running up the lake in our Whaler again, trying to find 'em. When we finally found them, it turned out they'd run the boat out of fuel. They were the most negligent parents I'd ever seen. They had this big hambone that they'd stuck in the corner of the windshield, and they were eating off that. The baby was poorly dressed, and sunburned, dirty diaper to the nth degree. We put them in our boat and gave them some blankets and then towed their boat in. We ended up calling Department of Health and Human Services with our concerns about that baby, because everything they did was totally delinquent. We were really lucky we ran into them, because we didn't know where they were, and we didn't have the radar systems that we have now.

Like so much of the real estate we deal with, Moosehead Lake is just a very dangerous piece of water. It's not just storms, either. It can get really foggy out on the lake. We had one night, it was in August, a bunch of teenagers, two boats, six or seven kids in one of them, had gone out on the lake, partying, and the fog had come in. Coming back to Greenville, they were lost. Despite the fog, though, they were going full throttle down the lake and they hit a rock.

They all went flying.

The driver of the boat went into the console and ended up seriously damaging his eye socket. One of the girls sitting in the front of the boat slammed up against the rock and broke her leg and her hip.

The boat split just like a peanut shell, broke right in two. Now they're all loaded into the other boat, they're lost in the thick fog, and they start calling for help. The best they could tell the wardens was that they'd just run into a rock, but there are many rocks in the lake.

So we go out in a brand new boat that has a radar system. We'd just gotten that boat, we'd had it maybe two days, and we'd never had a boat with a radar system on it before. We're out there, and the fire department's out there, we're all out there trying to find these kids.

Joel Wilkinson, who's now the colonel, was running the boat. He flipped on the radar, and I looked at it, and there was another boat, the fire department boat, coming at us full speed. We turned on all our lights and started hollering. If we hadn't had that radar, they would have run right into us for sure.

Finally, the kids popped up on the shore, at a camp, and we went there and dealt with it. Got the injured ones into ambulances and sent them off to Greenville. They were all underage kids and they'd been drinking. It was a mess. And driving back into town, I couldn't see to the next telephone pole.

Really. You just never know where it's going to come from. Things can go from everyday to life-threatening in a heartbeat. Talk about dangerous things that happen completely out of the blue. One day I was working fishermen on Brown Pond. I was on the backside of the pond, and there were some guys camping there, and I was just waiting for them to start fishing, and watching to see what they were going to do, and all of a sudden a guy at the camp grabbed his .357 revolver and shot it right in my direction. I heard the bullet whiz right by me. He wasn't shooting at me. He had no idea that I was there; I was in camo, and it's like HOLY MOLY! He fired a few more rounds, and by that time, I was scrambling to get out of there. So I came around, and I checked 'em, and I said, "What were you shooting at?"

And he said, "Oh, I just wanted to try my gun. I wasn't really shooting at anything."

And I said, "Right, well you were shooting at me. You almost killed a game warden today. Do you think it's a good idea to randomly just start shooting around the pond? Did you know there are three different trails that come into this pond? There could be people on any side of this thing. Do you have any idea how dangerous what you were doing was?"

And he said, "Oh. I'm sorry."

Such an idiot. A total idiot. Comes with the territory. I've checked guys where it made 'em so nervous they accidentally discharged their gun, fumbling to unload it. They get all nerved up and they pull the trigger and the gun goes off. That makes for a very interesting introduction. I'll say, "Why don't you hand me that? I'll hold it. Why don't you just catch your breath and breathe for a minute." Yeah.

The shootout in Brighton was like something from the wild west. I was in charge of this operation, so I didn't exchange gunfire. This whole thing started in Beaver Cove, north of Greenville. The guy's name, as I remember it, was Linwood Stewart. He had recently been convicted of a whole series of camp break-ins, I think it was eighty, and the judge sentenced him to something like six years in prison, and gave him two weeks to get his affairs in order before going away.

So they cut him loose, and Mr. Stewart decided that jail wasn't going to happen. He took off, and he started doing what he knew best. He went up to the Greenville area and started breaking into camps and stealing stuff. He was basically on the run. He'd also gone to New York

State to visit a family member, and gotten a speeding ticket on his way back, so police had a little information about his movements.

He wasn't alone. He was riding around with his girlfriend and her two children. They were going around breaking into camps when he hit a rock with his old beater car, broke his oil pan, and lost all the oil in the car.

He managed to get the car to Beaver Cove. It was at night. He went to a house in Beaver Cove, knocked on the door, said his car had broken down, could he use the phone. So, typical good Maine people, they let him in. He pulled out a gun, and demanded their car keys. His victims called the police, and the manhunt was on.

He took their Ford Ranger truck, picked up the girlfriend and the kids, and off they went, heading for Brighton, which is between Skowhegan and Greenville.

And the reason he headed to Brighton was that he had friends in that area.

I don't know how, but he got from Beaver Cove down to that country without getting caught. The search went on for about a week. It was getting into late August. Bear season was about to begin. They were having no luck finding this guy. And my Maine State Police detective chum Kenny MacMaster called me.

By this time, we had organized a whole lot of searches, for bodies and other things, worked together a lot, so when he called me, he said, "Do you think you guys could come down and organize this thing?" By "this thing" he meant helping to organize a search for this guy.

What they wanted us to do was organize search parties and bring a mobile command post down, so we'd have radio contact with everybody, and make a plan to catch this guy. I had to call the colonel to get permission (Tim Peabody at that time), and he said we could go, but that it would have to be a joint operation with the Somerset County Sheriff's office and Piscataquis County Sheriff's office, and Maine State Police. Everybody was to be an equal participant. We were not doing this alone.

I was trying to come up with a game plan. Knowing his MO, there are all these camps in the area, and we figured that he would be most likely tucked into a camp somewhere, collecting stuff as he went.

We got there early in the morning and we assigned teams. A major consideration of organizing this thing was safety. We anticipated that all of these camps were full of guns, so he would have access to plenty of firepower. We already knew that he'd told people that he would not be taken alive, and that if they were in a situation where they would get caught, he would kill everybody and then kill himself. So we had to anticipate how our teams might pull into a camp yard safely when we knew he might have a rifle and had no compunction about pulling guns on people.

My theory was that we couldn't sneak through the woods and go from camp to camp, because he would have the advantage and that would put our people at risk. My plan for sending out teams was to put two people in the back of a truck, with long guns, so that if they pulled into a camp and started taking fire, they could return fire and back themselves out of there. So we were sending out teams of three.

As we were sending teams out the door, an investigator for Somerset County Sheriff's Office came in. He had a lot of informants in the area, and he said, "I've got information. On this side road down here, in Brighton, there's a very suspicious campsite that looks like where these people might be hiding out. Kids, clothes, and a pile of fir boughs that might be used for covering a vehicle to hide it from the air."

So I sent a team in there. Kenny was one, Scott Thrasher (a warden), and two Piscataquis sheriff's deputies. They went into this area and they found the campsite, and there were fresh signs of food, some signs of kids being there.

As they were checking things out, the Ford Ranger pick-up pulled in. It had been spray-painted camo.

Everybody saw each other, and the chase was on. The guy whipped around and took off, and the officers in their vehicle were chasing them. They were calling on the radio that they were in pursuit. I was in the command post. What we had organized ahead of time was that as soon as we made contact with them, the MSP tactical team was going to deal with them from there. Our job was just to find them.

So, I was on the phone with the state police tactical team leader while this thing was flying down the road. The Piscataquis officers in the truck knew that he'd made threats against the children. So the Piscataquis deputy chief made the decision to take out the tires on the truck right away and not give him time to act against the children. They fired at the tires, but they were not successful.

The vehicle went around a corner, went off the road, and ended up in a ditch on its side.

The team that was chasing them pulled up and called for an ambulance. The driver of the Ranger crawled out the passenger side of the truck and started shooting at the officers. The first shot went through the driver's window, hit the back window, and went right between the two officers who were standing in the back of the truck. The next round glanced right off the roof of the pick-up and went off to the left.

Kenny called the command post and said, "We are going to need a helicopter." I didn't know why he needed this, but everyone was very excited. They were yelling, "We're taking fire." And once this went out over the radio, everyone heard it, and then everyone was on the radio, jamming it up, making it more and more difficult by the second to communicate. It was time for the dispatcher to call a Signal 1000, which locks everyone off the air except those directly involved in the incident.

By this point, after several shots, the officers had taken cover, and the guy got the woman and the kids out and they're traveling along the ditch. Periodically, he would pop up into the road and shoot at the officers.

Just ahead, there was an intersection, and we had no idea which way they went, right or left, up or down this road. Meanwhile, this event was happening right there in the road, with the potential risk of people driving into this area and maybe coming right up on this guy. I didn't want people getting shot, so I was trying to get everyone to stop, until we knew where he was.

I had about four wardens on the ground close to that area, and despite the general radio chaos, I could communicate with my people on our own frequencies, so I told them to set up roadblocks back away down the road, so we'd have containment and could stop people driving into the area.

After about ten or fifteen minutes—though it felt like forever—a guy in a gravel truck came from a side road inside the roadblocked area just bebopping along right through the middle of this thing. He stopped by one of my wardens, and he said, "Hey, are you looking for somebody? Because there's a guy hiding in the woods up on the hill here, just a little ways up on the hill, and he ran into the woods as soon as he saw me. Looked like a woman and two kids and this guy."

Now we knew where he was, so I moved everything in closer. He had a powerline right of way behind him, which was a great escape route. And he'd grown up in the area, so he knew it well. I was thinking, if this goes on too long, he's going to leave the woman and kids behind because they'll be too much of a drag on him.

I got in touch with the state police sergeant, who was in charge of the tactical team, and I said, "Sir, this thing is officially under your command."

"No problem," he said. And I handed off the mess.

Within minutes, the tactical team leader pulled into the scene. He could see the two checkpoints. And as he pulled in, the guy came out of the woods with the little boy tucked under his arm, and stopped in the road. He fired in one direction, then turned and fired in the other direction, then ran back into the woods.

This team leader was also a sniper. So he moved the teams to the side, where they wouldn't get shot, and he tucked in, and he waited, and sure enough, Stewart came back out again, fired one way, and when he turned to fire the other way, the kid was tucked off to the side. The sniper had a clear shot, and he shot the guy right through the ear.

The kid took off running down the road, and one of our guys picked him up.

When it was over, I got on the phone with the colonel, and I said, "I've got good news and bad news."

He said, "Give me the bad news first."

I said, "We've got a truck full of bullet holes, and one of our guys exchanged fire. When Stewart popped out of the truck and started shooting, Scott Thrasher returned fire. The good news is that it's over, the guy is dead, and we didn't do it, boss."

Then we had to secure and wait for the state police to arrive and do their investigation.

CHAPTER TWENTY-ONE

Banana Man and the Rock Collector

Over the years I've been driving these roads, I'm always on the lookout for people acting strangely, for suspicious activity, for vegetation that's been disturbed and places people have been that maybe they shouldn't. It's a habit that's become as natural as breathing. Stopping to check parked cars, to see if someone's in trouble, I've run into a lot of strange people. Just like we call it "the lemming point" because people wander off into the wilderness here, it's also a place where people kind of "wash up," by accident or on purpose. And with law enforcement thin on the ground up here, people tend to call the wardens when something is strange.

This particular story goes under the heading, I guess, of "unusually creepy." I was coming down the road to where there's a gatehouse that's a checkpoint for one of the lumber companies, and the gate attendant told me there was a brand new car parked on one of the little side roads just before the gate. Brand new car, with ten-day New Hampshire plates on it, backed right into the alders. She said, "I don't know where it came from. I've been here all day. And it wasn't here yesterday."

There are always concerns when a car is parked like that for so long. We worry that the subject might have committed suicide, or it's a stolen vehicle, or the person has gotten lost. So I went down the road. I had Rader with me, so I left him in the truck. I looked around a little bit and didn't see anything, so I called another warden who was working nearby, told him what was going on, and asked him to come over.

I took Rader out, put him on the road, and told him to track. We're going down the road, and all of a sudden Rader pops off the road, and there's the guy. He's just standing there. He's tall and thin, with a gaunt face and short hair, a very nervous type of person. He's got a little daypack with him, and he goes, "Oh, yeah, yeah, I was just hiking on the other side of the little ridge here, and I was just checking things out, and everything's fine."

I'm listening to this and my spidey sense is going. By the time we've walked back to his car, where I've got my truck, Dan Carroll, the other warden, is there, and he says, "We need to discuss the marijuana you have right on the center console of your car."

The guy had this funny look on his face, and Dan said, "See that joint sitting right there?" The guy unlocked the car and got the marijuana out, and Dan said, "So, do you have any more?"

The guy says, "Yeah, I've got some in my pack." He hands me the pack, and I set it on the hood, and I open it, and there's a piece of wood, like a cut-off piece of broom handle, about six or seven inches long, with some black tape where it was cut off. And I ask, "What is this?"

And he goes, "It's just a piece of wood. It's just a piece of wood," and he's getting all freaked out. I'm thinking the only thing in the world that that would be used for would be to plug a shotgun, to not allow as many rounds to be loaded in the shotgun. It's about that size, and I'm looking at it and the bag of dope in there and I pluck it out. Now, we're going to search the vehicle, because by handing me the pack and my finding dope in there, he gave us probable cause to search the car.

Dan starts pawing around in the back seat of the car, and all of a sudden he comes up out of the car, and he's white as a ghost, and he whispers, "We've got to put on rubber gloves, right now." I ask why, and he whispers, "There's a blow-up doll in the back seat."

I said, "You're kidding." And he said, "NO. Look in that bag right there." I opened it up, and there she was. She was deflated. So we popped the trunk, and it was full of porn magazines and these weird things, with lubricants, and a light bulb came on, and I realized what I was just holding in my hand—it was NOT just a piece of wood. I turned just as green as grass.

This guy was obviously as twisted as they come. I ran to the truck and I got some hand sanitizer and I put on rubber gloves. And then I started wondering: what if this guy abducted a child or something? Obviously, there was something wrong with this person, the way he was acting. He was from New Hampshire, and that's what a child abductor would do—run to a place like this.

We were getting really concerned, so we started interrogating him, and he didn't want to talk to us because we'd just found out his big secret—he kept all that stuff in the car because he lived at home with his mother.

I'll never forget the look on Dan's face when he came out of the back seat and said, "Blowup doll. It's in the bag."

What we surmised was this—it was a really windy day, and at the end of that road there's an overlook. We kind of figured his first date blew away in the wind and he had to come back for his other doll. I did take the dog and search that whole area, just to make sure there wasn't a victim out there.

Moral of the story? It's never just a piece of wood.

Sometimes, no matter how hard you try, you can't do much to help people. The systems just aren't there. Like with "banana guy." I got a call in Kokadjo, mid-April, from a Plum Creek forester who had found a gentleman sleeping on a log pile in the middle of nowhere. You don't drive around on woods roads at that time of year because the frost is coming out of the roads and everything's breaking up.

This gentleman told the forester that his car had been stolen, which doesn't happen too often up there. So I scooted up to the little Kokadjo trading post, where he was waiting, and I interviewed him.

He told me he was from Boston, and he was going to Baxter State Park because he wanted to go hike Mount Katahdin. There was no hiking on Katahdin that time of year. He said his car got stuck, he walked to look for help, and when he came back, his car was gone.

I figured what happened was he just got lost, so I had the plane go up, and we found his car right away. He'd burned out the transmission after he drove it up a snowmobile trail until he found a point where he went through and sunk it.

The whole time I'm interviewing this gentleman, there's something wrong. He's not dressed to go hiking. Things aren't adding up, and he's being evasive in a lot of his answers. So after we talked for a little bit, I said to him, "What do you have for gear? I want to see your gear."

So he opened his trunk, and said, "I've got it right here." He had one of those fifteen dollar Walmart summer sleeping bags. And a banana. That's what he had for gear.

He had a little daypack that he clutched in his hand the whole time. He wouldn't let go of that pack. Finally, I said to him, "Are you on any medications for anything?" He said no.

I said, "You're not on any kind of medications? What do you have in that pack right there?"

He said, "Just some stuff I need."

So I told him, "I need to see what's in that pack." I opened the pack and there were about fifteen prescription bottles. So now I knew I had to figure this out. It wasn't safe for this guy to be out here in a wilderness area like this. I started making calls. I wanted to blue paper this guy, because he was obviously a danger to himself. (Blue paper is the law that lets you hospitalize someone involuntarily if they are mentally incapacitated to the extent they're a danger to themselves or someone else.) I figured he's driving up snowmobile trails with a banana, didn't even have a bottle of water to take his meds, something bad was going to happen to this guy. I needed to do something.

I did my best, made my calls, talked to doctors and everyone, and no one was going to blue paper him. So I called a tow truck to get his car out of there, and when the wrecker showed up, he jumped in with the driver. The last time I saw him, they were headed south out of Kokadjo.

Then there was the lady with a wheeled suitcase on the Golden Road. The Golden Road is the east-west road that connects Millinocket to Québec. It's the main access logging road for lumber to go either to Canada or out to the mills in Maine. There are no towns. It is just a road through the wilderness.

We were getting reports of this lady with a little pull-suitcase on wheels—the kind you associate with airline stewardesses—walking on this road. People are talking with her and she says she's just going for a walk. Now, this is not normal behavior. She's got no camping gear, no food, no anything. Over the course of a couple days, several people called headquarters to say they're really concerned about this lady.

Finally, we got a call from some people who have a camp up there on Caribou Lake, and they said, "Look, she's going to die out here." She was complaining she had a really bad earache. This was not the place for her to be.

So I called over to the hospital—we have a pretty good working relationship with people at the hospital, because we're in there all the time with accident victims—I talked to the doctor, and he said, "Go get her. Because if she has an earache, she has a medical issue that certainly could be part of the reason she's disoriented. We'll send an ambulance."

I drive up there with the ambulance crew, and we go right to the camp, and they do an assessment and they put her in the ambulance, with the suitcase, and bring her to Greenville, so she doesn't just die out there with no one knowing what happened to her.

Once again, I was wishing they'd blue paper her, but I knew, from past experience, that the whole blue paper thing is a very difficult barrier to cross. My goal was to get her out of that environment. Once I got her to Greenville, it was going to take her at least a week to hike all the way back up there. So at least I was buying time, and hopefully during that time we could get in touch with someone. Unfortunately, we couldn't find out anything about her. She was there about a week and they treated her earache, and about a week later, I saw her walking south, out of town, pulling her little suitcase, heading up over Indian Hill.

Then there was the guy picking rocks. It was November, and we had a lost hunter up near Rainbow Lake country, an area with no road access. The guy had been missing overnight. It was pretty early in the morning on a Sunday, and I was on a woods road, and I came around the corner, and there was a truck parked there. The gentleman was behind a pickup with a cap on the back. The rear window was open, and when he saw me, he shut it really quickly and acted nervous and flustered as I pulled up to him.

I immediately knew something was wrong. I was thinking he'd shot a grouse on a Sunday and he'd just thrown it in when I came along. So I stopped real quickly, because I had to get to where I needed to be. I got out and I talked to him briefly, and I asked him if he was all right, because he was parked, literally, right in the middle of the road. And he said, "Yes, I'm fine, I'm just going up around the corner to get my prescriptions."

It kind of went over my head at first, because I was focusing on whether there was a crime. So I said to him, "What did you just put in the back of your truck?" and he said, "Oh, I'm collecting rocks, because it's going to snow."

It was a clear day. So I asked, "Where are you going again?"

"I'm going up around the corner to Rite Aid to get my prescriptions."

I said, "Can I look in the back?" I looked in there, and there were these pebbles. Little tiny pebbles. And I thought, *What the heck?*

So I asked him, "Where are you right now?"

He said, "I'm in Lewiston." And he had soiled himself.

So I said, "Why don't you get in my truck for a minute," and I got on the radio and I called the Piscataquis County dispatcher, and I said, "I have a problem. I'm headed to a search, and I've got a gentleman here who's completely disoriented, and I'm going to need an ambulance crew." I gave 'em his plate number and I gave 'em the name. And while waiting, I was talking to this guy, and he told me about going to Canada to get prescriptions on a bus. And then his story changed and he began telling me about going to the Walmart parking lot to go on the bus to Canada.

Piscataquis called me back and said, "Yeah, this guy left home, and he's suffering from severe dementia, and so they've been looking for him." So I said, "Well, I've got him, but I can't sit here all day because I've got a guy missing." I had to wait there until they came and took him in the ambulance, and then we beat feet up to Rainbow Lake to go find our lost guy.

We found him very quickly. He was way out by Second Roach Pond and Six Roach Pond. We were able to pick him up with the airplane and fly him out of there. Just another day in the freezing November woods of Maine. But a lot of people would drive down that road and they wouldn't see any of these things. Or they wouldn't want to get involved.

One last one, in that same area, was the guy looking for a bride. Funny how some areas seem to collect these people, like a low spot that they kind of roll into. Spring of the year again. Breakout time. April. A logging crew stopped by our headquarters and the guys said, "Look. Something strange happened yesterday that you need to know about. There was a guy in an El Camino, dressed in a three-piece suit and an overcoat, and he stopped and asked us some really bizarre questions. And when we asked him what he was doing up here, he said he was looking for his bride. She was around here somewhere."

He was a gentleman in his fifties. They said the guy got in his car, all confused, and drove away, and that morning when they came back, the car was parked where it had been the day before, and there was no one around. This was April and it had snowed a little overnight.

So we got there, and we ran the plate. The guy was a chemist, worked for the state out of Augusta, and he'd been reported missing. He hadn't come home from work. Now at that time, Folsom's Air Service in

Greenville had a helicopter, and we needed something fairly quickly, so they flew a warden up in a little jet ranger, and they spotted the guy about four hundred yards from his vehicle. He was standing in snow up to mid-thigh, and he'd stayed there all night. It had rained hard, but fortunately he had that raincoat. Otherwise he would have died.

I got to him, he was obviously hypothermic, and I said to him, "What's going on?"

And he said, "I'm collecting firewood. I'm bringing it back to camp."

I said, "Where is your firewood?"

He said, "It's right here." And he had a whole row of little fir needles, lined up, and a little pile of them.

He couldn't walk very well. We basically got under his arms and sort of fireman carried him out of there. We had snowshoes on, but it's hard to carry someone out when you're wearing snowshoes because the shoes are big and they get all tangled up, causing an instant face-plant.

When we got him out to the ambulance and they peeled off his pants, his legs were purple from standing in the snow. What had happened was he'd gone to work, started home, and something had snapped. He didn't know where he was or what was happening. Just thought he was getting firewood for camp. And the day before he'd been looking for a bride.

He ended up having an inoperable brain tumor. At least he didn't die in the middle of the woods.

Sometimes, even when the death isn't a homicide, there's plenty of mystery and investigation involved, as well as complicated logistics. There are lots of places in Maine where you don't just get in your truck and drive there and sort it out. And sometimes, because of the way information comes to us via multiple organizations, it can get as twisted and confused as a child's game of telephone.

What happened was this. We got a call that an elderly lady had passed away way up near the Canadian border, near Saint-Zacharie, a little town on the Canadian side. There are all these roads on the American side and all sorts of maple sugar camps, and our information was that this elderly Canadian lady had passed away at one of the camps on the American side. It was an unattended death. The county sheriff in Somerset County didn't have anyone who knew the area, so they asked us to take care of it.

A sugar camp would consist of two or three buildings for people to stay in and the main building to boil the sap, the sap house, and a garage. Just a little encampment of five or six buildings that they would use exclusively in late March/early April. Most of these are Canadian operations located in Maine, and there are more than a dozen of them along the border.

So, being bilingual, I got asked to jump in the plane and fly up there to Baker Lake. The warden stationed up there was going to meet me, and we'd do the proper investigation for an unattended death. Well, I knew better than to do that by plane, because I'd done the plane thing up there before. The weather socks you in and you can't get home, so I said, "I'll drive. It'll take more time but I'll have more control." So I drove up there from Greenville—it's about three hours—and I talked to the husband at customs at Sainte-Aurélie.

I found out from him that the dead woman was not an elderly lady; she was a woman in her mid-forties. She hadn't died of natural causes, but he had no idea what she had died of. She'd gone there to do all the painting that was needed in preparation for the year. He'd dropped her off and come back a week later, because he was allergic to paint fumes.

Now, when Somerset gave us the information, they said she was dead at the kitchen sink in the camp. I assumed that all the information was correct. I assumed she'd died in the camp and her husband had come in and found her there.

This happened in August. The husband stayed behind at the customs house and we went on into the camp, about ten or twelve miles in. By the time we got there, it was getting dark. There was a series of little buildings. We could hear a radio playing somewhere, and it was playing in French. We got out of the vehicle and went to the first camp, totally expecting to find the body, because that's where they'd told us she would be.

There's always an elevation of emotion, looking for a dead person that you know is there, so we kinda crept into the camp, ready for a body, and there was no body. Nobody. Her stuff was there. We could see her bedroll, and food on the table, and that eerie radio was playing. But no one was there.

We had just assumed we knew, from the information we'd gotten from the Somerset County sheriff, that she was dead at the kitchen sink. There were three or four little cabins in this cluster. We started going camp to camp, building to building, as we realized that the husband had never told us where she was. Each time, what we would do was one guy would go in, and the other one wouldn't, so that if there was some kind of poison, the other guy could pull you out. We went to cabin two. Nothing. One thing we knew was that the Canadians would sometimes use formaldehyde in their sap lines to keep the tree from scarring. It was illegal to do, but a lot of these camps had old formaldehyde kicking around. So, not knowing her cause of death, we were a little concerned about that.

We went from building to building until finally we got to the last building, the one that had the big tank for collecting and storing the sap. The big tank was elevated about ten feet off the ground. We looked inside the building. Nothing. We were standing there, wondering what the heck was going on and what to do next, and all of a sudden, we both noticed a ladder against the side of the tank, leading up about ten feet.

It was the creepiest thing when we started realizing what was going on. The place was totally deserted and the radio was playing. There were no lights on. And we'd been right on the edge. Every step. Looking and looking. And then we both looked at each other and we're thinking, *Oh no, she's got to be in there*, because that was the one place you wouldn't want to have to deal with a body.

I climbed up the ladder and looked in the tank and there she was, right inside that tank. Dead. She was on her knees, painting on some paint remover, and she just fell right over. She still had the paintbrush in her hand and the can of paint remover between her legs.

We couldn't read the label, which was in French, from where we were, but we didn't need to read it to know that if we went in there, whatever killed her was going to kill us, too. So we got on the phone to the Environmental Protection folks because they had the hazard gear to get her out. Piecing the story together from the evidence in her camp, we could figure out how long she'd been dead. We looked at her food supply and the trash. We could see where she'd had three breakfasts and three lunches, and two dinners, and her husband had been gone for five days. It looked like she'd gone in and had lunch, and then gone back to work and the fumes had killed her.

We—Jarrod Herrick and I—ended up spending the night at the Sainte-Aurélie camp. It was lunch time the next day by the time the environmental people got up there, along with Pat Dorian and the Maine State Police.

The environmental folks got her out and she was just as green as my truck, because she'd been there for a week. Now, since she died in Maine, we had to get her to the Maine medical examiner's office. The quickest way to get her out of there was to drive over into Canada and back into the United States, which was a little problematic, after 9/11, hauling bodies around.

We couldn't get a hearse up there through those logging roads, so we put her in a body bag and put her in the back of my truck. Then I had to call customs and explain to them that I had a dead person, who was a Canadian, that I needed to take through the border into Canada and then bring her back into the United States to get her to the ME's office.

Fortunately, my brother-in-law was at the helm of US Customs, and he had an officer come and escort us down through. It was really strange driving through Canada with a body. When I rolled into customs, they asked me what I had to declare, and I said, "I've got a body." We got her back into the United States, and the autopsy confirmed what we'd assumed: fumes from the paint remover had displaced the oxygen in the tank, and basically, as the fumes built up, it just pushed the oxygen above her head and she went unconscious and just dropped right there.

Pretty amazing that her husband never gave us any of that information about where she was and what had happened. And yeah, it was bad.

I could tell stories like this all day—the sad ones, the strange ones, the people who just kinda come up here and fall off the edge. The many places we find bodies and the complexities of getting them out of the woods. And then there are stories that are just plain strange. This isn't about a car parked by the roadside. This one is about an airplane crash. I'd just consider it one of the mysteries of the warden service.

We had a plane that went down on a Friday night. It was awful weather, we were really socked in with thick, thick fog, so we couldn't get our planes up to search. We didn't know exactly who was on that plane, but Saturday afternoon, we had a bunch of important FBI guys and a whole busload of Massachusetts State Police troopers, champing at the bit to find that plane.

We got hold of the air force base that tracks all the airplane activity, and we were able to get the three last radar ticks that gave us a line and it also gave us an elevation. We looked at that elevation, and said what's the elevation that's going to be higher than that because that would give us the point of contact. We pinpointed the most likely search area and we started working teams into those areas. It was very remote. When you're trying to run a coherent search, you can't have a bunch of people just milling around, so we paired up the Massachusetts troopers with our wardens, and sent them out to search.

Well, that didn't work very well. Those troopers were getting nervous in the thick brush, and they would fire their guns ahead of them to scare the bears and stuff, and we were getting calls back from the wardens, saying "Hey, we need to disarm these guys before they kill somebody." So, at the end of the first night, Saturday night, I don't know if he was the colonel or a major from Massachusetts State Police, rounded up all the troops that he had and he said, "I want all the guns. All your weapons are going to be put right here. Because if you don't do it, these game wardens are going to feed you to the bears." So all their weapons went back on the bus.

What we were waiting for was a little bit of blue sky to fly. We had the area pinned down fairly well, but it was big, and remote, and we needed to be able to see from the sky. Meanwhile, one of the guys from the FBI, like second or third in command at the FBI, shows up. At that point, our phones were completely overwhelmed, so he says, "You guys need more phones," and he adds, "I'll have the helicopters here in about another hour or two with the rappel teams." That was crazy, because the fog was so thick you couldn't see across the bay.

Sure enough, about two hours later, this truck pulls in and boom, boom, boom, we have phones in our airplane hanger, about nine phones all hooked up and then two helicopters land right at our head-quarters with two rappel teams.

This was likely a recovery mission. Based on our experience with plane crashes, with the ticks being in a straight line and no evasive maneuvering, we didn't think we were going to find someone alive. So finally, we get a ground team in the area.

Back up a little bit, so you can feel the mystery here. On Saturday night, when all our search teams came in, we regrouped and laid out our search plans for the next day. At this point, I was in charge of mapping the search areas, figuring out how many searchers we had, how to deploy them, and where. We knew, in the morning, that the skies were going to clear. It was just a question of when. I'll never forget this: we had this great big guy in his blue pajamas from Civil Air Patrol (their blue jumpsuits look like pajamas) and he was kinda stomping around, saying "We have control of the air in the morning."

At that point, we had warden service aircraft, state police aircraft, forestry helicopters, FBI helicopters, and everybody wanted that first chance to get into the air when the fog cleared. So, we were in this room, I was in the back corner, and our lieutenant was there, and we watched this battle start over who has the first flight time, who gets the first swing at finding the crash site.

Never mind sending the people who have the most experience in this region. That was irrelevant. So it started swirling around. We, as warden service, knew our place, because at that time an airplane crash was under the jurisdiction of Maine State Police, so we were an assisting entity to help state police, but ultimately, the investigation belonged to the state police. We knew our role was to stand down and let the battle ensue.

It was spinning pretty hard, everyone trying to get a piece of it, and the FBI agent in charge of recovery operations—his name was Trom or Tron—he did the most brilliant job of negotiating I've ever seen. I watched him haggle for fifteen minutes of airtime before the fog was going to clear. We knew the fog was most likely going to lift around eight-thirty, nine o'clock. And he negotiated a fifteen-minute slot before eight to get his choppers in the air.

He got everybody to agree to this sequence of who was going where and how. It was phenomenal. He must have been a hostage negotiator or something. And part of his discussion was, okay, if we find the aircraft and they're deceased, it's going to be a Maine State Police criminal investigation, that's the way it will go. So whoever finds it, it will be secured, MSP will take over the investigation.

The FBI sat there and agreed to everything, said they had no problems. Eight a.m. comes, the FBI fly their birds for about fifteen minutes. Can't see a thing. About nine-thirty, ten o'clock, the sky starts to clear a little bit. We have ground teams sweeping that area where the last tick came in. There's a pretty good elevation right there, so we figured it would be right off that last tick, so we worked our way up the ridge. A forestry helicopter, flown by the same guy who ended up saving me when I had the big confrontation at the bottom of my driveway, Otis, was in the air and he zipped right over and boom! They find it.

This is where it gets very interesting. So, the word came in that it had been found. Our ground team was within two hundred to three hundred yards at that point, and the warden in charge of that team left his team on standby mode. He went over to the crash site, found the occupants both dead, and called it in. Then he secured the scene.

In theory, this didn't have anything to do with anybody anymore except MSP, with the wardens to assist. It's a recovery, not a rescue. Everybody else can go home. But I suspect that MSP and FBI were having a kind of very quiet, backroom discussion, because all of a sudden, as soon as we got the confirmation that they were deceased, the FBI said, "My guys are going to be in the air." Boom, their chopper went up, and their whole rappel team was there.

Now MSP is in charge. They were out on the highway, about two miles from the crash site. And they said, "We're all set, we're going to let the FBI go in to secure the scene." Which didn't make any sense, because the scene was already secured.

Well, one of the senior wardens had a video camera, and he was in the helicopter that found the body and was still around while they made arrangements for removing the bodies and all. He watched those guys go down, and when they came back and got loaded, they had this big black bag. That's all. Go in, grab that bag, and they're done. Once they were loaded in the helicopter, they were gone. No sign that they were ever there except this line of phones we had no use for now.

It was the strangest thing and MSP just shrugged. I've been around Maine State Police my whole career and I've never seen them . . . uh, let's just say they don't share well. Something that is theirs is theirs. I was at the command center in Greenville and that plane was just gone! You would think that those guys were gonna hang around, during the process of getting their comrades out, but all they were there for was that bag.

I'll always wonder what was in that bag. What we heard was they were going on a white water rafting trip for a team building event. I don't think that's what they were doing because the plane went down at ten or eleven o'clock at night. And when we were interviewing people about the crash, they had heard another plane coming from the north, into Greenville, to the airport, turn their landing lights on, circle a few times, and head off north again. One of them, a pilot, told me, "Man, I heard that plane that night, and I couldn't figure out what they were doing, flying in that kind of weather." They flew right over his house, very low, and then the plane left, flying north. So we knew there had been two planes up, but the FBI, and Maine State Police, they never mentioned that second plane. There was a lot of speculation, but we'll never know.

PART VIII

KATRINA, PTSD, AND BEYOND

CHAPTER TWENTY-TWO

Searching for Bodies in New Orleans

In November 2005, right in the middle of hunting season, the warden service got a request from FEMA to send a couple of cadaver dog teams down to New Orleans to help with the recovery of missing persons. That request, and the two missions that followed, put me on a dark track that nearly ruined my health and my career, and ultimately left me changed forever.

How it came about was MEMA (Maine Emergency Management) allocated its resources to FEMA. All the states have their resources catalogued and ready to go, so if any state has a crisis, they contact FEMA, FEMA sends its feelers out to its branches, and they send their resources. FEMA needed cadaver dog teams in New Orleans, we had that resource, and so we were called upon to go.

Foreshadowing doesn't happen only in books; it happens in real life. The night before Warden Wayde Carter and I left for our second tour in February of 2006, we had a mission out on Moosehead Lake where a kid and his dad on a snowmobile had gone through the ice up by Kineo Point in the middle of the night. They were heading up the lake to a friend's camp for the night and they came around that point where there's a place that the lake never freezes and they just drove out into open water.

The kid got out onto the ice and was trying to get his dad out, and he couldn't. The kid actually jumped back into the water and tried to push his father out onto the ice, and hypothermia got him so quick he couldn't do it. Finally the father said, "You've got to let me go and get yourself out."

The kid crawled up on the ice to get out and kept slipping back in. He was stumbling and reeling, he was just like an ice cube, and another snowmobiler just happened to come by and got a glimpse of him, picked him up, and brought him back into the camps. So we took the airboat up, there, and drove around, and we found the father. He was floating. So we loaded him, and got the airboat up onto the ice, and it just stalled out. We couldn't get it to start again.

It was getting close to zero, and that airboat froze right solid to the ice. We ended up taking the father's body out by snowmobile. The next morning, we had to go back with axes and come-alongs and chip the airboat out.

I spent the night before heading out to New Orleans dealing with that boy, maybe sixteen, seventeen, who'd done everything in his power to try and save his dad. I knew that for the rest of his life he would be carrying the memory of his dad saying, "You've got to let me go, you've got to get out of here." That's some tough stuff. It really stirred up my memories of losing my own dad in a water accident when I was about the same age.

My job has involved first-hand contact with so much injury and death, but this one hit me hard. The son losing his father thing, I guess. And two years before, I'd had another one of those. I was out in Katahdin Iron Works country, out by Baker Pond, when a radio call came in for a potential drowning situation on the Kennebec River at the east outlet from Indian Pond. The river comes in there with quite a current. As fast as I could go, it was about forty-five minutes away, and that was really stomping on it. About halfway there, it came across the radio that what had happened was two men in a canoe paddled up into the current, dropped the anchor, and the rope caught and spun the canoe around quickly and capsized them.

The two men were laughing and thought it was funny. But as it was happening, the canoe was floating downstream, and what the stern-man didn't realize was that he had the anchor rope wrapped around his leg. With the anchor down and the boat drifting with the current, one moment he was laughing and the next, the rope tightened and he'd gone under.

The guy with him realized that his friend just went down, and he couldn't find him.

This was happening right by the campsite, and the kids were on the shore, seeing this all unravel.

So a guy fishing at the mouth of the river came over and jumped in. He had a knife, so he cut the rope, and they got the guy back into the boat. I got there, and there was another boat there that took me out to where they were. They were just getting the guy's body into the boat and trying to do CPR. I had an ambulance coming right behind me. We grabbed him and headed for the landing, and the ambulance loaded him and he was gone.

I knew, because I've been there before, that the guy was dead. But no one said it. I went back with the boat and picked up the mother and the children—it was two couples, and two children, a boy and a girl. It was the boy's dad who drowned. I picked up the moms and the kids, and a guy loaned me his vehicle because I couldn't take them all in my truck, and I ended up driving the vehicle with everybody in it to the hospital in Greenville, about twenty minutes away.

The little boy and the girl were talking, trying to process this, and I heard it; it was just gut-wrenching. This little boy, about seven, was saying, the whole time, "I hope Daddy's okay." And it hurt, because I knew his dad was not, and I had to keep my thoughts off my face and just keep driving. And his mom couldn't say anything; she was just totally distraught. So we got to the hospital, and they'd pronounced him dead.

Now this wasn't a rescue anymore, and I had to deal with the death. I had to get statements, track down the other fishermen who were there, and get statements from them. I was dealing with people at the hospital. I had to make a bunch of phone calls, and I had to interview the guy who was in the canoe with him, and the mom. I came into the room, and they were all sitting there praying.

It was a very defining moment. They were obviously very religious people, and they weren't praying about their loss, but about him going home to the Lord, and to help them and grow. It was incredible.

This guy also was an organ donor. Because the people at the hospital knew me and knew I'd developed a relationship with the family, they wanted me to go and talk to the family about organ donation, and they needed me to do that immediately. That's about the last thing that I wanted to talk to them about just then, but it needed to be done. The family said, no problem. Do it.

This little boy didn't know it, but he and I shared the same thing—losing our dads in a canoe accident. I was out mowing my lawn that night and just bawling my eyes out because that same thing that he was saying, verbally, was what I'd been thinking when they were looking for my dad. I knew exactly how that little boy felt and how huge a loss that was going to be in his life. This would have happened a year or two before Katrina happened, and I can see it on the timeline when I look back. That these two drowning incidents were kind of setting me up for everything else that came along. That whole incident was very difficult for me. It brought me back to that place—the loss of my father—that I had so conveniently tucked away. Having ripped open that scar, I was vulnerable to the big crash. Those boys and their lost fathers—that was what I was carrying when we got in the truck and headed south.

We went down to New Orleans twice, on two missions. Four weeks in the Ninth Ward with my dog, Rader. It was a total train wreck.

Katrina happened in August 2005. The first trip we made was in the third week of November. I drove down with Wayde Carter—he's out in the Machias area and corporal of the K-9 team—with my dog Rader and Wayde's dog, Buddy, a hundred-pound German shepherd.

On the outskirts of New Orleans, they were still clearing the highways. It looked like a giant weed whacker had gone through and just cut the tops off all the trees. It was incredible. Everything was decimated. It was clear long before we got to New Orleans itself that we were driving into disaster.

As we got closer and got to the bridge that crosses Lake Pontchartrain, the bridge was gone on one side; the whole side facing the ocean was no longer there. All that destruction was really driving my anticipation of what we'd find when we got there, and it kept getting worse and worse. Then, as we started driving into the city, the first thing we realized was that there were no signs. Signs are the first thing to go down in the wind. Three months later, there were still no signs. No traffic lights. No nothing. Luckily, we were used to working with GPS.

We got onto Canal Street, where we were supposed to meet everybody at the DoubleTree Hotel. We were replacing a team from Virginia that had been working there for about ten days. We were going to overlap with this team; they were going to train us and then head home. We got to the hotel, ditched our gear, and met up with them. They actually had set up a house with some cadaver stuff in it. I think they wanted to see how good our dogs were. That's just how cadaver guys are. We're always testing and training.

We were there maybe half an hour and we were going through the house, testing our dogs for them. The dogs just nailed it.

We then started in on the Ninth Ward, and right away, our concern was how the dogs were going to work effectively in that scent environment. There were dead dogs and dead cats and rotting food in the refrigerators and sewage and dead fish and chickens and birds and guinea pigs. The only way to describe it was just a soup of death. We train our dogs not to indicate on anything other than human cadaver scent, and we constantly mix new dead things into their training, but never in this volume and mixed the way it was. But the dogs had absolutely no problem. None at all.

Right from the start, we also had concerns with the way they were organizing the searches. Instead of working by blocks, so we could search and clear an entire area—the kind of searching we were used to planning and carrying out—they had lists of missing people and their addresses. We would go to that address and search in the general area. Often there weren't houses at those addresses; everything in the Ninth Ward was just so spun and turned. Sometimes all the houses for a whole street would have been swept into a huge debris pile. Even when the houses were standing, they might have been moved some distance off their foundations. And inside the houses that were still standing, water had come in and it had worked like a washing machine; everything was spun to the walls, and then the insulation and ceilings fell down on that, so often when we stepped into a room we couldn't see any of the floor, and we couldn't see what we were walking on.

We had a team. There were five, some days six, people who were assigned to us, three or four firemen and a police officer. We figured out, after a couple of days, that their main job was to get us out if something collapsed on us because they were more attuned to the structural dangers of working around collapsed buildings than we were. We learned pretty quickly, though.

While we were working the dogs, they would be searching around for pill bottles or other things with a name that might indicate we were in the right debris field for that particular residence. As we worked the dogs, much of the time, we couldn't see them. The dogs would work underneath the buildings, underneath the debris, below the collapsed ceilings and walls, places we couldn't go.

Initially, we tried to put stuff on them to help them, harnesses, protective booties to protect them from nails and glass, all that stuff, but that made it more dangerous for them because they'd get stuck in places or pull stuff down on top of them. We ended up just putting bells on them so we could hear where they were and letting the dogs work. The dogs learned to be conscious of what they were walking on. It took a day, and they had to slow down.

They figured it out pretty quickly, but it was seriously nerve-wracking for us because of all the risks to the dogs. These were dogs we'd spent years training and years working with, and we were putting them in serious danger every day. But we also knew these were working dogs. They were there to do a job just like we were. So we'd stand in a corner and, by listening, try to make sure the dogs covered the room as best they could. In most buildings, we could see the dogs maybe 10 percent of the time. We knew as long as they were moving, they were fine. It worked unbelievably well.

The second thing we learned was that every house once had a fence around it, and that often, the houses had floated over the fences while the fences stayed intact, so to get into many areas, we had to pick the dog up and throw him over the fence. I mean many, many times a day. To go thirty yards, you'd have to pick up the dog and throw him over the fence at least three times. We're talking about an eighty-pound dog and a hundred-pound dog. It was a lot of physical work. Most dogs don't like to be picked up, so it was amazing how quickly they adapted to it. It was like, *all right, throw me over again*. And sometimes, the houses had tipped onto their sides, and we'd have to put the dogs in through the windows.

We found a lot of body parts. We would work debris piles and we would mark them if the dogs indicated there were human remains there. We would mark them, but we would never know if anyone came and did follow-up and looked at them or if there was actually anyone in there. There was a guy with an excavator who was supposed to be working on searching through those debris piles. He came down and worked one day for a couple of minutes. And that was all.

What Wayde and I figured out, really quickly, was that while we were trying to do good work for FEMA and the people of New Orleans, FEMA wasn't really interested in our mission. They were using us a part of their public relations campaign. We were a press magnet in that environment. We'd come to work in the morning and there would be a line of different news affiliates waiting for us.

There was another team from Georgia, and the guy who was our boss, so there were five teams of dogs, after the handlers from Virginia went home. We would pull up in the morning and there would be these news people waiting to take their turn to go with us. I don't know if there was five minutes while we were working that wasn't recorded. It was a real nuisance trying to work with them there. They even wanted to put microphones on our dogs so they could hear the sounds of the search.

We were there trying to be professional and help out, but just the way they organized the searching, it was very frustrating to us. By not working a grid, but instead being brought to a specific debris pile or the remnants of a house, it was very haphazard. We wanted to do it the way we would work in the woods, systematically clearing a block of land. They wanted to do it by street address—when there was no street address anymore, and the person who had lived there could have been anywhere in the area.

I remember one day, we got into this area, and both dogs alerted on this debris pile outside a house. I can't remember which news crew was following us, it might have been CNN. Anyway, they both hit, and the firemen went and got some chainsaws, and cut up the trees, and we brought the dogs back in, and there was this big poured cement pad, like you'd use as the base for a post, and both dogs were digging on that real hard. Whatever was down there, it wasn't something from Katrina, not with cement poured over it.

So Wayde crawled into the hole and flipped the cement pad over, and you could see this big hunk of skin. And Wayde, being a game warden and used to telling human from animal, sniffed and said, "Yeah. I think it's human." That's all on camera.

We found lots of parts and pieces of bodies. What had happened was that they didn't even look for the bodies for weeks after the storm. The temperatures right after the hurricane went into the hundreds, so you had this rapid decay, and then a second hurricane came in and flooded that area again. Add in how the dogs and cats that survived were eating off whatever they could find. So we were finding fingers or pieces of feet or just fragments.

By the time we got there, other teams had been in the Ninth Ward for two weeks or more. We were searching the same places that had already been searched, not because that was the best use of us as a resource, but because politically, that's where they wanted us to be.

Another thing we kept running into that accounted for our finding so many pieces of bodies was that when they had collected the bodies earlier, they hadn't collected all of them; they'd just kind of scooped them up, and arms and legs and other pieces were left behind. So we'd work a debris field, and the dogs would just go over and find a bone or a part of leg or a finger.

Then there was the voodoo stuff. The dogs would be hitting on a cupboard and we'd pop it open and there would be all this voodoo stuff that was definitely human. We found that a lot. One place we found leg bones—human leg bones—braided with wire.

So you've got this voodoo culture, you've got human remains that are naturally mixed in with this culture. You've got the cemeteries that are like crypts, and they all got flooded. You've got parts of bodies that were left behind. And then you had real people who hadn't been found.

It was nasty. The whole city was out of control. No traffic lights, no controls, roving gangs and gunshots all night long. I had one of the scariest moments of my life while I was down there, the story that I tell in the prologue to this book. It wasn't the only scary moment— New Orleans was a scary place—but it left an indelible mark on me.

To this day, I get goose bumps remembering that event. I've been in a lot of pretty hairy situations, but this one is etched in my mind forever. We were within seconds of it going down, as the guy came around the edge of that car door, in that trench coat with his hand tucked into it, and turned that dead-eyed stare on me. And all for absolutely no reason.

Another time, we were in a different part of the city. We were checking a house, and all of our vehicles—warden truck and fire department truck—were parked in the middle of the road. Now you didn't see traffic in those sections, and suddenly this car came skidding around the corner, coming at us, and right behind them was this Louisiana State Police trooper with his blue lights and siren going.

They stopped because they couldn't get by us. And the trooper jumped out, gun out; he was doing a felony stop. A felony stop is a method of extracting people from a vehicle who are armed and dangerous. The trooper was alone, and there were three people and a lot of activity going on in the car. As a police officer, when you see that kind of activity, one of two things are going on: either they're hiding their dope or loading guns and getting ready.

The trooper was screaming at them from behind the door of his vehicle. Seeing this, Wayde and I went out wide, one on each side of the road. We didn't want to distract him or get in his line of fire, so we came out at angles, and when we got to within thirty yards of him, we just waved to him so he saw us, because he was in tunnel vision. And when he recognized that we were in uniform, he waved for us to come in. So we went in and we assisted him and helped him get the guys out of the vehicle. Once there were three guns there, then we had the upper hand, so we extracted the driver from the vehicle and searched him; the guy had two ChapSticks and a pocket full of condoms.

He was in a jumpsuit, like a convict, and I asked him "Where are you going?" and he said he was going to work. I always wondered what kind of work he did.

Wayde and I, we had this one place we would go, it was right on the bank of the Mississippi River, behind a high school. We would go and stand on the lawn. Nice green grass. We could stand with our backs to the debris and look out onto the water, the only place we could look and not see devastation and mayhem. We'd just go there and stand for fifteen minutes or so, trying to get ourselves reoriented to normal. Then we'd turn around, take a deep breath, and go back into it.

I really got to hate brick buildings. Those were the absolute scariest things, because the walls would be bowed, and we'd be crawling inside these houses, and we knew if we just touched that wall, it would collapse. And we didn't get to say no, we weren't going in because it was unsafe, because everything was unsafe. There was nothing that we didn't go in.

Going in, we couldn't look at all that danger and still do our job as a dog handler. We just had to focus on our dogs and what we were there for, and say, that's *their* job—the firemen we had with us. If this thing falls on me, they're going to come and get me. If we worried about that, we'd have gone crazy. So we purposely didn't look. We'd just crawl through there. Fall through panes of glass. Listen for those bells. Heft our dogs over fences, screen out all the chaos and filth and debris and concentrate on our mission. And even that was harder because so much of this job is reading the dogs and that dog and handler connection, and we were so often working in the dark without that visual.

It was amazing that the dogs didn't get seriously injured. The first trip down, we had a veterinarian and a vet tech immediately available to us as part of the package. When we would come in, at lunch time and at the end of the day, they would bring the dogs in and they would wash the dogs, and then the vet would check them all over, check their pads and look for any sign of injury. It was the vet who found that a small fragment of metal had pierced Buddy's eye. They anesthetized him and took that out and bandaged him up, and he was okay.

They took good care of us, too. We'd come in at the end of the day, our clothes just nasty from mold and slime and dirt, lifting the dogs and crawling through rat-infested, chemical-filled buildings. And they had laundry, and meals. We were in good shape all the way around.

We were down there to work, but it felt like to FEMA, we were there to show the media that something was being done. I think that's why they kept making us go back to the Ninth Ward over and over, even though it had been heavily searched and there were other places that needed us more. Because of the TV coverage. That's how we got to know the guy from CNN, Sean Callebs, and the folks from the Jim Lehrer's *PBS NewsHour*, and had the interview with Anderson Cooper.

For whatever reason, our dog teams became the ones they wanted to follow. I don't think we took a single step on a single day that they didn't follow. We were kinda being used as a media prop to show the world that they were doing something, when in actuality, we were just kinda spinning around in circles. There were a lot of other areas that we could have searched and gotten something done, but they kept us right close to the command post so that they could get good film clips. It was really frustrating to have traveled all that way and brought them this valuable resource, and to not be used more effectively.

CHAPTER TWENTY-THREE

New Orleans Again and the FEMA Fiasco

At FEMA's request, we went down again in February. The political situation was changing and everything went wrong. Everything. They'd made the same promises about veterinary resources and the facilities we'd had on the first trip, and nothing came through. Everything about the trip was a disaster. The bad news started even before we got to Louisiana and ended with a housing fiasco and a FEMA screw-up that ended up on the national news.

We stopped in Fort Payne, Alabama, and parked two spaces over from the front door of the hotel. We were in Wayde's truck, and he had a roof rack with a pump shotgun and a rifle. We knew, this time, that we wanted our long guns with us. We'd had that felony stop, and I'd had that guy in the street who wanted to kill himself a cop, so we knew that we wanted more firepower with us. We brought our dogs inside for the night, because they're service dogs, so we had them in the room with us. We came out in the morning and the side windows were busted out.

Our fire power was gone. They stole my digital camera; it was a state camera. They'd pulled my computer out of the bag, and what it really looked like was they didn't see the long guns until they were pulling things out of the truck and then they dropped the computer and busted the rack to get at the guns. All this was going on right in front of the hotel door and nobody noticed or called us or the police.

The Fort Payne police came up and made a report, but they never found anything. At least we still had our handguns. Now we needed to get the truck repaired, because we were not going into New Orleans with a busted window. That sent us on a mission to find Bobo the Window Guy. At the hotel desk, they told us he was just down the road. We went to see him, and as we were going through the door, we saw that he had a sign over his office that read: GOING SHOPPING WITH YOUR WIFE IS LIKE GOING FISHING WITH A GAME WARDEN. We walked in and said we needed a side window for a warden truck from Maine. So we sat there for hours, waiting, and when the guy showed up with the window, it was the wrong window. So Bobo said, "You're going to have to go to Birmingham."

We ended up in this old warehouse. It's the kind of place where they've got guard dogs inside the fences, and people were looking at us strangely. We found this guy, and he put the window in. This took us four or five hours.

We had planned to get to New Orleans around noon, and now we were pulling in after midnight. We didn't know it, but it was the last day of Mardi Gras, and there were literally thousands of people out who were being pushed off the street by police on horses. Everybody was in costume. Everybody was mad, dumb drunk. And we were driving the wrong way down Canal Street.

Before it even clicked what was going on, we had people trying to flip the truck over. That's where Buddy saved my hide the second time, because when people would start pushing on the vehicle, Buddy decided to light up the world and let them know they weren't coming any closer.

We couldn't back up. We had to keep going. Finally Wayde called in to our boss, and he said, "Just put on your blue lights and drive up the trolley lane."

I remember I had my gun in my hand the whole time. Everyone was in costume. Most of the costumes were voodoo and skeletons, all scary stuff. And this was the middle of the night on Canal Street. I said to Wayde, who was driving, "I'm going to get at least one of them before they get us."

Once we put our blue lights on and went up the center, we got out of the fray a little bit. But before that there was about a mile of total mayhem surrounded by all these people in costumes. It was like being on another planet and being overtaken by aliens. The trash in the street was amazing, a foot thick in places, and people were vomiting everywhere. It was horrid. Horrid.

We checked into our hotel, got instructions from our boss, and went to work, but the resources we'd been promised were not there. One of the biggest snafus in the second trip was that they had promised us a vet and they didn't have one. We were really concerned about that because we knew the kind of environment we were going to be working in. If a dog got hurt or fell through a pane of glass, we couldn't get him out of the city to get to where there was a vet in time. There were still no traffic lights. It was just a nightmare trying to drive there.

But we were there to do a job, so we went out and worked. The same stuff as before, working in the Ninth Ward, constantly trailed by reporters. Still working according to FEMA's crazy rules for finding the missing. It wasn't just the way they structured the searches, which was irrational, but the whole way FEMA behaved. Like this one day, these guys showed up with the white hardhats and they were going to move some buildings out of the road, and they decided that we couldn't be there because we weren't HazMat certified. We had gone through all of those buildings and cleared them all, but that day it was a hazardous site. It was FEMA silliness at its best. This was right at the end of our second tour. We'd been there for almost four weeks at that point. But now the president was coming so everything got to be more formal.

One day, about two weeks in, we had a big find. This day, we were sent to check out a house in the Slidell area, an area the levee had breached the morning after the hurricane had passed, catching people off guard. The house we went to search had already been searched several times. Its occupant was missing and was believed to have perished.

Unlike the homes in the Ninth Ward, this house was not torn apart and spun around. We could see that the water had gone up to the roof line but the current hadn't pushed everything around like in the Ninth. The front wall of the house had the familiar X painted on it to signify the last search that was done there, a few days earlier. The X is a search and rescue symbol that records what has taken place at the house, search effort wise, or if any bodies have been found there. Each side of the line has designated info: date, team, find, etc.

Wayde and Buddy went in first, and Buddy began to alert as soon as he went through the door. Buddy's alert was high as he was climbing the walls near the bathroom area toward the middle of the small brick house. Wayde took Buddy out and I brought Rader in to confirm. As I entered the house, the firemen with us had pulled the fold-down attic stairs and had started to go up. Rader and Buddy's alerts would have put the body to the right side of the attic entrance. A large air duct ran along that side of the stairs. When we checked the attic carefully, the body was found tucked up against the duct so that someone doing a casual scan of the attic would tend to look right over the top and not see it on the back side of the duct. The victim had been trapped in the attic and most likely died from the intense heat and lack of oxygen. Like most of the victims we found, he was not wearing any clothes.

CNN had been filming with us earlier in the day and was quick to show up and start filming this. As soon as they got the news, the New Orleans police parked a cruiser with a K-9 logo in front of the house, which was funny because they had missed the victim only a few days earlier, the second time the house was searched. And there was no NOPD K-9 involved. The officer had no reason to be there except for media purposes. This recovery led to a live interview with Anderson Cooper and the whole ungodly mess with FEMA that followed.

The next day, we came back to the hotel at the end of the day, our dogs and ourselves filthy as usual, hot and sweaty and needing to shower and care for our dogs, and we found we couldn't get in our rooms. Our keys didn't work. We went to the front desk to see what the problem was, and the manager said, "Well, you need to speak to those people over there."

He pointed to some women sitting at a little desk. They had a banner that said: FEMA Community Relations Team.

These were not the people we'd been reporting to. There had been a flyer stuck under our door saying that if you were a refugee from the storm, you needed to meet with these people on this date to fill out your affidavit for benefits. But that didn't pertain to us, so we didn't pay attention to it. So I walked up to these people, in my uniform, and I said, "We need to get into our rooms."

One woman said, "Well, you need to fill out this affidavit."

I looked at it, and it was an affidavit requesting federal aid. I said, "Ma'am, you don't understand. I'm here as part of the cadaver dog team. I have nothing to do with being a refugee. I'm helping recover bodies."

"Well," she replied, "if you don't sign it, you're not going to get authorized to go in."

So I said, "Who is your supervisor?" And she told me her supervisor was around the corner in the bar. So I went into the bar and there was this lady sitting on a stool. I introduced myself and explained, and she said exactly the same thing—we had to fill out the affidavits.

I said, "Ma'am, I can't fill it out. That's falsifying official information. I'm not a refugee."

She shrugged and said, "I don't know what to tell you."

Now I didn't know what to do. We were being held hostage. All our gear was in our rooms. We were filthy, our clothes were filthy, and we had these dogs that hadn't been cleaned, so we called our supervisor and he said he'd come in.

Sean Callebs from CNN had invited us to dinner at their complex that night. And the night before Wayde and I had been live on Anderson Cooper. So we're kind of standing around in the lobby, standing in front of the desk, and I said, "We've got to call Sean Callebs and let him know we're not going to make it for dinner."

We were dialing the phone, trying to let him know we'd run into a snag. We were Maine country boys, not even thinking about how we were standing there calling a national TV news reporter like Sean Callebs and saying, "We're probably not going to make it to dinner." But the manager behind the desk, his wheels clicked as to who we were, and as we hung up, he said, "Gentlemen, this is obviously a misunderstanding that's going to get cleared up. Here, take your keys and get cleaned up." Because he could see the writing on the wall.

So we were thinking, *Oh great. It's just a misunderstanding. It will all get straightened out.* We called Sean back and said we probably would make it after all, we might just be a little late. It was gonna be a rib night. That was a big deal, because food was very important in the midst of all that bad stuff.

So we got the dogs cleaned up, got showered, and the phone rang. Our boss was downstairs, and he said, "I need you guys down here right now."

We got down to the lobby, and there were all these Federal Protective Service police there with their guns and assault rifles. We knew most of the guys who were there, from working with them, and now we were wondering what was going on. We got to our boss, and he said that while he had his back turned, dialing high command to try and sort the room issue out, these FEMA community relations people called 911 and said he was brandishing a firearm and threatening them.

So now, the FPS guys don't know what to do. Fortunately, our boss had the presence of mind to ask for the lobby videotape and was able to show the FPS guys what had really happened: that after he talked to the FEMA people, he turned his back to make a call, and while he was on the call, these two ladies were kind of snickering behind his back and taking out the phone to dial. A stupid, disgusting, juvenile waste of everyone's time, as if what was going on in New Orleans was all a big joke.

Then we had to write reports about the incident. We did finally make it to dinner with Sean Callebs and the CNN people. They had their own building with a big parking lot underneath, down toward the commercial end of the city. That's where Buddy almost ate a little poodle on the street. I guess he was feeling stressed, too.

We were late, but we got there. And I'll never forget—after the stupid, ugly snafu at the hotel—one of those little things happened that kind of made the moment. We went through the door. There was a security guy there, and he said, "Guys, I've got to clip these IDs on you." He said, "If I don't give you these, I'll be speaking through the clown."

I looked at him and I said, "What?"

And he said, "You know, boys, speaking through the clown."

"What do you mean?"

He said, "The McDonald's clown. Can I take your order?"

What a riot. We needed that little bit of humor just then, because the room issue was not really resolved. I had made calls to the major, back in Maine, saying we had a big problem with the room. We were given basically that night and then we had to be out of there, and the solution for housing us that we were hearing was they were maybe going to put us in a camper-trailer in the Ninth Ward. We knew from the gang activity that had gone on around there and the gunshots we were hearing all day during the day that it was not going to be a good place to spend the night. And we'd have no electricity or water to clean up the dogs or ourselves.

What we were realizing was that on the one hand, the government was showing a face of caring, but on the other, FEMA was pulling its resources out of New Orleans and the city was making an attempt at taking itself back. We were caught up in that transition where the two weren't working together on this process; things were just happening randomly as they were going along and we were in the middle.

So we went to dinner. A phenomenal dinner. We had ribs and kicked back a little bit. Later, after we got back to our room, I made some phone calls, and we concluded that it was not worth remaining there without them having a clear and reasonable plan about where we were going to be staying. Not just for us. Wardens are used to roughing it. We had to be able to clean and take care of our dogs. They were our working partners. Way too much had gone into making them valuable resources to put them at risk down here, and the solution we'd heard discussed was definitely risky.

We decided we were going to pull out and go home. That was going to be big news because everything on the news at that point was how FEMA had screwed up.

Think about it. The day before, we'd found a missing body in a house that had already been searched three times. We'd had news crews following us everywhere we went. We'd been on the national news a number of times.

For a couple guys from Maine, going down there, and dealing with the corruption that was going on, and dealing with the constant danger, it had been a complete horror show. Where we were, in the Ninth Ward, there were gangs fighting for turf, primarily to establish who could go in and clean that place up. There were all these people who were off their medications who were out of control. We were crawling around inside things that could collapse on us at any second. We lived and breathed on the edge the whole time we were there. We'd just put up with it, trying to do our job. That was the warden way. Keep a low profile, do your job, and go home. And now they'd locked us out of our hotel room and called the police on us and thought it was funny?

It was definitely time to go.

When we got down to the lobby in the morning to load our gear, the cameras were already there waiting for us. And now we knew it was going to ripple, it was going to be a media event. They were filming us loading our gear, and spinning it hard about the good we'd done and how FEMA was treating us. The FEMA issue put us in the spotlight. We became kinda the symbol for FEMA's dysfunction at a time when the media was being very critical.

I was interviewed by, I think it was, CBS. I'd been told not to say anything bad about FEMA. Not to dis anybody. Just to say that the resources we needed weren't available and we didn't feel comfortable, etc., find some fandango way to say we're leaving without dissing anybody, which was almost impossible to do.

So they were all filming us leaving, and talking about why, and as soon as we were underway, I was on the phone with the major again, telling him be prepared, it's hitting the fan. I tried to give him the picture and I could tell that he doesn't understand how big this was, that this was national news. I think he said they got something like three thousand phone calls in Maine at headquarters that morning, which totally shut them down, including people from home, and across the country, offering to pay for our rooms so we could stay in New Orleans.

That prompted a phone call to us about mid-morning from headquarters saying that they were going to refer all the calls to us, since we were just sitting in a vehicle driving. Then the phone started ringing and ringing. At one point, we were eating lunch in Tennessee, and there we were on the TV news, loading up the truck. And the news was saying FEMA screwed up again. Couldn't get anything right. Their best dog teams were leaving because they couldn't even get 'em a room to stay in.

We drove all night and we got back to Maine, and this thing had caused such a firestorm that we had to do a press conference when we got back, saying things without saying anything. One of the quotes that really caused problems was when our boss in New Orleans spoke to the major at one point, and he used the term FUBAR. Then the major used that term in the local press conference.

The colonel was still MIA. He was away at a conference and no one could reach him; the major was using FUBAR on every news station. I figured he thought the "F" stood for fouled. It was bad.

Shortly after that, we were notified that they were not going to pay us our overtime that we had accrued. The colonel said that we would have to file a grievance with the union. No one ever said "you guys did a nice job" or acknowledged what we had been through and done down there (aside from a single photo op with the governor). No one really *had* any idea what we'd been through. We had a debriefing scheduled, but that basically fell apart because everyone had to go out on a search for a missing child. So all that had happened to us was never discussed or acknowledged.

And it went straight downhill for me from there.

CHAPTER TWENTY-FOUR

Migraines, PTSD, and Beyond

I didn't know it at the time, but the events in New Orleans and those that followed when I got home brought on a case of PTSD so bad it nearly destroyed me. The violence, the chaos, the filth, and the corruption created a perfect storm of all the things from my life all coming together. You don't go to suicide scenes and into armed conflicts or see all this human tragedy and death and not carry a piece of it away with you, no matter what. You do. Sucking it up and carrying on, that's the warden's way. Our job is to be there for others. To be strong for others. To keep people safe. We're supposed to be able to deal with what we see. Handle it. Some people deal with it better than others, but when you deal with it day in and day out, every day, it's a pebble in your bucket until the weight of it can just break you.

I didn't recognize what was happening for the longest time. That's too often the way it is with law enforcement, even though we're trained about it, warned about it. But far too often, we don't see it. To the warden service's credit, they did a lot of training on the issue because we're exposed to so much death and mayhem, but when it happens it is not some big cataclysmic, overnight thing; it's very subtle in the way it grabs you. Then, when it has you, you can't see through the fog. You can't figure out how to get out or help yourself. That's when it pulls you apart, one block at a time.

Looking back now, I call it a perfect storm because it was a conjunction of events—all the stuff I carried from my work that I didn't know was affecting me, plus problems with my mother's care and a serious conflict and break-up with the congregation at my church—that worked together to bring on a total personal disaster. New Orleans was the catalyst that finally brought it on.

I had gone down to New Orleans that second time carrying the vivid memory of the boy whose father had drowned the night before, his words about how hard he'd tried to save his father and his father's admonition to let him go and save himself echoing in my brain. I knew what he was going through, and how it would weigh on him. I'd been there.

I'd done two tours in New Orleans under incredibly dangerous conditions, crawling through mold and filth and rat-infested buildings. Listened to gunfire all day long, watched roving gangs. I'd faced down that man in the trench coat who planned to kill me just because I was standing there, alone, wearing a uniform. And the whole thing had ended with me standing in a hotel lobby, a tired, filthy man with his filthy dog, having just risked my life all day, while FEMA personnel tried to make me falsify documents, then snickered and called the police, like it was all some big joke. And I'd done that—Wayde and I had done that—under the unrelenting gaze of TV cameras.

I had come back to Maine to find a wall of disapproval and no support or understanding of what it had been like down there, back to the lost, the bodies, the perpetual random call-outs that ran my life. While I'd been busy just doing it, the job had changed so much. For decades—like that one tranquil spot Wayde and I had found in New Orleans, where we could look away from chaos and disaster—getting out into the woods and doing my job had been the refuge that kept me sane. Now, between policing boaters and off-road vehicles, searching for lost people and homicide victims and evidence, along with the increasing volume of paperwork, there was little time for that.

I began to have these headaches, seriously debilitating migraine headaches, which I'd never had before. At first, I thought it was from something I'd been exposed to in New Orleans, some kind of poison, because I'm talking serious headaches here, headaches that laid me right out. Then the medicine I got for them made me feel ten times worse. I was getting sicker and sicker and sicker and they were giving me more and more painkillers until I was spiraling into a cycle of total destruction. And that's what happens, you know. You're just trying to get by and function day-to-day with no way to see the big picture. I saw no correlation that the migraines and PTSD were intertwined.

Another thing that threw me, when I got back from New Orleans and I started getting migraines, was that things that had strong smells, like soaps and scented candles, would trigger an instant migraine. It was almost as though my system had become so sensitive that any little thing would throw it off. I got extremely photosensitive, so I couldn't go outside. I had to wear sunglasses in the house. I was just a mess.

One particular thing that was going on involved the smell of death. Death has a very unique smell—I'm talking fresh death, not decomposed. And at the height of my PTSD, every time I got into a situation where the adrenaline was kicking in, I could smell that smell. I could smell death. That's very unnerving because the death smell triggers all the other emotions that come with a situation where you're dealing with a dead person. Your brain is reacting, your mind is remembering all those other times. You get into that realm, you start smelling that, and you're at very high alert. It's like you drank ninety-five cups of coffee and someone put the record player on seventy-eight. High, intense alert like someone has punched the go button and you can't find the off. And you can't come down from it.

All of a sudden, I no longer had the ability to concentrate. My memory, my concentration, my judgment, my stamina, everything I'd relied on in myself to do my job was gone. I couldn't read a single sentence without my mind going in three or four directions. My ability to read the woods and to read people, to comprehend and see things around me was gone.

I couldn't read a paragraph. I would have to read a paragraph six, seven, eight times before I could understand it. And what came along with that was absolute fear. The fear that I had when it finally gripped me, the state my mind was in, I can only compare it to people with severe hypothermia who've reached the point where they can no longer make a decision. I would think I was comprehending and functioning when I was just spiraling in circles.

My stress levels were through the roof, and my way of dealing with it was to go to work, 'cause I could jump in my truck and I could drive around and not have to deal with the world. Realistically, I couldn't really work because my fuse was too short. I couldn't train the dogs because I had no patience. The walls were caving in, and things were just getting worse and worse and worse. I kept trying to get on top of it, to master it and get back under control, and I couldn't. Then fear kept building inside me because my whole world was uncontrollable, my reliably good memory was gone. I took refuge in sleep, or trying to sleep. Or I'd go out and try to work and just burn myself to the ground.

My decision-making skills were off; I wasn't making good decisions. Paranoia was really setting in. I had conflicts with the administrators that really slammed me. My wife, Jolyne, and my daughter could see the problem and suggested that I meet with my boss. I said I didn't need that. I was impossible with them, to the point where they didn't know what would set me off. My family was tiptoeing around me, as worried as I was, and with no idea what to do or say.

I begin to feel that I couldn't function on the job, but I didn't know what to do because, like so many people with PTSD, I didn't understand what was going on inside me. I really didn't want to admit, even to myself, that there was something happening, that there was anything wrong. When you get to that point in your world, that's when bad things start to happen.

My entire emotional response system had gone kaflooey. Just trying to get through each day was a battle. My inability to function brought on this incredible fear and paranoia as well as this awful, jittery sense of being out of control. It was as if someone completely unexpected stood in front of me and raised a big knife and *whoosh*, I was just flooded with adrenaline. It was recurrent and random and I couldn't predict when it might happen. When I wasn't on a paranoid high, I just started taking naps—taking long naps.

When those adrenaline spikes would happen, it could be hours or days before I could get myself down again. When I had migraines, I'd lose my capacity to think, to absorb information, or to function. With PTSD, though the person in the midst of it can't see it, there's this whole hiding thing that goes on where you are trying desperately to get hold of yourself and you can't. You're in yourself everyday so it's not like you can escape it and not try, but on the other hand, you can't see that you've got to get the help you need. You keep telling yourself you can deal with it and you'll make things better tomorrow. That's where a whole lot of people fall down, because someone's got to intervene. At some point, someone's got to be able to recognize it. And the person who has it, he'll be the last one to know.

Lucky for me, someone did intervene. While I was in the middle of this, two of my fellow wardens, Sergeant Kevin Adam and Sergeant Ralph Hosford, came over to the house. They just drove in and came inside and they sat down with me and said, "Look. You're done. You can't function. You've got to take some time off to fix yourself."

Jolyne was crying with relief in the other room.

At that point, I was fighting everything. I was fighting my bosses and my family and even myself, trying desperately to stay afloat. But when they came into my house and they did that, I didn't fight them. I was exhausted from trying to hold myself together. I didn't have any more fight left. Just like they'd said—I was done. I knew both of those guys well enough, they'd worked under me, and worked with me, and all, and those were probably the only two people in the whole department who could have had that conversation with me. Anyone else, I guarantee you, I would have resisted and been in denial and it wouldn't have gone well.

So I really appreciate Kevin and Ralph coming to the house and saying today's the day that we're going to deal with it. When that happened, it took a million pounds off my shoulders. It broke through my resistance, and I started to feel hope.

A short time after that visit, I ended up in the emergency room with a terrible migraine. While there, I experienced symptoms resembling a seizure. I involuntarily curled into the fetal position and my whole body jerked with tremors. In the midst of this episode, the doctor was quick to reassure me that it was not a seizure. He said that my being totally coherent about what was happening was a good thing. He explained what was happening: this was a serotonin spike. My body was finally giving in to its need to just stop, and it was using the combination of medications and life's stressors to do that. I must have been given some medicine because it stopped, and I was released to go home.

Once home, I was exhausted and took a nap. Upon waking and returning from a bathroom trip, I had another episode. My knees just went out from under me and I was totally helpless. Jolyne got me the few steps to the bedroom, yelling at me the whole time not to fall, to help her. I don't remember much about that whole thing. Jolyne had to call an ambulance. By the time it arrived, along with our neighbors and the local cop (who had heard about it over the airways and was concerned for me), I had experienced quite a few of these non-seizures. I can't even imagine how my wife got through that.

I had a couple more of those episodes during the following three days in the local hospital. All my meds were taken away and new ones prescribed. I remember the ER doctor continuing to check in with me while I was in the hospital. I liked him.

So now it was absolutely clear that my life had to change. Not just my work, but my whole life. My cousin, who was an ENT surgeon in Cleveland, got involved. He connected me to a doctor who specialized in migraines at Dartmouth–Hitchcock Medical Center in New Hampshire. My cousin pulled strings and got me in within two weeks, and the guy took a look at me and said, "Okay, we've got to get you off everything you're on." That's where I learned a whole lot about migraines and how they're the body's way of shutting down to remove you from the stress machine you're on. As it develops, the triggering mechanism gets easier and faster until you reach the point where you're living with a migraine every day. I'd gone months just completely shut down.

After I was treated at Dartmouth–Hitchcock, I found a good therapist in Bangor, and I started to work my way back.

From all of that—the intervention, a good therapist, and the migraine specialist—I finally got some help. But I can see now why a lot of officers commit suicide, because when you're in the middle of that, you're in the biggest, darkest hole and there is no light. Because you're looking down into it, you're not looking behind you or looking up. You don't see a way out. And it's a scary place.

It was awful, and it changed me forever. But I also got lucky, because I found good doctors who could help me. And because wardens do try to have each other's backs, when I was in the middle of the whole thing, a couple of my fellow wardens intervened.

A lot of people helped me get back on track, and back to work, because I didn't want to leave the warden service on that note. I wanted some more good years doing what I loved.

Now I've been trained by a professional counselor how to cope with the triggers and how to assess the situation and bring it down to reality. But I have to work aggressively at not getting myself into that same trap. Because now, when I get really stressed, I can feel it climb right back up, the overactive adrenaline, the anger, the inability to focus, the lack of concentration—the whole syndrome. Now I have the tools to recognize what's happening, process it, and bring myself back down.

There are still certain things that I can't fix. Like that death smell I talked about? Even today, if I'm in a bad situation, I smell death. I couldn't describe what it's like in a million years, but I've handled it and dealt with it a lot, and when I get into high danger mode, I smell the smell even though it's not there. It's my brain's reaction, and what it's doing is taking this scenario and putting me in this elevated state to compensate for what I don't have. It's intense, to say the least.

With PTSD, if you're lucky and you get help, you get over that part— the fear, the paranoia, the disjointed intelligence; but it physically changes you forever. And it changes your personality. It takes a lot out of you. They don't talk much about that. I'm not as optimistic, or as carefree, or as resilient as I was before this happened. I can't just be the go, go, go, live my life, optimistic, happy-go-lucky, adventurous Roger.

I have to manage it. I have to be vigilant.

The good thing was that the road back was easier than I thought, thank God. A lot of it was just learning to look at things, to stop and assess things and not make big piles of rocks where they don't need to be. I have learned to deal with my symptoms and recognize the triggers. I still have migraines, although they have become less and less frequent and more manageable. I still have them to this day when stress rears its ugly head and I am not so vigilant to my triggers.

And once I got to that point where I stopped aggravating this thing, I started going into the healing mode. It was like seeing color for the first time after being blind for years, you know. It reminded me, *Oh, this is why I'm alive.*

CHAPTER TWENTY-FIVE

Survivor

When I started on with the warden service, I remember that senior officers would often earmark their tenure by the number of falls they had worked. If you would ask them how many years they had on, they would answer, "I've worked twenty-three falls now," rather than the number of years from the date they got hired. It was a way of earmarking something that you'd survived, because each season was a milestone. The fall season meant countless hours of no sleep, people with guns, and marathons of investigations combined with lost and injured hunters. The season tested your mettle and at its end left you completely drained and worn out, taking its toll on you. Then when it was over, you would eagerly wait for it to come again.

Today I work at a much different pace. Though it can still get hectic at times, I don't feel the pressure to save the world that I did. I still do on occasion look for the missing with my cadaver dogs. A year after I retired, I found myself on a search for a missing woman in Western Maine who had disappeared from her camp after losing her battle with depression. She left a note that confirmed what she had left to go do. I was working for Merrill's Investigations & Security Dog Detector

Team when I was approached by the family to try to find her after the Maine Warden Service and State Police exhausted their resources looking for her.

After careful study of what areas had been searched, I identified several potential areas that needed a closer look. My hunch was right, and I found her the first day. That was such a bittersweet event; I was happy that the mission was a success but sad for the family who now had to deal with their loss. Those bittersweet endings have been a theme throughout my career—so often, I have been "successful" in finding someone, yet I have found them dead or had them subsequently die.

After retiring, you tend to have this time of finding yourself again in a new world without a gun, without a badge. It's a very interesting time as you feel new freedom but are challenged by a lot of unknowns.

While I was floundering around and discovering that the original plans I'd made weren't working out, my good friend, and former warden colleague, Allen Stehle, made me a unique offer: to help him teach at Beal College, where he was president. He wanted me to teach in the law enforcement program. Being from the school of hard knocks rather than the world of academics, stepping into the realm of higher education was very intimidating. Walking into a classroom was not foreign to me. I'd done plenty of it over the years, teaching wardens. But these were not officers, they were students from all walks of life. Finding common ground was going to be a huge challenge.

I remember my opening speech to the Conservation Law class, a group of about fifteen students. I told them to look around the room. I said, "Maybe one of you will make it to the colonel's interview for a job as a Maine Game Warden. It's going to be the hardest thing to which you will ever commit yourself. Only the few who can keep their eye on the prize will get a chance to try out, let alone get hired." I remember the surprised looks on their faces. That was not what they expected me to say. There were also some blank looks coming from them. I don't think they had considered how difficult a challenge this was going to be. Of this group only one did make it.

Over the next few months, teaching classes like Patrol Procedures, Police Patrol Tactics, or Fish and Wildlife Identification reminded me of all the skills I had accumulated over the last twenty-five years. I'd forgotten that I'd once had to learn them, because after so many years, using them was like breathing. In my zeal to ensure that my students were well prepared, my teaching spilled over onto weekends, and I found myself designing trials and leading them out into the woods in the same way I'd once led rookie wardens out to learn about basic wilderness survival and investigation.

Beal College was a very small school and I quickly got to know my students on a personal level. To this day, I am still in contact with most of them.

I absolutely loved working with these kids, but I kept hearing the call to work my dogs again, and the call of the world outside the classroom. When another close friend of mine offered me the opportunity to do private investigator work and K-9 work, the call to keep hunting the bad guys and working dogs was too great; I couldn't refuse. I ended up getting my private investigator license and working dogs for detecting cadavers, bombs, and bed bugs. Yes, bed bugs. It may not sound exciting, but it's a super efficient way for a college to be sure its dorms are bed bug free. Dogs are faster and better than human searchers. And working with Gator, the bed bug dog, was quite an adventure.

My most challenging expedition recently took me to Panama, to a small island area called Bocas Del Toro, to look for an elderly man from Toronto, Canada, who had disappeared during October of 2012. The logistics of going to a foreign country with dogs were an absolute nightmare. Traveling with K-9s is very difficult at best; getting them into a country that doesn't want them there is even harder. The irony of it all was that after all the formal documentation, health certificates, and permissions from the embassy, we got there only to find wild dogs running everywhere with every kind of disease known to man.

Getting our dogs to Panama wasn't the only hurdle. Foreign governments are not friendly to searchers from afar, especially in the case of a missing tourist. The search could generate bad press and affect their tourism, so our challenge was to build a bridge of trust with the local officials and explain to them our mission was only to bring the victim home. No press, no breaking stories, just get the victim back to his family.

The way they keep you out is to bury you in red tape and impossible deadlines and keep putting up barriers so you eventually get the message and give up. Being a determined, resourceful lot, and with the family's tremendous determination to recover their missing father, we finally made it to Panama. We quickly found out that the local law enforcement investigation was skewed to make the problem go away. Their goal was to close the investigation as quickly as possible so they simply wrote down that the victim wandered off into the jungle and was most likely suicidal, while all the elements of the investigation were contrary to that. The most obvious possibility, that of criminal activity regarding the victim, had been, for the most part, ignored.

The story was that the man habitually walked into town in the morning and had disappeared along the route. The police reports we reviewed focused the search to the north based on a possible sighting, which unfortunately drew all the resources to one area. As experienced law enforcement personnel know, this is a very easy trap to fall into, which can cost precious time and give you tunnel vision as to what really could have happened.

The jungles of Panama are very thick, hot, humid and full of poisonous things. Working with K-9s in this environment was very difficult. The dogs seemed to adjust much quicker than we handlers did, but after only a few hours each day, the teams were exhausted. Our team of four managed to reach our objective. We cleared the area the police had identified and debunked the theory that the victim had headed north into the jungle, hoping it would give the police the tools they needed to keep the investigation open.

After five days of hard searching in extreme heat, we cleared our objective and opened the door for the police to look at the other possibility—the very likely prospect that he was a victim of foul play. The "Law of Shifting Probabilities" comes into play here. The more blocks you clear in what you believe are your best places, the more the stats are telling you to move on, you're wrong. Emotion verses logic. In your mind, the tendency is to keep searching the likely places over and over again, but the science is telling you to move on.

In this case, as we cleared the jungle trails, our results were telling the police that their theory was wrong. We hoped that our actions would give local police the information they needed to keep the investigation open, but that didn't happen. As soon as we left, they closed the investigation, saying that everything possible had been done.

For the victim's two daughters, this was a very painful process, and seeing their anguish brought back a lot of memories of the time I spent looking for my dad and how it felt, that frustration and the pain of not knowing.

The tough part of this work is that you can't take the reins and do the law enforcement work for them, and they don't really care about one missing tourist from Canada. To the family, it's a crushing blow. To their credit, they will never give up the search for their dad. Always that bittersweet thing. Since that search, new information has come to light which makes much more sense. But how to finish this search, or whether they ever let us finish the job, only time will tell. I would go back if I could.

I started writing this book because people always told me I was a great storyteller, and that I ought to write my stories down. Every game warden across this great land has a million stories to tell, a million funny moments and situations that we get from sitting in the front row, watching nature's unfolding story and how humans interact with it. So often, too, we see people going hunting, or fishing, or off into the wilderness kind of like a lab puppy chasing a tennis ball for the first time, all wide-eyed and ramped up, forgetting all else around them, chairs, furniture, other people, heedless of anything but the pleasure they're chasing.

Along the way, as I began to write about my two and half decades in the warden service, I realized that I had another story to tell as well. A story about what it's like to be on the front lines in a world where there is so much careless indifference, a world where everyone carries a gun. A world where there is so much human tragedy. A world where people are visibly changing an environment they often don't even see. Wardens have lots of funny, human encounters. We also see the havoc people sow, how people will destroy everything to get the prize, forgetting all else. People taking risks that have huge consequences, leaving all the common sense behind. And we see bad things happen.

When I started this journey, I was eager to protect Maine's fish and wildlife resources so they would be available for my children, and my children's children. My dreams were about catching the bad guys and saving the day just in the nick of time. (Dudley Do-Right was my favorite cartoon growing up.) I never gave any thought to all the human tragedies I would encounter. Despite my experience with my own father's drowning, and the lasting impact that had on me, I never imagined that the job would involve so much death and tragedy. I certainly never imagined the cumulative impact so much death and tragedy would have on me.

The rule in the public safety world is to protect yourself. We are trained to hold the things we deal with at arm's length, to box it up, not dwell on it. We are taught that we cannot let the events we deal with become personal, because all that bad stuff will erode us and make us unable to do the job. I thought I could do that. I believed that I could apply the lessons of my own life—be the steady and compassionate person that others needed in bad situations—and keep walking away unscathed to do it again another day.

I was wrong. Over the years, I found that those situations never left me. I would relive their final moments and in my mind, die their death, never forgetting a single one. All the details were locked inside and saved forever in my mind. Like many other public safety officers I've seen over the years, I didn't see it coming. I came back from the wallow of filth and death and corruption in New Orleans and fell into a black, black hole, the circumstances of my life creating a perfect storm that would have the potential to destroy everything good in my life.

Looking back, I know that three things saved me from that black abyss: my faith, my family, and my friends. I have been blessed with these special gifts: that those who could love me continued to do so when I wasn't lovable, and that my family and friends stood beside me when I was pushing them away, often just supporting me by being there, saying nothing. They were there on the journey with me, steering and steadying the canoe, keeping me moving forward through the storm.

So many times in my journey, I looked up to the heavens and said, "God, I can't do this alone," and each step from then on would be more focused, more directed. The exhaustion would wane and my strength would return. Over the years, I saw so many times that had I not had Someone watching over me, I would have and should have died. My relationship with my Lord and Savior grew, and over time I came to realize that God doesn't waste pain.

Those horrible things in our lives, the things that seek to destroy us, are the things that will bring us to our knees and overwhelm us; they also bring us closer to the place where God can reach our hearts and we can lay our huge burden of human anguish and worry at His feet, give Him the reins, and watch the impossible happen. Faith is where I realized that the whole time I thought I was driving, "Dad" was really holding the wheel. His foot was on the gas and in control of the brake; I was just tugging at the wheel.

As I came into the end zone of the writing process, I realized that I couldn't leave my story without talking more about PTSD. I realized that my pain, my journey, and my battle could all be used to help others going through the storms of life; maybe they'd realize that if I made it, they can make it too. There is hope. My vision is to have people reading this understand that you can survive PTSD, but you have to acknowledge it and deal with it and not just try to limp along and survive day to day.

Depression and PTSD thrive on you when you are trying to take on the fight by yourself. They force you to stay in a place that causes you to shrink inside yourself and disappear in a black hole that will eventually swallow you up. It forces you to ignore all of the hope and help that is at arm's reach, and it keeps you looking at the world through a pin hole, not seeing anything but the inside of the little soup can you put yourself in. Your family's and friends' arms are reaching for you and you are so self-absorbed you can't see them.

I have seen men and women made of steel taken down by this. You are not impervious or immune to this. At some point in your life, you will be taken off your feet and tipped upside down. Your canoe will upset in the rapids and you are going for a ride over which you have little or no control. You may grab a rock in the middle of the river, but you are not on shore. You will need help to get there: faith, family and friends. They will get you home. You are not alone.

PTSD isn't something to be "gotten over," it's something you adjust to, because it changes you. In all the law enforcement training that we had, PTSD was a big part of it; what they didn't tell us is that it changes your life forever. That's the reality. You don't go back to what you were. It's not like an illness where you get sick and then you get better. You have to cope with it for the rest of your life, so you have to learn the mechanisms and the things that help you get steady again. And it's always a challenge, because your brain wants to go back to where you were, and you can't physically do that. So you're always running into conflict and frustration and learning to say "Slow down." That is the hardest thing.

I am the only living survivor of my working game warden class-mates. Three of us stayed with it: Daryl Gordon, Rick Stone, and I. Both Daryl and Rick have died. Daryl in a plane crash and Rick of cancer. Both of these great men loved the Lord, their families, and being game wardens, in that order. They left behind legacies of honor, pride, and service. As I sit here and write this, it humbles me that they were my brothers, both in service and in faith; it is my duty to never forget them and for what they stood.

My favorite Bible verse is Isaiah 40:31, "They that trust in the Lord shall mount up with wings as eagles. They shall run and not grow weary and walk and not grow faint." As many times over my career that I looked up and said, "Help, I can't do this alone," I survived.

The journey isn't over, far from it.

I have taken new paths and journeys since retiring. I've spent time teaching Conservation Law Enforcement at Beal College, training K-9s for work in the private sector as well as law enforcement, and occasionally going on missing person searches.

Looking back, despite my troubles, I wouldn't change a thing. I believe I was made for this journey. Everything I did as a kid unknowingly prepared me for this great adventure. If I have one regret, it's that I didn't spend more time with my own kids. They've grown up way too fast.

Today, the trail is not as steep as it was, and I get to pick the paths I like that work for me and live life at a slower pace. The challenges of the past still haunt me and some days are harder than others, but I just have to slow down and breathe and look back on the trail and say, "I made it!" I survived twenty-five falls as a Maine Game Warden. I am a survivor.